TRANS-ATLANTIC CONSERVATIVE PROTESTANTISM IN THE EVANGELICAL FREE AND MISSION COVENANT TRADITIONS

See last pages of this volume for a complete list of titles

TRANS-ATLANTIC CONSERVATIVE PROTESTANTISM IN THE EVANGELICAL FREE AND MISSION COVENANT TRADITIONS

Frederick Hale

ARNO PRESS
A New York Times Company
New York • 1979

Editorial Supervision: Steven Bedney

First publication in book form 1979 by Arno Press Inc.

SCANDINAVIANS IN AMERICA
ISBN for complete set: 0-405-11628-4
See last pages of this volume for titles.

Manufactured in the United States of America

Library of Congress Cataloging in Publication Data

Hale, Frederick.
Trans-Atlantic conservative Protestantism in the evangelical free and mission covenant traditions.

(Scandinavians in America)
Originally presented as the author's thesis, Johns Hopkins University, 1976.
Bibliography: p.
1. Evangelical Free Church of America--History.
2. Evangelical Covenant Church of America--History.
3. Pietism--United States. 4. Pietism--Scandinavia.
5. Revivals--United States. 6. Revivals--Scandinavia.
7. United States--Church history. 8. Scandinavia--Church history. 9. Disseaters, Religions--Scandinavia.
I. Title. II. Series.
BX7548.A4H34 1979 289.9 78-15183
ISBN 0-405-11638-1

TRANS-ATLANTIC CONSERVATIVE PROTESTANTISM

IN THE EVANGELICAL FREE AND MISSION COVENANT TRADITIONS

Frederick Hale

PREFACE

An earlier version of this study was submitted to The Johns Hopkins University as a doctoral thesis in 1976. It is an investigation of the religious currents which influenced Scandinavians on both sides of the Atlantic during the nineteenth century and gave the antecedents of the Evangelical Free Church of America and the Evangelical Covenant Church characteristics which have persisted in those two traditions and are now regarded as "conservative." The research on which the study rests has also been trans-Atlantic, begun at Harvard University in 1969 and completed in Scandinavia in 1977.

The use of the term "Scandinavian free churches" in this study requires a word of clarification. "Scandinavian" refers only to Sweden, Norway, and Denmark and to emigrants from those three nations to the United States. It does not include either Iceland or Finland, because immigrants from those countries did not play any part in the formation of the two Scandinavian-American religious traditions under consideration. It should also be mentioned that "Nordic" is synonymous with "Scandinavian" in this study. The term "free churches" designates the various communions within these two traditions, namely the Mission Covenants of Sweden, Norway, and Denmark, and their counterparts in the United States. Many other nonconformist denominations either arose in or were transplanted to the Nordic countries during the nineteenth century, of course, but except where other dissenters are specifically mentioned, as in Chapter III, use of the term is limited to the Mission Covenant and Evangelical Free traditions.

The research for this study could not have been conducted without the assistance given me by many people and institutions on both sides of the Atlantic. In Scandinavia, Ingulf Diesen of the Norwegian Mission Covenant, Ragnar Widman of the Swedish Mission Covenant, Professor Niels Knud Andersen of the University of Copenhagen, Professors Nils Bloch-Hoell and Ingrid Semmingsen of the University of Oslo, Dr. Andreas Ropeid of the Institute for Folklife Research in Oslo, and Peder A. Eidberg of the Baptist Theological Seminary in Stabekk, Norway gave me countless research hints and assisted in procuring pertinent source materials. Sigurd Westberg and Erik Hawkinson of the Evangelical Covenant Church and Arnold Olson of the Evangelical Free Church performed similar services to facilitate my research in the United States. I also received help from the staffs of the Royal Library in Copenhagen, the Minnesota Historical Society, the Chicago Historical Society, the libraries of Chicago Theological Seminary, Harvard Divinity School, Trinity Evangelical Divinity School, North Park College, and the Universities of Copenhagen, Oslo, Chicago, and Minnesota, as well as the Norwegian State Archives in Trondheim and Kristiansand. Generous fellowships from the George C. Marshall Memorial Fund in Denmark, the Lilly Endowment, the Oslo

International Summer School, and the Norwegian Emigration Fund defrayed the costs of conducting research on both sides of the Atlantic.

A special debt of gratitude must be expressed to the many men who have taught me in the field of ecclesiastical history during the past decade. I wish especially to thank Professor Ernest R. Sandeen of Macalester College, who not only supervised my thesis there and guided my early investigations in American religious history, but who also facilitated much of my own research through his pioneering studies of millenarianism in the nineteenth century, and my adviser and thesis director at The Johns Hopkins University, Professor Timothy L. Smith, who supported my search for research funds, offered interpretive help and, with deft strokes of his editorial pencil, transformed my most chaotic lucubrations into readable prose.

TABLE OF CONTENTS

CHAPTER I

INTRODUCTION

For several decades ecclesiastical historians and other scholars have sought the origins of modern conservative Protestantism in the United States. Their efforts have shed considerable light while also casting many shadows on the history of several denominations and religious groups, but they have failed to illuminate this complex tapestry as a whole. The sheer size and variety of conservative Protestantism have foiled all attempts to comprehend it with simplistic theories which fit one of its segments, but fail to unravel the rest. Compounding the task is the fact that immigrants have added innumerable threads to the pattern; many of these have remained invisible to historians who are unable or unwilling to conduct research in Scandinavian, central European, and other pertinent languages. As a result, the heterogeneity of the fibers constituting its warp and woof has not been fully appreciated.

Perhaps nothing has been a greater hindrance to the process of analysis than the loose and usually undefined term, "fundamentalism." Ernest R. Sandeen may be correct that Curtis Lee Laws coined "Fundamentalist" in 1920 as a result of the World's Conference on Christian Fundamentals,[1] but semantic etiology is not so simple. Never precise theological parlance, the words "fundamentalism" and "fundamentalist" quickly became terms of opprobrium when the so-called "modernist-fundamentalist controversy" erupted in the 1920's. Laden with negative connotations, "fundamentalism" was indiscriminately applied to such diverse denominations as the Southern Baptist Convention, the Jehovah's Witnesses, and the Seventh-day Adventists. The fact that these Christians held widely diverging views on many central matters, including eschatology and the sacraments, did not prevent their more liberal detractors -- themselves a heterogeneous lot -- from relegating them en masse to a primitive wasteland where they supposedly lived in ignorant harmony subscribing to a common five-point creed. In the 1940's Carl Henry and other conservative Protestants founded the National Association of Evangelicals, an organization which eschews the "fundamentalist" label but has nevertheless grown to encompass many of the denominations which have often been so designated. The NAE has advocated use of the word "evangelical" to denote conservative Protestants, but its leaders' and others' use of this term has often been so inclusive as to preclude precise definition. In the meantime, however, "fundamentalist" has persisted in the vocabularies of both conservative and liberal Protestants, church historians and scholars in various other theological disciplines.

Consequently, since at least as early as the 1930's the historiography of conservative Protestantism in the United States has suffered. Stewart G. Cole's seminal History of Fundamentalism, published in 1931, may have been the only study of that period to place the controversies then rocking several denominations into a historical context. This work, however, reflects a liberal bias and deals with a relatively small number of religious groups. Moreover, Cole mistakenly stated that the Niagara Bible Conference, an important, perennial North American Protestant gathering, produced in 1895 a five-point creed to which most if not all subsequent conservatives subscribed. His blunder echoed and re-echoed in the historiography of American religion until 1970 when Sandeen applied the needed corrective by pointing out that the Conference's creed was written in 1878 and contained fourteen points, some of which conflicted with the doctrinal statements of other Protestant groups.[2] Cole's error distorted other historians' perception of conservative Protestantism in two ways. First, it gave the impression that the conservatives of the late nineteenth and early twentieth centuries were merely seeking to preserve traditional Protestantism from such radical intellectual currents as Darwinian evolutionary theory and German Biblical scholarship. No less significantly, the theory of a common creed among conservatives gave the mistaken impression that they were a relatively homogeneous lot. Cole, in fact, tacitly denied or ignored the great diversity which can be found among these Christians.

A decade later H. Richard Niebuhr presented an equally odd picture of the movement which he identified as "Fundamentalism," claiming that it was characterized by "conservatism with regard to beliefs" and conducted "aggressive efforts to impose its creed upon the churches and . . . schools of the country." Mimicking Cole, the noted Yale theologian defined its creed as the "five points of fundamentalism," and numbered "the inerrancy of the Bible, the Virgin Birth of Jesus, the supernatural atonement, the physical resurrection of Jesus and the authenticity of the Gospel miracles" as the bastion walls of that phantom pentagon of faith. Niebuhr went beyond Cole to analyze the social sources of the movement, asserting that they lay chiefly in the rural South and other ostensibly isolated communities which were "least subject to the influence of modern science and industrial civilization." His image of anti-intellectualism meshed well with his statement that hostility to evolutionary theories was "the central question of the fundamentalist controversy."[3]

Norman Furniss' The Fundamentalist Controversy, 1918-1931,[4] despite its limited chronological scope, was widely recognized as the standard work on modern conservative Protestantism in America prior to the 1970's. Like most preceding scholars who attempted to analyze this topic, Furniss indiscriminately applied the "fundamentalist" label to many postwar reactions to the vicissitudes of religious and secular modernization. He further tried to delve into the psyches of the "fundamentalists," where he claimed to find a "vaguely defined fear" stemming from a need for certainty in a rapidly changing world. Furthermore, these ostensibly paranoid Christians displayed anti-intellectualism, egotism, a high rate of illiteracy, and a tendency toward mental and rhetorical violence.

Sandeen's The Roots of Fundamentalism marked a new departure in the historiography of conservative Protestantism. Its author analyzed the trans-Atlantic origins of "the Fundamentalist movement, now calling itself Evangelicalism and rallying behind national leaders such as Billy Graham. . . ." The book differs from most preceding studies in several respects. Whereas several earlier historians treated the subject with general condescension and occasional hostility, Sandeen shows both respect and sympathy for the Christians whose movement he analyzes. This attitude allows him to consider in detail the dimensions of their thought which are generally thought of as conservative. Sandeen finds the primary root in trans-Atlantic millenarian movements "which gave life and shape to the Fundamentalist movement." The geographical context itself is new; earlier students had tended to focus their attention on the so-called "Bible Belt," a poorly defined region which included the South and perhaps other areas of the United States. The second most important root, Sandeen explains, was Biblical literalism, especially the theory of verbal inspiration of the "original autographs" of the Scriptures which was taught at Princeton Theological Seminary. In terms of chronological emphasis _The Roots of Fundamentalism_ also differs from previous studies which asserted a continuity between nineteenth and early twentieth-century evangelical Protestantism but were preoccupied with the controversies of the 1920's. Sandeen also traces links between the Victorian era and the twentieth century, but he emphasizes the former period and states unambiguously that neither the Princeton theology of Biblical literalism nor the millenarianism which he analyzes was simply a manifestation of traditional

Protestant orthodoxy. Rather, he insists that "no such theology [of Biblical literalism] existed before 1850" and finds untraditional elements in some of the nineteenth-century eschatologies which have influenced profoundly conservative Protestantism in our own time. No scholar acquainted with the conservative Biblicism which Ernst Hengstenberg developed at the University of Berlin during the first half of the nineteenth century will accept the former statement at face value, although Sandeen is apparently limiting his assertion to American religious history.

Other historians quickly acclaimed The Roots of Fundamentalism, but also recorded their reservations. George Marsden accused Sandeen of creating an "imbalanced perspective" by focusing on millenarianism.[5] "Might there not be more than one root?" he asked rhetorically. The answer, as Sandeen makes clear by devoting a great deal of attention to Biblicism in addition to eschatology, is a resounding Yes. Having set up and bowled over this straw man, Marsden proceeded to describe the plurality of continuities between "the theological and religious tradition of evangelical Protestantism in nineteenth-century England and America" and conservative Christianity after the turn of the century. "Fundamentalists, for instance, tend to emphasize individual religious experience, personal ethics, and freedom as in making 'decisions' for Christ, and to identify with free-enterprise capitalism," he wrote, "all tendencies which seem to have definitely nineteenth-century origins." Marsden's reasoning, however, is faulty, because he failed to distinguish between a similarity and a root.

It is correct, of course, that most self-styled "fundamentalists" and other conservative Protestants espouse personal ethics and the other characteristics which Marsden assigned to them. But all of these attributes antedated the nineteenth century in which he found their genesis, some by several centuries. Moreover, many Protestants on both sides of the Atlantic whom nobody would label either "fundamentalist" or "conservative," including, in fact, some Unitarians, have displayed the markings which Marsden seems to believe are the unique domain of "fundamentalists" and their immediate spiritual ancestors.

Two intimately related factors which church historians have never adequately treated are the European backgrounds of twentieth-century conservative Protestantism in the United States and the role which European immigrants played in weaving the present evangelical fabric of this country. Studies such as those by Cole and Furniss make no mention of immigrants, while Sandeen only briefly refers to a few British newcomers, such as George Needham. Owing to Sandeen's groundbreaking work, historians of conservative Protestantism can no longer afford to ignore the trans-Atlantic context into which their subject falls, but his bifocal study of millenarianism in Great Britain and North America is not sufficiently inclusive to explain why many European immigrants were both Biblical literalists and millenarians long before they reached American shores. This gap in our knowledge cannot, of course, be blamed entirely on historians of religion; their counterparts in immigration history have also neglected to explore many of the religious ideas which influenced European-Americans both before and after they left their homes in the Old World. Perhaps the chief offenders have been those who have written the chronicles of individual immigrant denominations. All too often they have focused their attention narrowly on the particular communion in question without casting more than a rare glance at the other immigrant and native American religious groups with which the subjects of their inquiries interacted. One result has been the distorted impression that "fundamentalism" was either a uniquely American or Anglo-American phenomenon which had nothing to do with the spiritual life of European immigrants and their cousins who remained in the Old World.

The antecedents of the two American denominations in the International Federation of Free Evangelical Churches are the subjects of the present study. The records reveal that at least two kinds of conservative Protestantism gave rise to twentieth-century "evangelicalism" among Scandinavian-Americans.[6] The progenitors of the Evangelical Covenant Church, long known as the Evangelical Mission Covenant of America, traced their spiritual roots to pietistic revivalism in Sweden a century ago and the search for a pure visible church. The parallel denomination in their homeland is the Swedish Mission Covenant, founded in 1878. The Evangelical Free Church of America, on the other hand, had several forebears which merged in 1950 to form the present denomination. These antecedent organizations were composed of Swedes, Danes, and Norwegians who in the 1880's and 1890's shared the trans-Atlantic expectations of the imminent Second Coming of Christ. They included Swedish immigrants who opposed formation of the Mission Covenant of America in 1885 and returned to Scandinavia to proclaim the return of Christ and to help inspire the formation of the groups which became the Mission Covenants of Norway and Denmark. In the United States, millenarian Swedes organized the Swedish Evangelical Free Church of America in 1884 and those of Norwegian and Danish backgrounds formed the Eastern and Western Evangelical Free Church Associations in the 1890's. In 1912 the two regional bodies united as the Evangelical Free Church Association, which existed alongside the Swedish-American group until they all merged at mid-century. The Norwegian and Danish-Americans in this tradition have always felt a close affinity with the Mission Covenants of Norway and Denmark. Although these two latter denominations have practically the same name as the Swedish Mission Covenant, their theology more closely resembles that of the Evangelical Free Church of America than that of their large cousin in Sweden. Because of the confusing nomenclature, it is essential to remember that the three denominations in Scandinavia represent two Protestant traditions which, although they overlap, have important differences which I shall analyze in several chapters.

The International Federation of Free Evangelical Churches, officially constituted at Bern, Switzerland in 1948, is a loose confederation of fifteen denominations which regard themselves as conservative Protestants. These communions are found in Canada,

Czechoslovakia, Denmark, Finland, France, Germany, Greece, The Netherlands, Norway, Spain, Sweden, Switzerland, and the United States and stem, for the most part, from nineteenth-century revivals. To a certain degree they are a heterogeneous group. Some, but not all, stress the infallibility of the Scriptures. In those countries which have established churches, they are nonconformists, although not all insist that their members leave the state churches. Some of these denominations anticipate the imminent Second Coming, while in others this hope is less predominant. The constitution of the Federation guarantees this latitude by stating that the "sole requirement for church membership is spiritual life through personal faith in Jesus Christ as the Son of God, Savior, and Lord." Of the denominations considered in this study, the Mission Covenants of Denmark, Norway, and Sweden as well as the Evangelical Covenant Church of America were charter members. The Evangelical Free Church of America, which had not yet been born in 1948, joined in the 1950's.

The present study falls into four general sections. In the first, I sketch with broad strokes the nineteenth-century background of the Scandinavian free churches in the revivalist movement which swept across the Nordic countries. Moreover, these communions were made possible by the larger movement of religious toleration which came to Scandinavia and many other European countries in the nineteenth century. In all the Scandinavian lands, dissenting sects co-existed more freely alongside the established churches. The coming of toleration allowed them to function as legally recognized bodies, whereas they had earlier been compelled to keep low profiles and endure civil harassment. But no less significantly, most of the nonconformist traditions came from abroad, bringing new religious ideas and institutions to these Lutheran lands. Religious toleration thus allowed Scandinavians to share more readily trans-Atlantic movements which were not indigenous to their own countries and Lutheran heritage. The next chapter covers Biblical scholarship in Scandinavia, focusing on the reactions of Nordic churchmen to the "higher criticism" of the Scriptures which came from German universities to northern Europe after about 1880. The spiritual ancestors of the Evangelical Free Church and the Evangelical Covenant Church have always been quite Biblicistic; their devotion to the Scriptures antedated radical Biblical scholarship and made them oppose that intellectual current, often with arguments borrowed from English and American Protestants. The final chapter of the background section deals with the millenarian streams which flowed from British and American sources to Scandinavia, where they influenced profoundly both the established and the free churches. Millenarianism became a crucial part of the theology of the Danish and Norwegian Mission Covenants, as well as of the various Nordic immigrant communions which coalesced to form the Evangelical Free Church of America.

After analyzing the main currents which influenced conservative Protestant nonconformists in Scandinavia, I describe the origins of the Mission Covenants in Sweden, Norway, and Denmark, and trace the development of these traditions among Scandinavian-Americans to about 1885. These three chapters will reveal that two kinds of conservative Protestantism developed among these Scandinavians on both sides of the Atlantic, one springing from Lutheran roots in Sweden, the other imported from the United States in millenarian revivals.

In the mid-1880's immigrants of both traditions began to cooperate with American Congregationalists, who gave them educational and financial assistance. This period of cooperation, though short-lived, made an important impact on the Scandinavians. They soon perceived liberal tendencies in this Yankee denomination and, in defense of their own conservative faith, severed many of their ties with the Congregationalists. Before doing so, however, the Nordic immigrants debated vigorously the wisdom of remaining under the wing of these often nationalistic Americans who were urging them to assimilate rapidly American ways. The controversy among these newcomers, especially the Swedes of the Mission Covenant, reveals something of the links between their conservative faith and their continuing attachment to Old World culture. The debate over Americanization and resistance to coerced assimilation is the subject of the third part of this study.

The fourth section, Chapter XI, deals with the period following the immigrants' assertion of spiritual independence from the Congregationalists. It describes the zenith of their Biblicism and their responses to millenarianism around the turn of the century. At that time, and indeed during the last ten or fifteen years of the nineteenth century, these Nordic-Americans displayed the same reverence for the Bible and opposition to higher criticism as nonemigrating Scandinavians of the corresponding denominations. Moreover, they were caught up in (or, in the case of the Swedish Covenanters, generally opposed) the eschatological currents of the times.

Because the documents reflecting the early history of the Evangelical Free Church are sparse, I have chosen to limit this study largely to a consideration of ideas. It would be interesting to know more precisely what kinds of Scandinavians, both in the Old World and the New, became adherents of these two traditions. While much can be learned from the archives of the Swedish Mission Covenant and its American counterpart, the materials pertaining to the Evangelical Free Church's forebears yield little information about their social class, age, or sex.

This study, then, is largely one of trans-Atlantic religious continuities which demonstrate that conservative Protestantism in the United States cannot be regarded merely as an outgrowth of American Christianity. No simple theory of "fundamentalism" explains the origins of the divergent Mission Covenant and Evangelical Free Church traditions. Neither developed as a reaction to liberalizing tendencies in Protestantism in the United States or in Europe or produced a five-point creed. Neither was rooted in the American South or nourished by anti-intellectualism. Their members were not paranoid individuals seeking certainty in a changing world. Finally, the Sandeen theory of the role of millenarianism does not adequately explain the genesis of these two traditions. Rather, they grew out of pietistic and millenarian revivalism and Biblicism decades before the "modernist-fundamentalist controversy" erupted in the 1920's; moreover, millenarianism was a hallmark of the Norwegian and Danish Mission Covenants from their inception in the 1880's. Like-minded immigrants developed analogous denominations which were by 1900 clearly progenitors of two vital wings of modern conservative Protestantism in the United States.

CHAPTER II

THE PIETISTIC REVIVAL HERITAGE

Revivalism has characterized the Mission Covenants of Sweden, Norway, and Denmark since they came into being nearly a century ago. All three denominations are historically rooted in long traditions of awakening birthright members of the Scandinavian state churches from merely nominal Christianity to a living faith. The Nordic immigrants in the United States who organized the Mission Covenant of America and the sects which eventually coalesced to form the Evangelical Free Church brought the tradition of revivalism with them. It was not something which they first confronted in the New World. This fact is important to an interpretation of these denominations' conservative roots. In much American religious historiography, especially that which grew out of the progressive school and the Turner frontier thesis, revivalism is presented as an almost uniquely American phenomenon, indeed, one which was born on the western frontier.[1] Such a provincial interpretation ignores the various types of revivalism which had flourished in Britain as well as in many European countries since the seventeenth century and became one of the strongest religious currents in Scandinavia during the years which witnessed the exodus of more than two million of that region's inhabitants to North America. While some Scandinavian churchmen viewed revivalism as a threat to their ecclesiastical stability, awakenings occurred repeatedly both in the state churches and among the dissenting sects. These revivals led to the formation of the Mission Covenants.

Admittedly, not all of nineteenth-century Scandinavia's revivalism can be traced to European pietism. Returned immigrants who had worked with the eminent American evangelist Dwight L. Moody in Chicago brought his techniques back to the Old World. Through these individuals, who played important roles in the formation of the Danish and Norwegian Mission Covenants, Moody indirectly left his mark on those twin denominations. Their revivalism was consequently more enthusiastic than that of the Swedish Mission Covenant. But even in Norway and Denmark the revivalistic wave of the 1880's which produced the Covenants there drew on a tradition of awakenings which was more than a century old.

The spirit of pietism brought the first significant challenges to Scandinavia's religious homogeneity more than 150 years after the Reformation had introduced a close alliance of the Swedish and Dano-Norwegian monarchies with their respective Lutheran state churches. Between 1690 and 1740 nearly all varieties of German pietism came to these countries. As in central Europe, the predominant forms were the "Halle pietism" associated with August Hermann Francke, which stressed conversion experiences, and the Moravian Brethren's more communitarian "Herrnhut pietism," which Count Nikolaus Ludwig von Zinzendorf founded during the 1720's.

Halle pietism posed little threat to the social order during the age of absolutism. Many clergymen and lay people throughout Scandinavia welcomed its emphasis on the Holy Spirit and experiential religion as a refreshing change from the rigid Lutheran orthodoxy of the seventeenth century. Halle pietism eventually characterized state church Lutheranism in the Nordic countries until the Enlightenment began to make headway in northern Europe later in the eighteenth century. Part of the movement's success in Scandinavia can be attributed to monarchs and their ministers who sought to imbue their realms with its fervor. This was especially true in Denmark, where Frederik IV and his son, Christian VI, tried to anchor the pietistic spirit within the state church. Their efforts also found expression in secular life. The poor law of 1708 aimed at improving social conditions and advancing the country's weak educational system. After the plague of 1711 ravaged Denmark, the government opened an orphanage modelled after Francke's famous institution in Halle. Strict Sabbath laws in the 1720's and 1730's curbed works on Sundays, forbade entertainment on holidays and on the Sabbath, and prescribed penalties for those who failed to attend worship services. Bibles remained in short supply, but inexpensive devotional literature proliferated throughout the kingdom, despite the low literacy rate of the Danish people. True to the absolutist tendencies of the century, the government did its best to keep the resultant awakenings within the established church.

This type of pietism also dominated in Sweden, where Francke and Philip Spener, another important German leader of the movement, had contacts in the 1680's and 1690's. Swedish pietists founded social institutions, promoted revivals, and distributed devotional literature. As in Denmark and Norway, the established ministerium was divided in its attitudes toward this new current. Some actively participated in it, while others pressed for legal measures against what they regarded as a foreign threat to the nation's ecclesiastical stability.

Zinzendorf's Herrnhut pietism also enjoyed royal favor for several years. The count, whose travels eventually took him to North America in the 1740's, visited Copenhagen in 1731. The Danish royal family and other prominent individuals listened attentively to the young nobleman, sharing his plans to organize more religious refuges on the Herrnhut model.[2] Herrnhuter societies sprang up in Denmark and Norway during the next few years. The leading figures in them were usually laymen, although Zinzendorf also had a small number of followers among the clergy.[3] He visited Sweden in 1735, but the Moravians did not reach the apogee of their influence there until the 1750's and 1760's, when they led awakenings in the province of Skåne in southern Sweden.

Much of this mid-century activity violated the Conventicles Edict of 1726, through which Swedish opponents of lay-led pietism had tried to inhibit extra-ecclesiastical religious gatherings. The Edict's notorious second paragraph was directed at colporteurs and läsare, or readers, laymen who conducted worship services in private homes. It read in part:

> But that in private houses men and women, old and young, known and unknown, few or many should have the freedom to congregate under the pretext of practicing

> their piety and particularly to worship and that in these places there should be preaching and exposition of the pericopic texts as well as the explication of prayers and novel prayer practices -- this we consider neither useful nor needful but rather a dangerous novelty, which destroys good order in our Christian congregations and ultimately, under certain circumstances, leads to self-will, abuses, and many serious disorders.[4]

But not even the power of the absolutist state could completely smash lay pietism in Sweden. In Stockholm and a few smaller towns separatist congregations temporarily flourished, and bitter criticism of the established church continued. Nevertheless, the Conventicles Edict and related laws promulgated during the 1730's and 1740's seriously hindered religious meetings outside the state church until the nineteenth century. As we shall see, the dissolution of this legislation allowed numerous dissenting sects to prosper in Sweden.

Some Danish and Norwegian pietistic conventicles also criticized the established clergy, who replied with legal force. A decree of 1732 forbade Biblical exegesis in conventicles in Denmark and Norway (which the Danish Crown ruled until 1814), but it proved to be unenforceable. The Herrnhuters became increasingly radical; some refused to have their children baptized and to participate in the Eucharist with parishioners whom they regarded as unawakened. A few openly separated and organized free congregations. Despite his ecumenicity, Zinzendorf gained a reputation as a separatist in the eyes of the Danish church. Christian VI broke off his relationship with him in 1735. A more telling blow was struck when the Conventicles Edict of 1741 directed the clergy to supervise private religious gatherings and to assure their subordination to the church's regular worship services. Members who failed to appear in church on Sundays forfeited their right to attend conventicles. Pastors were encouraged to gather awakened individuals in their parsonages for supervised Bible readings. At these meetings individuals were allowed to express personal opinions insofar as they did not provoke disputes.[5]

As in Sweden, however, radical pietism erupted in defiance of the law. Harsh criticism of the state church and refusal to participate in its sacraments crested in the 1740's. In the southern Norwegian town of Drammen, for example, Søren Bølle, who had studied theology at the University of Copenhagen but refused to be ordained, led a radical movement called the "Zionites." In 1741 he and several of his followers separated from the Dano-Norwegian state church to form their own free congregation. They denied the efficacy of infant baptism and began to practice believers' baptism in the Drammen River. Their movement soon spread to nearby Christiania (before 1624 and after 1924 called Oslo) and other southern Norwegian communities. But the banishment of Bølle and several other Zionite leaders soon broke the back of separatism, reducing it to a handful of tiny, scattered congregations.[6]

Explicit sectarianism remained negligible for approximately 100 years. Legal reforms in the middle of the nineteenth century brought some measure of toleration, though not complete religious freedom, to those Scandinavians who could not find spiritual homes in their state churches. A few small Quaker meetings, for example, appeared after 1814 when Norwegian sailors who had been incarcerated in England during the Napoleonic Wars brought the faith of the Friends back to Norway. But the brief history of these meetings only emphasizes the Norwegian government's intolerant stance on religious heterogeneity. Persecution of these Quakers forced many into exile; nineteenth-century Norwegian emigration to the United States began in 1825 when Friends and others took the ship "Restauration" from Stavanger to New York City.

During this long period of intolerance, and indeed for several years after the governmental grip on religious life was relaxed, many Scandinavian Lutherans became disenchanted with the condition of their churches. The arm of the law was not sufficiently long to reach all who denounced the cold formalism of the clergy and liturgy. Nor did the pastors' moral turpitude no uncriticized. A Swedish farmer wrote in 1868 that the three divines in his parish included an alcoholic, an avaricious individual more concerned with private business transactions than with preaching, and one reasonably well-behaved but clownish pastor. Even the Swedish archbishop corroborated this estimation of his clergy. He accused them of being profane, heretical, blasphemous, dishonest, lewd, and sacrilegious.[7] Norwegians and Swedes who lived in the sparsely populated northern provinces often lacked even the services of these unsatisfactory clergymen.

The most serious charge levelled at the Scandinavian state churches, however, was that they failed to turn people into Christians. This indictment was rooted in the essential difference between high church and low church ecclesiology. Lutheran national churches since the sixteenth century have regarded themselves as inclusive bodies in which citizen-members are born. This high church inclusiveness remained intact despite criticism by some pietists. Low church ecclesiology, on the other hand, has generally viewed the church as a communion of born-again Christians who have undergone conversion experiences. In this type of church a central duty of the pastor is to make conversions. But to the state church clergy, with some notable exceptions, this was unnecessary. From their viewpoint the church's birthright members were already Christians.

At the beginning of the nineteenth century, therefore, the evangelistic task which most pastors consequently ignored often fell into the hands of lay revivalists. Clearly the most influential of them was the itinerant Norwegian evangelist, Hans Nielsen Hauge. Born in 1771 on a farm near Tuve in the southeastern province of Østfold, he experienced conversion in 1795 and embarked on lengthy revivalistic journeys which took him through much of his homeland and twice to Denmark. Hauge's efforts to reinvigorate the spiritual life of Norway soon prompted the civil and ecclesiastical authorities to invoke the Conventicles Edict against him. Arrested ten times and imprisoned from 1804 until 1811, Hauge died prematurely in 1824. Although his protracted confrontations with the guardians of clerical prerogative left Hauge a broken man, his preaching and books made a tremendous impact on both contemporary and later followers, the Haugianere. Einar Molland has characterized Norwegian church history in the nineteenth and twentieth centuries as the gradual victory of the lay movement which stemmed from Hauge.[8]

It should be noted, however, that despite his frequent clashes with the established church and its clergy, Hauge was avowedly non-separatistic. Although he placed less emphasis on the sacraments than was customary among Lutherans, he implored his adherents to remain within the national church and not organize formal religious societies. Norwegian revivalism heeded Hauge's admonition and remained largely within the established church during most of the century. The absence of a strong, separatistic revival tradition was probably one factor which limited the success of free churches in Norway even after most of the legal barriers against them had fallen.

In the other Nordic countries, however, especially in Sweden, the revivalistic base was broader and encompassed both Lutherans and non-Lutherans, ordained clergymen and lay preachers. In the frontier province of Norrland many conventicles had survived the 1726 Edict; the low ratio of clergymen to parishioners forced awakened laymen to take the initiative in organizing worship services. But even here in the distant North a small number of pastors led the evangelistic work. Lars Levi Læstadius (1800-61), a learned but folksy clergyman, worked among the Lapps, preaching the gospel as well as temperance. He also served non-Lapp Swedes. The followers of Læstadius, who were not representative of Swedish revivalism, became known for their glossolalia and hallucinations. More typical revivalists were Peter Sellergren (1769-1843) and Pehr Nyman (1794-1856), who led more subdued Lutheran awakenings in Småland, Skåne, and other southern areas of Sweden. Their popularity was enormous; even Swedes who lived outside their parishes frequently heard their sermons.[9]

The influence of these latter evangelists was matched by that of George Scott, a Scottish Methodist minister who came to Stockholm in 1830 to serve as a chaplain for British workers in that city. His mission, though, soon spread beyond its original bounds. Scott became fluent in Swedish and began to preach revivalistic sermons to the natives of Stockholm. He helped organize the Swedish Mission Society in 1835 and cooperated with Peter Wieselgren and the American Robert Baird in founding the Swedish Temperance Society. But Scott's direct influence on Swedish religious life was doomed in 1841 when, during a fund-raising trip to the United States, he added his popular voice to the cacophony of criticism of the Swedish church and clergy. This offended many who were still loyal Lutherans, and after he returned to Stockholm, Scott found it impossible to conduct services without being interrupted by hostile mobs. He left Sweden shortly thereafter.[10]

Scott's successor as Sweden's leading evangelist and editor of the widely read newspaper, Pietisten /The Pietist/, was Carl Olof Rosenius (1816-68). Although critical of the state church, Rosenius believed it could be reformed from within and consequently did not condone separatism. Through his publications, Sunday schools, and preaching, he exercised an influence which quickly spread beyond Sweden's borders into Norway and Denmark, where he had followings. The Danish Møllerianere were but one of the groups which either stayed in the state church or returned to it because of his prompting.[11]

In Denmark, the revivalism of the early nineteenth century was even more closely linked to the pietistic heritage. As in Sweden, circles of laymen continued the movement after many of the clergy had followed the Enlightenment into rationalism and become more concerned with reading philosophy than effecting conversions. Several of the lay evangelists who led revivals and organized "holy assemblies" around the beginning of the century had themselves been awakened under the influence of pietism years before. One of the more prominent of these men was Peder Frandsen, a native of Jutland whom pietist pastors had converted in the 1750's. At the close of the century he led a movement which sharply differentiated between awakened and unawakened individuals, often consigning the local clergymen to the latter group.[12] About the same time Herrnhuters constructed their community, Christiansfeld, in southeastern Jutland. From this center lay preachers and colporteurs spread out to all regions of the kingdom. They made their greatest impact on the central island of Fyn, although Brethren congregations were also organized in other areas, including Copenhagen.[13] An undetermined but undoubtedly small number of the Danish clergy also engaged in the evangelistic task. Bone Falch Rønne, a former rationalist and a pastor in Lyngby north of Copenhagen, organized in 1821 the Danish Mission Society, which he modelled after English societies.[14]

The Scandinavian state churches, however, often stood in opposition to these varieties of revivalism. As we have observed, Hauge and Bølle went to jail on account of their lay preaching. In all of the Nordic countries the Conventicles Edicts were used to halt countless other unordained evangelists and dissipate private religious gatherings. Pulpit persuasion was also used against evangelism. Pastors harangued their flocks to stay away from revival meetings which, as in the United States, allegedly induced powerful spasms, jerks, and other manifestations of the "preaching sickness." To opponents of revivalism Satan, not the Holy Spirit, was at work whenever preaching led to these results.[15] Nor did pastors who became evangelistic avoid their more conservative colleagues' criticism. The rationalist Bishop Plum, for instance, joined like-minded clergymen in Zealand in denouncing Rønne's Danish Mission Society.[16]

Revivalism was thus a major factor in Scandinavian religion for several decades before the second half of the nineteenth century, when the free churches began to proliferate rapidly and employ its various forms to win converts. The magnitude of the evangelical impulse is indicated by the fact that E. J. Ekman devoted more than

1,000 pages of his comprehensive study of revivalism in Sweden to the period between 1800 and 1850.[17]

But even the present brief survey of these phenomena in Scandinavia reveals several facts of obvious significance to the subsequent history of free churches in northern Europe. Many Christians were clearly dissatisfied with their state churches and sought spiritual fulfillment outside them. Lay initiative tried to fill some of the gaps which the disenchanted perceived among the clergy. Both Lutherans and non-Lutherans participated in revivalism, although the number of free churches remained minute prior to about 1850. Finally, although most of the revivals appear to have been quiet meetings, some emotional excesses alienated and antagonized state church opponents. For this reason, when British and American forms of evangelization came to Scandinavia later in the nineteenth century, their Lutheran detractors could rely on a rhetorical tradition of long standing when confronting them. But the outsiders could also count on a general familiarity with pietistic revivalism to provide grist for their mill.

CHAPTER III

THE COMING OF RELIGIOUS TOLERATION AND HETEROGENEITY TO SCANDINAVIA

Some measure of religious liberty was a necessary precondition for the birth of the Mission Covenants in Sweden, Norway, and Denmark. Although most of their adherents remained *de jure* members of the established Lutheran churches, the events which led to their founding, such as lay preaching and private communion, would not have been allowed to develop into well-publicized movements in previous times. Scandinavia's steps toward spiritual liberty also facilitated the entry of British and American ideas and practices, and eliminated old barriers to the foreigners who introduced these elements to northern Europe.

Scandinavia's course to religious toleration in the nineteenth century was not an unbroken path, however. Freedom proceeded slowly in all three countries. In retrospect, it sometimes seems to have taken alternating forward and backward steps. By 1860 most Swedes, Norwegians, and Danes could worship as they saw fit, but many state church pastors, some lay leaders, and other individuals who clung to the ideal of religious conformity in a corporate state vociferously opposed all measures which benefitted those whose spiritual roads did not lead to the Lutheran parish churches.

The Swedish constitution of 1809 paid lip service to the principle of religious freedom, but in practice little was changed from the preconstitutional period of absolutism. Indeed, in some respects legal codification further restricted liberties. Civil servants, for example, were required to be Lutherans. During the 1850's another piece of legislation restricted sacramental liberties. It forbade individuals from receiving communion from clergymen who were not their own parish pastors and also prohibited laymen from administering the sacraments.[1] Efforts to enforce these laws, however, together with the deportation of several Swedes who had converted to Roman Catholicism, aroused indignation both at home and abroad. Yielding to criticism, the Swedish government abolished the Conventicles Edict in 1858. A year later the sacrament law was also struck from the books over the protests of the clergy. In 1860 a further measure of religious freedom was granted; Swedes were allowed to withdraw from the state church, but only if they transferred their affiliation to another religious society which the dissenter law recognized. Seceders did, however, get certain reductions in their church taxes.

In Norway, which in 1814 gained independence from Denmark only to be subordinated in a personal union with the Swedish Crown, religious liberty came only slightly more rapidly. As Einar Molland has pointed out, the principle of spiritual freedom contended with the desire to create a religiously united nation-state at the Eidsvoll constitutional convention in 1814.[2] The latter emerged victorious and the Lutheran church was established as the official religion of the land. Initially there was no provision for leaving it, and parents were required to have their children baptized as Lutherans. The constitution also explicitly excluded

Jesuits and monastic orders from Norway, and further prohibited the admission of Jews. Moreover, as in Sweden, all civil servants were required to be members of the established church, a stricture which gradually disappeared during the nineteenth and twentieth centuries. Finally, although Norway was no longer subject to Danish rule, the 1741 Conventicles Edict remained in force.

During the next three decades, however, liberal reforms undermined this rigid ecclesiastical structure.[3] Liberals like Søren A. W. Sørensen called for a law granting freedom of worship to all Christian groups. On the other hand, the conservative jurist Claus Winther Hjelm (1797-1871) drafted in 1840 a law which prescribed stiff penalties for proselytism and public worship by non-Lutherans, separation from the established church, and various other manifestations of religious freedom.[4] Owing to widespread opposition, however, including that of Jens Lauritz Seip, who subsequently became bishop of Christiania, this proposal was handily defeated. Over the opposition of the theology faculty at Christiania's new university, a large number of pastors, and other governmental officials, the liberals and Haugian pietists succeeded in getting the Conventicles Edict abrogated in 1842. The following year Roman Catholics gained the right to form a church in the nation's capital, although their religious processions remained forbidden and prejudice against the denomination continued to be strong.[5] An equally important piece of legislation was the 1845 dissenter law.[6] This act made it possible for Norwegians, for the first time in history, to quit their state church. In contrast to its Swedish counterpart, the law did not stipulate that those who withdrew had to establish membership in a recognized free church. The dissenter law also made it possible for all Christian societies to hold worship services and distribute religious propaganda. It stated, though, that these freedoms were contingent on the dissenters' willingness to remain within the bounds of common morality, a provision with which Mormon polygamy came into conflict during the 1850's. Finally, those who severed their ties with the state church were relieved of the church tax burden. Few, however, left the Lutheran establishment, despite the pecuniary motivation for doing so. According to the census of 1865, only 5,105 people were outside the state church.[7] It may be significant that Haugian farmers, despite their indigence, generally opposed adoption of the 1845 law.[8] They cherished national Lutheranism more than the ideal of religious freedom.

Denmark's experiment with a liberal monarchy and spiritual liberty was more dramatic. It began in March, 1848, when a revolution in Copenhagen terminated the nation's age of absolutism. The Danes received their first constitution a year later. It maintained the established status of the Lutheran church, but granted basic religious freedoms in harmony with general nineteenth-century liberalism. "The citizens have the right to unite and worship God in accordance with their convictions," stated Paragraph 81, "but nothing may be taught or done which violates morality or public order." Those who seceded from the state church were freed from church taxes only if they joined recognized free churches. Paragraph 83 stated that a law would be passed to regulate the nonconformist communions, but such a dissenter law was never enacted. In practice, however, the government recognized some churches, such as the Methodists, and empowered them to conduct marriages and other legal functions, but refused to recognize others, including Baptists, Mormons, and the Catholic Apostolic Church.

Foreign sects lost little time before they began to proselytize in Scandinavia. Unfortunately for subsequent dissenters, the Church of Jesus Christ of Latter-day Saints became one of the first groups to do so in the 1850's. Mormon missionaries incurred the wrath of the Scandinavian Lutheran clergy, making the religious establishments in all of the Nordic lands even more hostile to nonconformists than they had been previously.

The history of Mormon missions to the Scandinavians can be traced to the 1840's when the Saints began to work among Norwegians and Swedes in northern Illinois. This early proselytizing was interrupted, however, when mob action forced the Mormons to abandon their temple city of Nauvoo, Illinois and begin the 1847 trek to Utah. Missionary activities were resumed aften an 1849 conference in Salt Lake City resulted in the commissioning of Erastus Snow, Peter Hansen, and John Forsgren for work in Denmark and Sweden.[9] Hansen, who had emigrated from Denmark in 1844, translated the <u>Book of Mormon</u>

into Danish at the behest of Brigham Young and returned to his native land in 1850. He began the barrage of Latter-day Saint propaganda in Scandinavia with a brief tract titled En Advarsel til Folket [A Warning to the People], which was published there the same year.[10] Within a few months of his arrival in Copenhagen, Hansen gathered a Mormon congregation of fifty members and gained permission from the city's Board of Magistrates to hold worship services.[11] Forsgren, on the other hand, was less hospitably received when he returned to Sweden, where the Conventicles Edict and other laws restricting lay religious activity were still in force. He was promptly arrested and deported after baptizing a group of farmers in his hometown, Gefle. Fleeing to the less oppressive political climate of Copenhagen, Forsgren began to proselytize among Zealand Swedes.

The work of these two men marked only the beginning of a long and, in some respects, successful campaign to win Nordic converts to the Church of Jesus Christ of Latter-day Saints. The focal point of Mormon proselytism among Scandinavians remained in Denmark even after missionaries had gained footholds in Sweden and Norway. Most of the early Mormon literature was translated into Danish before it appeared in the other Scandinavian languages, and prior to the 1880's no more than six of the church's missionaries worked simultaneously in Norway or twelve in Sweden. The number of Mormons sent to the Danish field easily outstripped these figures. Some headway was made in Sweden during the last two decades of the century when the

Swedish government further relaxed its restraints on proselytism,[12] but 50% of the Scandinavians who converted to the Mormon faith between 1850 and 1905 were Danes. Of the other half, 36% were Swedes, and only 14% Norwegians.[13] During the same period approximately 21,000 Scandinavian Mormons emigrated to North America, 12,350 of whom were Danes.[14]

Neither the Lutheran state churches nor the Scandinavian governments accepted passively these Mormon incursions. Both legal means and the rhetoric of the pulpit and the press were marshalled against the unwanted proselytizers. In Norway, for example, the Supreme Court declared the Church of Jesus Christ of Latter-day Saints to be a non-Christian religious society and as such outside the protection of the 1845 dissenter law.[15] Sporadic police action against Mormon missionaries resulted. In Fredrikshald (now Halden) a trio of them were arrested in 1867 and fined for conducting "illegal religious activities;" one of the three was further sentenced to twenty days in jail on bread and water.[16] Harsh punishments of this sort, however, appear to have been the exception rather than the rule.

More frequently, Lutheran clergymen lectured on the Mormons or debated them publicly. The latter practice set a precedent, and was used quite often as a means of confronting subsequent proselytism by Protestant free churches. In Norway, it began at least as early as February, 1855, when the Grundtvigian pastor Ole Vig did verbal battle with the Latter-day Saints in Christiania.[17]

A still more frequent method of attack was through the printed word. Like their counterparts in the United States, Scandinavian Protestants quickly penned a body of anti-Mormon literature which equalled the American material in vituperativeness, if not in quantity. Bearing such titles as _Et Aar i Utah eller En Dames Rejse til Mormonstaten, hendes Ophold dér og Flugt derfra_ [A Year in Utah or a Lady's Trip to the Mormon State, Her Stay There, and Escape] and _Oplysninger om Mormonsamfundet i Utah, deres Løgne og Bedragerier_ [Information Regarding the Mormon Society in Utah, Their Lies and Frauds], thousands of tracts and books flowed from the presses from the 1850's until well into the twentieth century. Like the American anti-Mormon propaganda, it often focused on polygamy, easily the most emotional issue in the campaign. But Scandinavian foes of the Saints also devoted a considerable amount of space to the Mormon sacrament of baptism. Those unacquainted with Lutheran history may have difficulty understanding why the Mormon practice of baptizing converts who had already been baptized as infants in Protestant churches caused such a fervor. In the Lutheran tradition hostility to rebaptism is deeply rooted and can be traced back to persecutions of Anabaptists in the 1520's. Protestant dissenters who refused to recognize the efficacy of infant baptism also enraged Scandinavian Lutherans, especially the Baptists, who spread quite rapidly in Scandinavia after 1850 and soon became one of the largest nonconformist groups in Denmark, Norway, and especially Sweden.

The early history of the Baptists there reveals that religious freedom had not progressed uniformly in the Nordic countries. Like the Mormons, they owed their existence in northern Europe to foreign influences, although they drew on both the Anglo-American and European pietist revival traditions. Danish Baptism came into being in the late 1830's, before the advent of religious liberty in Denmark. Julius Købner (1806-84), a Jew who converted to Christianity and had already been baptized in Lübeck, came under the influence of the German Baptist preacher Johann Gerhard Oncken (1800-84) of Hamburg, who baptized him again in 1836. Oncken himself had been baptized by an American Baptist, Barnas Sears, in Germany two years earlier.[18] Købner returned to his native country and began to win converts to his new faith. Among them was the Copenhagen engraver, Peder Christian Mønster, who organized the capital's first Baptist congregation in 1839.

Although this society numbered only eleven members, it soon aroused the opposition of the Lutheran establishment. A royal decree of 1842 ordered Baptist parents to submit their children for baptism in the state church. Many refused to do so. The 1741 Conventicles Edict and a 1745 ordinance against separatists and Anabaptists were invoked against them. In a report to Bishop Mynster, Dean E. C. Tryde of Copenhagen revealed another reason why the state church opposed the Baptists. Their individualism and personal interpretation of the Scriptures, he wrote, threatened the unity and stability of the national church.[19] The 1849 constitution, however, recognized the existence of religious pluralism in Denmark and halted compulsory infant baptism. The sect grew rapidly after it gained legal toleration. By 1887 it had 2,299 members, a figure which climbed to 3,310 by 1894.[20]

Across the Øresund in Sweden, Baptists had considerably more conflicts with the law, and their fight for liberty did not end nearly so soon. A Danish preacher, E. M. Førster , baptized the members of the first congregation in 1848. Its early growth elicited strong clerical reaction. "Watch out for the Baptists," warned one Lutheran pastor. "They are so erroneous they are on their way to hell. . . ." Baptists' indictments of the state church were equally harsh. Some designated it as "Babylon" and called its clergymen "squires of the devil."[21] In 1850 Fredrik Olaus Nilsson, one of the first congregation's leaders and a returned emigrant who had partaken the free church spirit in the United States, was arrested for violation of the Conventicles Edict and deported. Court records reveal that from 1851 to 1854 637 people in the provinces of Hälsingland and Dalarna were fined because they proclaimed Baptist views.[22] But persecution did not check the denomination's advance in Sweden. By 1860 it numbered approximately 4,500 members, a figure which climbed rapidly to 37,601 in 552 congregations in 1894.[23]

As we have seen, most legal restrictions on religious liberty had fallen in Norway during the 1840's. Hence, when the Baptist faith first appeared there in 1860, it encountered fewer civil obstacles. Frederik L. Rymker (1819-94), a former Danish sailor from Odense who had become a Baptist during a revival in New York, gathered the denomination's first Norwegian congregation. Its eight members had seceded from Gustav Lammers' free church in Skien over the question of baptism.[24] Despite the relative weakness of legal hindrances, the denomination grew more slowly in Norway than in Sweden. in 1865 there were reportedly only 300 Norwegian Baptists.[25] The Baptist Union, formed in 1877, encompassed fourteen congregations during its first year. When the century drew to a close there were only 2,671 Norwegian Baptists in thirty-two congregations.[27] Nevertheless, the Lutheran press was alarmed and kept a keen eye on the Baptists, whom it regarded as a threat to the supposed homogeneity of Christianity in Norway. Newspapers like Luthersk Kirketidende also sounded the alarm whenever their editors detected Baptist advances in Sweden.[28]

The chief legal obstacle which Baptist proselytizers confronted in Norway was a provision of the 1845 dissenter law which prohibited people under the age of nineteen from leaving the established church. This paragraph did not, however, prevent Baptists from immersing minors, despite the legal harassment to which they were consequently subjected. As late as 1888 at least twenty-five Baptists were convicted for baptizing minors, and many of them served short jail sentences on bread and water.[29]

Denominations which recognized infant baptism were generally not quite so vehemently opposed in Norway, Sweden, and Denmark as those which did not. The Methodists, who were revivalistic and often accused of proselytizing, but accepted pedo-baptism, thus illustrate another aspect of trans-Atlantic and inter-Scandinavian religious influences.

The founder of Norwegian Methodism was a sailor, Ole Petersen (1822-1901), who had been exposed to Methodist preaching in the Bethel ship mission in New York in the 1840's. Shortly after his change of faith, Petersen returned to southern Norway and held revival meetings in Fredrikstad and Sarpsborg, then in 1850 went back to the United States and began to preach to Scandinavians in New York harbor. Three years later Petersen was ordained and sailed back to Norway. In 1856 he organized that country's first Methodist church, a congregation of forty-three members in Sarpsborg. American Methodists commissioned a Danish immigrant, Christian Willerup, to assist Petersen. Progress was initially slow, although legally unimpeded; during the first decade about eight Methodist churches were gathered. According to the census of 1865, there were 987 Methodists in Norway. By 1891, however, the number had risen to 8,187.[30]

After working with Petersen for two years, Willerup returned to Denmark and began to hold well-attended revival meetings in Copenhagen. The energetic preacher, who had begun his pulpit career among Scandinavians in the Midwest, soon organized a Methodist congregation in the Danish capital. Owing largely to his efforts, the government officially recognized the denomination in 1865.[31]

Only in Sweden did the Methodists encounter much resistance. Although most legal obstacles to free church activities had disappeared when the Swedish-American pastor, Victor Witting (1825-1906), returned to his native land to build up the infant denomination, his efforts and those of his colleagues occasionally became the targets of mob violence and legal chicaneries. Nevertheless, the Methodists gained official recognition as a dissenting denomination in 1876. At that time they numbered 5,663 members.[32]

This does not, of course, exhaust the list of foreign denominations which set up shop in the Scandinavian countries. In addition to the British and American millenarian sects which we shall examine in Chapter V, such diverse groups as Quakers and Unitarians also came to northern Europe, although they failed to make significant impacts on the religious life of the Scandinavian peoples. The Salvation Army marched into Sweden in 1882 and within six years had also entered Denmark and Norway. It still exists on an active basis in all three countries.

Not all of the free churches were imported from abroad. Despite their efforts to preserve religious uniformity, the state churches had themselves spawned dissenting groups in all of the Nordic lands. Some of these indigenous denominations retained the "Lutheran" label and regarded themselves, rather than the inclusive state churches, as the authentic heirs of the Reformation.

Others abandoned the Lutheran name and theology. Both types, however, fought rhetorical battles with the established churches.

Although Swedish Lutheranism did not experience any major schisms before the Mission Covenant came into being in 1878, the so-called "hyper-evangelism" associated with Fredrik Gabriel Hedberg (1811-93) divided part of the church into rival camps in the late 1840's. This Swede-Finn, who labored in northern Sweden, protested against modifications in the state church's hymnal and catechism which he regarded as steps in the direction of Arminianism. He accused Rosenius, who had cooperated with the Methodist George Scott only a few years earlier, of being a prophet of this deviation from the central Lutheran doctrine of justification by faith alone. Hedberg began to publish a newspaper in Stockholm, _Evangelisten_, to compete with Rosenius' _Pietisten_.[33] Some of his followers avowedly professed separatism from the impure state church and formed their own congregation in the Swedish capital. Under the pressure of the Conventicles Edict and compulsory use of the controversial hymnal and catechism, many emigrated to the United States. The Hedbergian movement failed to become a free church in its own right, but it formed a basis for the Baptists in Sweden.

In Denmark, on the other hand, a pair of free Lutheran denominations emerged in the 1850's and 1860's. Niels Pedersen Grunnet (1827-97) organized the first of these, the Evangelical Lutheran Free Church, in Copenhagen in 1855. Grunnet had been trained at the Basel Mission School, but after returning to Denmark came into conflict with the state church and fell under the influence of Søren Kierkegaard's harshest attacks on it. Following a heated controversy regarding his future as an overseas missionary, Grunnet severed his relationship with the established church and gathered his own congregation. Vigorous opposition from the Copenhagen clergy did not prevent him from assembling about a dozen similar groups during the next decade and erecting a sanctuary in Copenhagen in 1877. The denomination, which still exists, has never numbered more than a few hundred members. But it reached beyond Denmark's borders to establish relations with the conservative Evangelical Lutheran Free Church in Saxony as well as the Missouri Synod Lutherans in the United States. Its polity is congregational, while theologically it stresses loyalty to the Lutheran confessions and Biblical literalism.[34]

The Lutheran Mission Association, on the other hand, although originally an independent denomination, eventually became a society within the Danish state church. Like the Evangelical Lutheran Free Church, it traces its history to the 1850's, although it was not officially constituted until 1868. Peter Christian Trandberg (1832-96), perhaps the nineteenth century's most restless Danish pastor, formed a personal bridge from the Free Church to the Mission Association. Like many other young Danes who studied theology at the University of Copenhagen in the 1850's, he avidly read Kierkegaard's works and added his voice to the cacophony of criticism. Trandberg's disenchantment with the state church, however, did not alter his plans to be ordained one of its pastors in 1858. After serving for two years as a chaplain in

Viborg, Trandberg returned to his birthplace, Bornholm, a Baltic island far to the east of the rest of Denmark.

This rocky isle soon became fertile ground for religious dissent. Trandberg stirred the fervor of the Bornholmers through revival meetings, at which he demanded dramatic conversions and often lashed out at his more languid colleagues. Bishop Hans Lassen Martensen visited the island in 1862 and found Trandberg's evangelistic techniques "methodistic." The fiery revivalist responded by suggesting that the "Babylon" of Revelation included not only the Roman Catholic Church, but also the Danish national church.[35] One state church pastor returned the favor by terming Trandberg "a brother of the devil."[36] Fearing that Trandberg's revivals would divide their congregations, many other clergymen barred him from their pulpits. Their fears were not without foundation. On June 21, 1863, five months after he had opened a tiny seminary on the island, Trandberg held a large outdoor rally on Bornholm and announced his withdrawal from the state church. A week later he sailed to Copenhagen and joined Grunnet's Evangelical Lutheran Free Church. Upon returning to Bornholm Trandberg organized a free congregation with nearly 1,000 members.[37]

Tranquility never characterized the Bornholm free church. Born in controversy and subjected to the rhetorical abuse of the resentful state church clergy, it lost little time before tearing itself apart. In 1864 Trandberg and Grunnet quarrelled over a Swedish student whose questionable moral background bothered Grunnet, but whom Trandberg nevertheless allowed to preach to his congregation.

Grunnet protested vigorously; Trandberg overreacted by denying the Copenhagener access to the church's prayer hall. But not all of Trandberg's parishioners agreed with this rash action. A faction led by Hans Christian Møller (1834-1907), a blacksmith whom Trandberg was preparing for the ministry, sided with Grunnet. Only a few months after this crisis Møller discovered Rosenius' Swedish newspaper, Pietisten, and soon began to preach the Swede's doctrine of the atonement, which Trandberg rejected as non-Lutheran "cheap grace." An irreparable breach ensued. The majority of the Bornholm free church members supported the popular Trandberg. A large minority, however, heeded Rosenius' advice and followed Møller back to the Danish state church. These Møllerianere formed the nucleus of what became known as the Lutheran Mission Association.

Not all of the Danish free churches and religious societies, of course, professed to be heirs of the Lutheran Reformation. The churches which Mogens Abraham Sommer (1829-1901) gathered, indirect ancestors of the Danish Mission Covenant, denounced the Lutheran label.[38] Sommer, like Trandberg, was a restless character, but in contrast to his more famous countryman, was never satisfied with his lot in life. Born into a Jewish family which had emigrated from Germany to Denmark by way of Norway and Iceland during the eighteenth century, Sommer was baptized and confirmed in the Danish Lutheran Church. He underwent a conversion experience on Good Friday in 1849 and shortly thereafter began to offer free religious instruction, distribute tracts, sell Christian literature, and operate a free lending library. He conducted all of these activities in addition to his remunerative employment as a homeopathic physician and teacher in Haderslev, a community in southern Jutland.

In the mid-1850's Sommer began to read Søren Kierkegaard's periodical, Øjeblikket /The Instant/, and in 1855, shortly before the young philosopher died, went to Copenhagen to confer with him. When Sommer's fascination with Kierkegaard's assault on the state church brought him into conflict with the clergy in Haderslev, he resigned his teaching position and began his fateful career as a preacher and organizer of independent congregations in Denmark. Within three years Sommer had gathered several small churches in Jutland communities as well as a larger congregation in Copenhagen. In 1858 the Norwegian free church leader Gustav Lammers came to Denmark and ordained Sommer. For reasons which are not fully clear, however, the cooperation between the two proved to be short-lived. By 1860 the Dane had fallen out with Lammers. The following year he left his free churches in a state of disorganization and made his first trip to the United States. Sommer returned to Denmark and worked both as an emigration agent and independent revivalist, but resigned his position as head of "The Free Apostolic Churches in Denmark." His subsequent activities as a homeopath and evangelist brought him to the New World again for a longer stay and back to Denmark, where he joined the socialist party. But even here Sommer found it impossible to work harmoniously with other leaders, and was expelled from the rolls.

The Danish Mission Covenant was one of the heirs of this

stormy episode in the nation's religious history. A quarter of a century after Sommer dissolved his relationship with the congregations which he had gathered, the Covenant inherited some of the remnants of his movement. The denomination's historian has asserted that "many" of Sommer's followers affiliated with the Covenant when it was organized in places where the erratic Dane had led awakenings.[39] The absence of detailed records of these loosely organized congregations, though, precludes any systematic analysis of the historical link between Sommer's revivals and those which immediately antedated the birth of the Danish Mission Covenant in 1888.

The relationship between mid-century Norwegian separatism and the Norwegian Mission Covenant was a more direct continuity, although as in Denmark the chief agitator of the 1850's abandoned the free churches which he had organized. Gustav Adolph Lammers (1802-78) was born in Copenhagen, the son of a Danish military officer and his Norwegian wife. The family soon moved to Norway, however, and he received his education, including a theology degree at the new University of Christiania, in that country. Ordained a pastor in the Norwegian state church, Lammers served congregations in Trondheim and Bamble before being called to the southern Norwegian community of Skien in 1848. As one historian of the Norwegian lay movement has observed, the Haugian revivalist spirit had long pervaded this town.[40] Lammers meshed well with the community's mood and soon began an awakening. At his behest even Skien's dance halls closed. In 1853 Lammers organized a domestic mission society to distribute tracts, the first of its kind in Norway. The religious fervor which dominated the parish's life remained uncontroversial until the mid-1850's, when Lammers discovered Kierkegaard's periodical. Apparently impressed by the critical Dane's attacks on the state church, he held a lecture in Christiania early in 1856 in which he vehemently criticized the Norwegian ecclesiastical structure and clergy. This speech drew a sharp rebuke from Bishop Arup, who warned Lammers to restrict his public speaking to his own district. No longer inclined to take orders from his superiors, Lammers resigned his pastorate and, accompanied by twenty-three of his parishioners, withdrew from the state church. They organized "The Free Apostolic Christian Church in Skien" on July 4, 1856. Its constitution set this new congregation off from the state church in many respects. It denied the existence of a special clergy, although it urged that the chairman be a university graduate. It also provided that elders were to conduct the congregation's business. Finally, the authors of the constitution declared that "because faith must precede baptism, we dissociate ourselves from infant baptism."[41]

These two dozen residents of Skien were not the only Norwegians who withdrew from the state church in the spring of 1856. At the same time a farmer from Balsfjorden in northern Norway, Johan A. J. Bomsta, who had held revival meetings in his hometown and neighboring communities, and a group of his supporters seceded and formed an independent body which they called "The Apostolic Church."[42] In nearby Tromsø more than 100 people withdrew and organized "The Free Apostolic Christian Church in Tromsø."[43] The Norwegian Mission Covenant has always regarded these secessionists, and others in several other communities, as its spiritual ancestors.

It is not fully understood why these secessions occurred almost simultaneously in northern and southern Norway, although one apparent factor was Søren Kierkegaard's radical attack on the religious establishment. The Dane's pamphlet series, Øjeblikket, was read throughout Norway soon after it appeared. Writing in Theologisk Tidsskrift for den evangelisk-lutherske Kirke i Norge (an important state church periodical) in 1859, Hans Blom, rector of a school in Tromsø, attributed that town's religious turmoil to the popularity of Kierkegaard's works. A much-needed revival had renewed the inhabitants' interest in Christianity, he stated, but "in 1854 S. Kierkegaard's Øieblikket began to come up here, and it was read with enthusiasm by many people, both the privileged and the least mature." "Kierkegaard's acid pen," Blom asserted, "killed the last bit of love they had for the old church. . . ."[44] Lammers agreed that Kierkegaard's works had played a key role in creating an atmosphere of dissatisfaction with the state church in Tromsø.[45]

On the other hand, there is no direct evidence that Øjeblikket stimulated the secession which Johan Bomsta led in Balsfjorden. Indeed, when he described his withdrawal many years after the fact, Bomsta insisted that it resulted from six years of reflection about the nature of the church. He admitted, however, that only in 1855 -- the year Øjeblikket became available in Norway -- did the possibility of organizing a church on an apostolic basis become a "burning question" for him. Bomsta asserted that his decision to withdraw from the established church was made before he heard of Lammers.[46]

In any case, it is clear that these free congregations and thirty-odd others in Norway cooperated fairly closely after they were organized. Bomsta, for example, went to Norway soon after his congregation in Balsfjorden had been set on firm ground, and assisted in the organization of independent churches at Bergen and other communities.[47] No less significantly, Lammers helped gather several free congregations, especially in southern Norway, and in 1857 left his Skien congregation to spend a year with the previously pastorless group in Tromsø. He thereby served as a personal link between like-minded seceders in northern and southern Norway.

During his absence the question of baptism polarized the rapidly growing church in Skien. One faction, led by Søren Tufte, who served as the congregation's spiritual leader in Lammers' absence, insisted on believers' baptism. They argued that the constitution's explicit rejection of infant baptism justified their position. Despite this constitutional provision, however, the majority of the members apparently opposed Tufte's insistence on re-baptism. Lammers, who always retained many elements of his Lutheran theology, aligned himself with the larger faction when he returned from Tromsø, and Tufte was excommunicated. Nearly two dozen of his supporters followed Tufte out of the congregation. They formed "The Christian Dissenter Church," but adopted the constitution of Lammers' congregation as their own.

The departure of some of the best educated and wealthiest members of his congregation apparently disillusioned Lammers. Speaking to the remaining members in November, 1860, he admitted that it had been a mistake to withdraw from the state church.[48] Later that year Lammers re-entered it, but he was never again given a pastorate. Only nine of the seceders in Skien immediately followed him back to the established church.[49]

The loss of Lammers was an undeniable blow to the young free church movement in Norway. But most of the approximately three dozen "free apostolic" churches continued to offer an alternative to state church Lutheranism. They sought to consolidate their work through a series of national conferences in 1863, 1870, 1874, 1877, and 1882. These meetings, which were structural roots of the Norwegian Mission Covenant, confirmed the autonomy of the local bodies but united them in a loose confederation headed by a steering committee. Delegates discussed methods of increasing the independent churches' effectiveness in evangelization, but little appears to have accomplished before a Swedish-American, Fredrik Franson, ignited a new revival in Norway in 1883.[50]

State church Lutherans denounced the Lammers free church movement from its inception. When Lammers went to northern

Norway to lead the congregation in Tromsø, a local newspaper, Tromsø Tidende, warned its readers to avoid him. "We must suppress our curiosity and not run after things which do not concern us, but rather remain in our own congregation."[51] From Christiania the Lutheran press kept a sharp eye on events in Skien. In 1864 Luthersk Kirketidende gleefully reported that "a family which had been in the free congregation since its beginning, but has now allowed itself to be persuaded by the truth and has returned to the [state] church, presented three children for the sacrament of holy baptism on Sunday, December 27."[52] Two years later the same periodical informed its readers that Søren Tufte had died, and suggested that his small Christian Dissenter Church was hot on his heels toward the grave.[53] Furthermore, the Norwegian Lutheran press seldom passed up an opportunity to comment on free churchmen's occasional violations of the 1845 dissenter law, such as re-baptizing minors without parental consent.[54] The harsh diction used in these reports echoed complaints which could also be heard in Sweden and Denmark, where nonconformists were also threatening the monopolies which the state churches had on religious life.

In all three countries Lutheran leaders organized domestic missionary societies to occupy pastoral gaps which the free churches were either filling or threatening to fill. Rapid population growth in all of the Scandinavian countries created an increasingly critical clerical shortage. The ratio was widest in Norway, where by 1825 there were approximately 3,000 laymen for each pastor in the state church. By 1910 this ratio had widened to nearly 3,300 to one. In Denmark and Sweden clergymen were not quite so scarce, but nevertheless the average flock reached about 1,800 laymen in both countries by 1900.[55] The domestic missionary societies were conceived as one means of reaching the vast numbers of laymen who consequently had little personal contact with their clergymen. In Sweden the Evangelical National Foundation began this task in 1856. The Norwegian Luther Society came into being twelve years later with the Christiania systematic theologian Gisle Johnson as its chairman. In Denmark the Inner Mission began to play a similar role in 1861, adding an evangelistic third wing to Danish Lutheranism, which was already split into the romantic, nationalistic party identified with N.S.F. Grundtvig and the rationalist, Hegelian party led by Bishop Hans Lassen Martensen.[56]

The activities of all these societies were essentially similar, and perhaps most clearly illustrated by the Inner Mission in Denmark, where the challenges to the state church appear to have been most acute. It constructed churches, especially in rapidly industrializing Copenhagen. The Inner Mission also sought to divert the working class from socialism, which came to Denmark in the 1870's. Social work, including temperance campaigns and homes for children and unwed mothers, augmented this urban task. In the capital city this program was conducted through the Copenhagen Inner Mission after 1865.

Internationally, the Danish Inner Mission cooperated with the YMCA World Alliance until 1888 when chairman Vilhelm Beck discovered that continued membership in that organization required that non-Lutheran Danes be admitted to the Danish affiliate. Because this ecumenicity would have undermined one purpose of the Inner Mission, the Danes withdrew and established a Scandinavian Youth Fellowship.

Although the domestic mission societies existed to preserve the vitality of the state churches, some Lutheran clergymen resented the sometimes abrasive efforts of their leaders to prod the establishment to greater activity. Their use of colporteurs and lay preachers -- offices associated with the free churches -- also drew criticism. In a passage which reveals more about his own defensiveness than about the actual free church situation in Denmark, Vilhelm Beck of the Inner Mission retrospectively observed that "many pastors suddenly became prophets as a result of this new movement. They were especially fond of conjuring up the spectre of sectarianism. . . ." Perhaps oversimplifying the _raison d'etre_ of his organization, he added that "it is an incontestable fact that the Inner Mission has been a strong bulwark against sectarianism, which has made no appreciable inroads in Denmark. At the time when the Inner Mission was founded, the sects were about to gain a foothold among the people; but the confidence which the Inner Mission soon gained in our country made it difficult for them to make any headway." Beck explicitly denied that his organization was another sect in Denmark, remarking that the "Inner Mission always carried on its activities within the [state] church and gradually gained the cooperation of its believing pastors."[57] In Christiania, however, fourteen of the city's pastors declared their opposition to the analogous Luther Society before it was even officially constituted.[58]

Liturgical reform was another front on which some churchmen hoped to fight growing popular indifference to the established churches. Religious dissenters had frequently expressed dissatisfaction with the formalism of Lutheran worship, and usually made their own liturgies less structured than those of the state churches. When clergymen from all three Scandinavian countries convened in Copenhagen in 1871 for their periodic Nordic church council, they discussed the question "To what extent will modification of the Lutheran church's liturgy promote livelier participation on the part of the congregation?" All who took part in the discussion agreed that liturgical changes were desirable; one pastor suggested that a complete restructuring would be more appropriate.[59] Little action was taken, however, and the Lutheran liturgy continued to be characterized by a much higher degree of formalism and less lay participation than were found in most of the free churches. This proved to be a continuing liability in the state churches' struggle to preserve religious unity in Scandinavia.

Despite the enthusiastic claims of Beck and his colleagues regarding their successes in reinvigorating the established churches and staving off the advancing sects, neither of these goals was fully achieved. If church attendance can be accepted as one index of religious vitality, apathy grew steadily among nominally Lutheran Scandinavians. One historian has estimated that during the last years of the nineteenth century only 6,000 of Copenhagen's 160,000 residents attended worship services regularly. In Norway, laments about poor church attendance and widespread irreligiosity were frequent by the 1880's.[60]

The proliferation of sects also progressed unchecked. In addition to the Mission Covenants, such groups as the Jehovah's Witnesses and the Pentecostals either arose in Scandinavia or were imported around the turn of the century. In Norway, the Evangelical Lutheran Free Church sprang from the state church in the late 1870's. It remained the country's largest dissenting religious group until the Pentecostals surpassed it in the 1930's.[61]

The Norwegian Lutheran Free Church played an important role in preparing the ground for the formation in 1884 of the Norwegian Mission Covenant. It owed its existence largely to the dissatisfaction of two pastors with the state church. Johan Storm Munch (1827-1908) had been a pastor among Norwegians in the United States during the 1850's. While in the New World he appears to have been impressed with the revivalism which characterized much of American Protestantism at that time. After returning to his homeland, Munch bitterly opposed the inclusiveness of its established church, and suggested that the faith of its members be examined before they were allowed to participate in communion. Munch's superiors disagreed. He resigned his pastorate in 1875 and gathered a congregation of approximately 400 followers in protest in Christiania. Paul Peter Wettergreen (1835-89), one of his closest associates, also resigned his pastorate in the state church. The two men organized several other local bodies of dissenters, and in 1878 their movement won legal recognition as a nonconformist sect. Both Wettergreen and Munch had visited the Scottish Free Church, from which they borrowed presbyterian polity. The new denomination's theology, however, remained essentially Lutheran. Some of its early leaders, including Wettergreen and Peder Tallaksen (1843-1912) of Christiania, were caught up in the millenarian fervor which swept across the country in the 1880's. By 1898 the Lutheran Free Church encompassed twenty-nine congregations in three presbyteries, most of them in southern Norway, where the Norwegian Mission Covenant also had its greatest strength.[62]

Søren Kierkegaard's relentless attacks on the state church and its clergy echoed and re-echoed in all corners of northern Europe during the second half of the nineteenth century. But while the melancholy Dane regarded himself as essentially a defender of Christianity, many of his followers and other dissentients were prepared to dispense with orthodoxy or indeed with the Christian faith altogether. These iconoclasts sparked bitter verbal duels with defensive church leaders, who were already feeling the pressure of such secular forces of modernity as Darwinism and urbanization. The impact which these critics of Christendom had on religious life when the Mission Covenants were organized requires that we examine them more closely.

Søren Kierkegaard (1813-55) was born into a prosperous and pious Copenhagen family. During his student days at the city's university he came under the influence of two philosophy professors, Paul Martin Møller and Frederik Christian Sibbern, both of whom had declared their aversion to systematic philosophy. Sibbern, in fact, preferred to express himself through fiction. From the start Kierkegaard was a champion of the free will. He insisted that it is incumbent on each individual to make conscious, responsible choices throughout life. This central tenet of Kierkegaard's thought diametrically opposed the determinism of Hegelianism, the dominant European philosophy of that time. Kierkegaard would probably have remained a minor figure in the history of Christianity if many prominent Danish churchmen had not been advocates of "the system," as Hegel magisterially termed his own all-encompassing philosophy. To the young Dane, it appeared that his country's pastors had abandoned the uniqueness of Christianity by incorporating it into this system and had ruled out the possibility of faith by equating thought and existence in Hegelian fashion. Moreover, he believed that Denmark's clergymen, comfortable in their status as civil servants, better exemplified Hegelian etatism than the suffering of Christian discipleship.

Feeling called by God to expose this scandalous situation in the national church and explain to his countrymen the real meaning of the Christian faith, Kierkegaard launched his attacks in the late 1840's with such works as Sickness unto Death (1849) and Training in Christianity (1850). After the court preacher and professor Hans Lassen Martensen became Bishop of Zealand in 1854, Kierkegaard further honed his rhetorical rapier through Øjeblikket, a periodical which he published and to which he was the only contributor. So virulent did his attacks on the established church become that a petition was circulated among the Zealand clergy demanding that Kierkegaard be sentenced for libel. Even Vilhelm Beck, who subsequently became a sharp critic of certain tendencies within the state church, added his signature to the list.[63] In his Memoirs, however, Beck acknowledged his debt to Kierkegaard: "One thing remained with me from Kierkegaard's Øjeblikket: a complete contempt for pastors as the most pitiable race of men. This was not strange, for with the exception of a few pastors, particularly Grundtvigians, rationalists occupied the parsonages and preached in empty churches -- or did not preach at all, since there was no one to hear."[64]

Kierkegaard's early death in November, 1855 released him from the storm of protests which he had borne during his last years. His parting, though, hardly ended the controversy in Denmark. As we have observed, Mogens Sommer and Peter Christian Trandberg read Kierkegaard's works and responded by leading their flocks out of the state church. In Norway, Gustav Lammers and many like-minded laymen followed suit.[65] Most of Kierkegaard's works were published in Swedish translations shortly after they appeared in Denmark. Øjeblikket, in fact, was made available for Swedish readers in 1855, the same year it was written. The pamphlet series was one of several factors contributing to mid-century anticlericalism in Sweden.[66]

The best known critic of the Swedish Lutheran establishment at that time was not a Kierkegaardian, however, but a de facto Unitarian. Viktor Rydberg (1828-95) combined the personal religiosity of his boyhood home with a craving for spiritual and political freedom. As editor of Göteborgs Handels- och Sjöfartstidning he fought the "new Lutheran" reaction and its theological authoritarianism. His 1862 study, Bibelns lära om Kristus /The Bible's Doctrine of Christ/, in which Rydberg challenged orthodox Christology, made his name known throughout Scandinavia. He asserted that the Biblical Christ was not divine but rather, human; more specifically, Jesus was "the ideal person," or the "prototype of the human race" revealed in a worldly body. In subsequent books Rydberg questioned the validity of Pauline eschatology, the existence of hell and eternal damnation, and the value of all doctrines which did not harmonize with reason. His commitment to rationalism, however, did not make Rydberg a prophet of nineteenth-century materialism. Indeed, this humanist fought a two-front war against the encroachments of materialism in Scandinavia and creedal conformity in his Lutheran fatherland.[67]

Although Rydberg's attacks on orthodoxy aroused the Swedish clergy, they were relatively mild in comparison to the radical critiques during the fourth quarter of the century. Such organizations as the Uppsala student club, Verdandi, popularized foreign radical thought among the nation's intelligentsia. The famous dramatist, August Strindberg, performed a similar function. The works of this atheistic playwright conveyed the thought of Kierkegaard, Darwin, Marx, Lassalle, and Nietzsche to appreciative audiences.[68]

The challenge of cultural radicalism made its most rapid impact on Norwegian Christianity. In 1874 one Norwegian pastor and journalist, Thorvald Klaveness (1844-1915), observed that "the currents of infidelity, which have flowed through other lands, have not yet reached into our fjords or up our valleys." He added, though, that "this time appears to be almost past."[69] Indeed, it was. The next decade witnessed several controversies which brought attacks on orthodoxy to the forefront where they occupied the center stage of academia and religion for several years.

The most bitter of these confrontations was fought by Georg Brandes (1842-1927), a Danish Jewish litterateur who had also aroused opposition among some intellectuals in his own country. An atheist and a positivist who had made public his hatred of Christianity, Brandes gained recognition in Germany after being denied an academic position in Denmark. When he returned to Copenhagen, conservative forces still opposed his appointment. Bishop Martensen was only one of several churchmen who sought to defend their faith by resorting to ad hominem arguments against the Jewish scholar. The former professor of ethics asserted that modern Jews destroy Christian values through their individualism, capitalism, and lack of a permanent home.[70] When Brandes came to Christiania in 1878 to give a series of lectures on Kierkegaard, whose writings he used in ways which their author would have deplored, the university denied him use of its auditorium. He consequently delivered his lectures in the Student Society's Hall.

The following year Johan Christian Heuch (1838-1904), who spent much of his life fighting modern thought,[71] wrote a series of articles in the Norwegian Lutheran journal, Luthersk Ugeskrift, under the title "On the Occasion of Dr. Brandes' Appearance in Christiania." He denied Brandes' contention that the discoveries of Copernicus had seriously undermined the Christian faith and that Darwinism would spell the end of the church altogether. Like Martensen, Heuch attempted to bolster his arguments by attacking Brandes' ethnic background and suggesting that Jews have always hated Christ.[72]

Heuch's answer to Brandes was well received in Norway and abroad, although it had little effect. It was translated into German, and the Berlin court preacher and anti-Jewish agitator Adolf Stöcker cited sections of it before the Reichstag. But Heuch failed to check either the rising tide of infidelity or the influence of Brandes in Norway. In 1880 the critical Dane returned to Christiania; this time he was granted permission to speak at the university. In the meantime another positivist literary critic had been given a teaching position there. The same year a positivist journal, Nyt norsk Tidsskrift, began to appear in Christiania.[73]

Another indication of radical change in Norway's spiritual environment was the conversion of Bjørnstjerne Bjørnson, one of the country's leading dramatists, author of the lyrics of the national anthem, and a former Grundtvigian, to atheism.[74] Speaking to the Student Society in 1877, he echoed much of the American Unitarian Theodore Parker's well-known _non credo_ of 1852.[75] Bjørnson denied the existence of hell, the divinity and atonement of Christ, and eternal life. Six years later he published an anthology of the noted American infidel Robert Ingersoll's works, which he titled _Tænk selv!_ [Think for Yourself!][76]

In the United States the controversy over Darwinism is generally regarded as an important episode in nineteenth and twentieth-century religious history. In Scandinavia, however, the evolution debate was less heated. This was not, of course, due to Nordic intellectual isolation. Darwin's 1859 _Origin of Species_ was reviewed in Scandinavia within two years of its publication and appeared in Swedish and Danish translations in 1871 and 1872, respectively.[77] Nor was opposition to his theories lacking. His later book, _The Descent of Man_, appears to have met more clerical resistance than _Origin of Species_. Writing in _Dansk Kirketidende_ in 1871, Julius Lassen stated that Darwin's anthropology would "lead to materialism and is an unquestionable challenge to Christendom." He also observed that _Origin of Species_ had initially been poorly received in the international scientific community.[78] But Lassen and his co-belligerents were fighting a losing battle, as they soon realized. More in tune with the spirit of the new age, the University of Christiania defied violent clerical criticism and installed a Darwinist, Ossian Sars, as professor of zoology three years later.[79]

Nineteenth-century Scandinavians interpreted variously the development of religious toleration in their respective countries. To liberals like Viktor Rydberg, it ended a dark age of ecclesiastical despotism and paved the way for religious humanism. Many state church leaders, on the other hand, feared that spiritual freedom would destroy the Lutheran solidarity of northern Europe and open the door to countless heresies and allow modern secular thought to dominate religious life. But to free churchmen, including those of the Mission Covenants, the coming of toleration provided opportunities to practice Biblical Christianity which, they believed, the state churches had long since abandoned.

CHAPTER IV

BIBLICAL SCHOLARSHIP IN GERMANY AND SCANDINAVIA

The Genesis account of Creation was not the only Biblical idea which the winds of religious and intellectual change buffeted. Mosaic authorship of the Pentateuch, the value of the Gospel of John as a historical source, and several other traditional views fell victim to nineteenth-century Biblical scholarship. Much of this research was conducted in Germany, although the results of German scholars' investigations were quickly disseminated abroad, where their reception often sparked bitter controversies. In Europe and the United States groups and individuals who rejected much or all of the Teutonic theological fare generally became identified as conservatives. In the Scandinavian countries the debates about the Bible were most heated during the infancy of the Mission Covenants. They constituted an important part of the Nordic spiritual environment when these young denominations were in their formative years. The Scandinavian state churches eventually accepted what they now call "moderate Biblical criticism." In the United States the Congregationalists, with whom the Nordic free church immigrants under consideration briefly cooperated, accommodated most German Biblical scholarship. At their Chicago Theological Seminary, scholars like George Gilbert and Samuel Curtiss, both of whom had studied in Leipzig, openly championed it. For several decades, however, the Mission Covenants rejected the new ideas which ultimately gained acceptance among many

Scandinavian Lutherans in Europe and the United States, as a compromising of Scriptural authority. Their repudiation of them made a profound impact on the Covenants and set them apart from many of their countrymen on both sides of the Atlantic. Hence, an examination of German Biblical scholarship and its reception in Scandinavia is essential to an understanding of the Mission Covenants' theological conservatism.

Lutheran veneration of the Bible is as old as Lutheranism. To the Reformer of Wittenberg, the Scriptures were God's Word, a priceless gift to be protected jealously from the capriciousness of the papacy and the ever-shifting course of ecclesiastical history. To be sure, Luther himself frequently tampered with Scripture in ways which have embarrassed his most conservative spiritual heirs. He differentiated levels of value in the Bible, revering the Gospel of John and Paul's Letter to the Romans while flippantly casting aside Revelation with the remark, "It doesn't reveal anything." Moreover, Luther regarded Hebrews, Jude, and James as contrary to the spirit of the Gospel and relegated these epistles to the rear of the New Testament, where they remain in most German Protestant Bibles. Finally, he loaded his Biblical translations with terms and concepts common to central Europe and German peasant culture but foreign to the Middle East and the Vulgata. To Luther, this willingness to translate freely and juggle the canon did not debase the Bible. Rather, he did it to bring the Good News closer to those for whom it was intended.

Within a few decades after his death and that of his scholarly colleague, Melanchthon, Lutheran orthodoxy in Germany as well as in Scandinavia ossified into a rigid system which left little latitude for theological speculation or innovative theological language. The flourishing of Biblical scholarship during the first half of the sixteenth century appeared to have fallen victim to the alliance of throne and altar which characterized German Protestantism until the twentieth century. Critical investigation of the Scriptures lay dormant for more than a century until reawakened by pietism and the Enlightenment. When these contemporaneous movements roused the spirit of free inquiry, the protracted German domination of Biblical scholarship began.

Johan David Michaelis (1717-91) has often been called the father of German Biblical scholarship. He followed his own father's footsteps to become both an Orientalist and a theologian. Michaelis left his boyhood home of Halle, then an important center of pietism, and accepted a professorship at the University of Göttingen. Until his death Michaelis taught in the critical spirit of that Hannoverian institution. Lecturing regularly on Old and New Testament exegesis as well as ancient Hebrew culture and Middle Eastern languages, he taught his students to combine their disciplines and read the Old Testament as part of Israelite history. Michaelis was among the first to take this fateful step. Moreover, in contrast to most previous theologians, he was prepared to admit the existence of contradictions among the four Gospels. Finally, Michaelis, like Luther, maintained that different levels of inspiration could be found in the New Testament.

Because no claim to apostolic authorship had been made for Luke, Acts, Mark, James, Jude, and Hebrews, Michaelis did not regard them as canonical works on par with such books as the Gospel of John or the Pauline epistles.

While Michaelis labored in Göttingen to pave the way for generations of theologues who subsequently studied there, the Hamburg rationalist Hermann Samuel Reimarus (1694-1768) inadvertently began what has come to be known as "the quest for the historical Jesus." In a work which the young Gotthold Ephraim Lessing published a decade after his death, Reimarus contended that there had been no Resurrection. Rather, Christ's disciples, disappointed with his failure to become a political messiah, had stolen his body from the tomb, thereby opening the door to a soteriological, not a political, interpretation of Jesus. In this cynical way Reimarus sought to explain the origins of Christianity.[1]

Johann Salomo Semler (1725-91), the Halle theologian who no less than Michaelis deserves to be called a father of German Biblical scholarship, stridently opposed Reimarus' conclusions. Like Reimarus, he believed that the Bible should be subjected to vigorous critical investigation. But unlike his colleague in Hamburg, Semler tried to steer a middle course between uncritical literalism and rationalism's passionate attacks on the Bible. He argued that there need not be a contradiction between reason and revelation. Indeed, to Semler revelation broadened and confirmed the ability of the human mind to comprehend reality. With this premise he studied the Scriptures, confident that nothing in the

Bible could contradict reason.

Although the works of these eighteenth-century scholars stimulated spirited debates in German academic and ecclesiastical circles, they awakened relatively little interest in Scandinavia before 1800. Their importance to Scandinavian Christianity lies chiefly in the fact that they prepared the way for subsequent, more radical scholars whose works sparked controversies in northern Europe. The Enlightenment, of course, had come to the Nordic countries, and Scandinavian students had studied theology at German Protestant universities since the decades when Luther lectured in Wittenberg. But the cultural lag of the North, combined with a close relationship of throne and altar which often viewed German religious developments with suspicion, prevented such scholars as Michaelis from having direct, perceptible influence there.

During the eighteenth century Scandinavian conservatives' concern about the Bible was not so much an anti-intellectual struggle against rational critics as it was a demand for a return to exegetical preaching, which had been subordinated to or replaced by philosophical sermons in countless pulpits. In Sweden, for example, Olof Wallquist (1755-1800) became a leader in this fight after being appointed Bishop of Växjö in 1787. He demanded a return to preaching in the way common people spoke, so as to bring the Biblical message closer to the parishioners.[2] Illiteracy was widespread in Scandinavia before the nineteenth century, and few homes had Bibles. Samuel Ödmann (1750-1829), who studied at the University of Uppsala under the famous taxonomist, Carl von Linné, and later taught theology there, agreed. As a professor of both exegetics and pastoral theology, he realized that most Swedes knew little about the Bible. During the last years of his life Ödmann prepared a paraphrase of much of the New Testament, which was published posthumously in 1832.[3] The Swedish Bible Society supplemented his efforts after it was organized in 1816. By 1878 it had printed 273,238 Bibles and 650,100 copies of the New Testament.[4]

Similar efforts can be seen in Norwegian church history. At the University of Christiania, Svend Borchmand Hersleb (1784-1936) and Stener Johannes Stenersen (1789-1835) guided theology students "back to the Bible." Hersleb was one of the founders of his country's Bible society, and he later produced a translation of the New Testament. Einar Molland has summarized the two professors' impact on nineteenth-century Norwegian clergymen. "Before the lecterns of these men grew up a generation of theologues who bore the stamp of Biblicism and mild Lutheran orthodoxy."[5]

The Norwegian Bible Society, like its Swedish counterpart modelled after the British Bible Society, came into being in 1817. Andreas Aarflot has observed that

> the founding of the Norwegian Bible Society was among the most important factors in the renewal which took place in Norwegian church life after

> 1814. Interest in the Bible manifested itself as a subcurrent in church life whose most important results included an awakened consciousness of responsibility both in the life of the congregation and in organized lay activity during this period.[6]

Statements by nineteenth-century Norwegian Christians support Aarflot's assertion. In the mid-1850's, for example, one young lay evangelist from Balsfjorden near Tromsø attributed the recent revival in northern Norway to wider distribution of the Scriptures, and noted that the price of a Bible had just dropped to one-fifth of the previous charge.[6a] By 1878 the Norwegian Bible Society had distributed more than 351,000 copies of the Bible and the New Testament.[6b]

Germany continued to produce theologians who sought to turn back the theological clock to pre-Enlightenment Lutheran orthodoxy. Ernst Hengstenberg (1802-69), the most powerful of these figures, exercised a strong influence in Norway, where his *Repristinationstheologie* helped insulate theology students from radical currents for several decades. The son of a Westfalian Calvinist minister, he became a Lutheran in the early 1820's and spent the remainder of his life defending that tradition with the enthusiasm which often accompanies conversions. In 1826 Hengstenberg was appointed to the Old Testament chair in Berlin. Shortly after his installation at that city's university, he began to publish *Evangelische Kirchenzeitung*, which soon became the leading organ of theological conservatism in Germany. Hengstenberg would have no part of recent Old Testament scholarship. He accepted without question the integrity and Mosaic authorship of the Pentateuch and maintained a belief in the inerrant, literal truth of Scripture.[7]

Hengstenberg's impact on Scandinavian religious life was powerful but indirect. As we have noted, Hersleb and Stenersen maintained a traditional Lutheran view of the Bible while they taught in Christiania. In the 1840's the torch of Biblicism was passed to a pair of younger theologians, Carl Paul Caspari (1814-92) and Gisle Johnson (1822-94). These two men, prophets of renewed Lutheran confessionalism, kept the Bible before the eyes of theology students at Norway's only university for another forty years.

Caspari was an unlikely Norwegian Lutheran confessionalist. Born a Jew in the German city of Dessau, he studied Semitic languages at the University of Leipzig before converting to Christianity. Following his change of faith, Caspari transferred to the University of Berlin, where he studied the Old Testament under Hengstenberg's tutelage. He received a Ph.D. in 1842 and quickly won acclaim for his study of the prophet Obadiah. The Prussian government offered Caspari a professorship at the University of Königsberg, but this strict Lutheran declined because he could not conscienciously teach in a merged Calvinist-Lutheran theology department. Instead, Caspari accepted a call to Christiania where he spent the next four decades protecting old Lutheran orthodoxy from Grundtvigian romanticism. He was not simply jesting when he referred to himself as "a hard-boiled Hengstenbergian."[8]

Gisle Johnson, Caspari's younger colleague and a systematic theologian, was of similar persuasion. The son of an Icelandic immigrant and a graduate of the University of Christiania, he studied briefly in Germany, where he met Caspari and Hengstenberg. Johnson returned to Norway and joined the theology faculty in 1849. An authority on pre-pietistic Lutheran literature, he opposed Grundtvigianism both from the lectern and in the press. Together with Caspari and Tønder Nissen, Johnson began to publish the conservative organ, *Teologisk Tidsskrift for den evangelisk luthersk Kirke i Norge* /Theological Journal of the Evangelical Lutheran Church in Norway/ in 1858. Five years later he founded *Luthersk Kirketidende*. Both of these periodicals represented confessional Lutheranism and its traditional, literalist hermeneutics. Moreover, in the 1850's Johnson stimulated the revival associated with his name by giving public Bible readings in the Norwegian capital.

The position of the Bible in Danish Christianity before the arrival of radical German criticism is more difficult to describe. During much of the nineteenth century the country's state Lutheran church was divided into two, and later three, hostile factions. The party which dominated ecclesiastical politics was clearly high church, and claimed to be defending traditional Lutheran orthodoxy. Led by such authoritarian men as Bishops Mynster and Martensen, it opposed Enlightenment rationalism, but many of its adherents fell under the influence of Hegel, whose glorification of the state confirmed their own allegiance to an Erastian relationship between church and civil government. Despite their philosophical leanings, however, these pastors professed loyalty to the Bible. They paid it more than mere lip service. Mynster, for example, was a dedicated student of the New Testament. While he was Bishop of Zealand the Danish Bible Society was founded; the British Bible Society, with which it cooperated, continued to function in Denmark until 1895. The proliferation of Bibles during the century coincided with a sharp rise in Danish literacy after a public act of 1814 mandated seven years of education for all Danes.[9]

N.S.F. Grundtvig (1783-1872), the versatile theologian, historian, psalmist, and educator, led the other major faction. For more than a decade following his ordination in 1811 he was one of the most Biblicistic clergymen in Denmark. Grundtvig's orthodoxy and 1816 book, Bibelske Prædikener [Biblical Sermons], set him apart from many of his colleagues. But his so-called "matchless discovery" of 1825 started Grundtvig on a new course and launched the school identified with his name. In that year he defended a group of Danish revivalists who, despite their inability to read the Scriptures in Hebrew and Greek, had been quite successful in awakening their countrymen, especially on the island of Fyn. To Grundtvig it seemed ironic that the erudite clergymen should ridicule these successful lay preachers merely because they had neither studied theology nor learned the Biblical languages. Seeking a simpler foundation for Christianity, he subordinated the Bible to what he called the "living word," by which he meant the Apostles' Creed and the words of institution at communion. Grundtvig did not reject the Bible, but he insisted that without the sacraments, which have always been central to Lutheranism, it is an inert text. The Grundtvigian party soon became influential in Denmark, where it still exists. Grundtvig also had followers in Norway and, to a lesser degree, Sweden. But their demotion of the Bible drew the fire of more Scripturally-oriented groups in Scandinavia and among Nordic immigrants in the United States, to whom "Grundtvigian" was a term of opprobrium.

In these controversies the Scandinavian lay movements almost invariably opposed Grundtvig and maintained a strong Biblicism. This is perhaps most clearly seen in Norway. Hauge's reading of the Scriptures made him aware of certain inconsistencies in the texts. But he did not allow them to dampen his allegiance to the Lutheran principle of _sola scriptura_. To Hauge the Bible remained "a secure rock on which to build and the clearest way by which God will lead us to His kingdom."[10] Olaus Nielsen (1810-88), at mid-century the most influential man in the Norwegian lay movement, continued its loyalty to the Bible. As editor of _Kirkelig Tidende_, the only lay-edited Norwegian religious newspaper at that time, he waged rhetorical warfare against the Grundtvigians. Disenchanted with more recent translations of the Scriptures, Nielsen also printed 15,000 copies of a 1744 pietistic Bible, "inspected and corrected" by himself.[11]

Meanwhile, however, German Biblical scholarship was becoming increasingly radical in its rejection of traditional ways of belief. Although conservatives like Caspari prevented it from having an immediate impact on Scandinavia, the new direction in German Biblical research eventually rocked the churches of the North.

Wilhelm de Wette (1780-1849), whose liberal views cost him his professorship at the University of Berlin, made one of the first waves in the century's tempestuous theological waters. In his dissertation of 1805 on Deuteronomy he rejected the traditional view of Mosaic authorship of the Pentateuch. De Wette established the view that the second codification of the Law was a late phenomenon in Jewish history. He argued strongly that it had probably been composed shortly before it was discovered during the reign of Josiah in Judah (ca. 640-609 B.C.), thereby driving an early nail into the coffin of the Mosaic authorship legend.

The controversy which de Wette's treatment of the Pentateuch occasioned, however, was mild compared to the furor of the "Strauss debate."[12] In 1835 a young instructor at the University of Tübingen, David Friedrich Strauss (1808-74), published his seminal work, Das Leben Jesu. Strauss was thoroughly disenchanted with the efforts of New Testament scholars to piece together disjoint Gospel pericopae into biographies of Jesus. Moreover, he had only scorn for the attempts of such rationalists as Heinrich Paulus to explain away Christ's miracles as natural phenomena. As Strauss pointed out, their use of stones under the surface of the water on which Jesus walked and "Essene confederates" to replenish the supply of loaves and fish with which he fed the multitudes did violence to the spirit of the Gospels, which constantly stress the supernatural essence of Christ. Strauss' conclusion was succinct: the life of Jesus cannot be written, at least not as a traditional biography.

This conviction, however, did not prevent him from undertaking his own lengthy attempts to present Christ in a manner which would avoid the pitfalls into which the rationalists had stumbled. The *via media* between uncritical supernaturalism, which Strauss perceived to be succombing to modern science, and the rationalists' fancy footwork around the miracles of Christ, was what Strauss called "the mythical." As Stephen Neill has pointed out, the Tübingen theologian never clearly defined what he meant by "myth."[13] But for the most part, he used it to denote the commitment to and expression of an idea which cannot be demonstrated empirically. Those who wrote the Gospels, according to Strauss, were unable to prove that Jesus was the Messiah. But this incapability did not negate their conviction that he was in fact the Christ, a belief which they strove to convey to others through ahistorical accounts of his appearance and majesty. Strauss, in short, held that the idea of Christ can and indeed must be divorced from the historical Jesus, about whom very little can be known.

Orthodox churchmen, unimpressed by Strauss' pleas that he was saving Christianity from rationalism as well as modern science, were immediately alarmed when Das Leben Jesu appeared. They feared that if cut loose from its historical moorings, the Gospel might simply drift away. A bitter debate over the historicity of Jesus and the quality of Strauss' scholarship ensued, and the enfant terrible was expelled from his academic position in Tübingen. Unable to secure employment at another university, he returned to his home of Ludwigsburg, where he continued to fuel the fires of controversy by writing sequels to his work of 1835.

Das Leben Jesu was soon translated into several other European languages, including Swedish and Danish. In Sweden it precipitated a heated debate in the 1840's. George Scott reported from Stockholm in 1842 that Strauss had followers in the country who were seeking to spread the skepticism of his anti-biography of Christ.[14] Several German political and religious leaders sought unsuccessfully to have the controversial book suppressed. As a more positive reaction, opponents of Strauss wrote a new flurry of biographies of Jesus. On the other hand, Bruno Bauer (1809-82), a radical Hegelian on the theological faculty in Berlin (and from 1839 until 1842 in Bonn), suggested that Strauss had not gone far enough. He attributed the four canonical Gospels to the influence of a single, anonymous Urevangelist who was the real originator of Christianity. Concomitantly, Bauer doubted that Jesus had ever existed as a historical person. As in the cases of de Wette and Strauss, Bauer's academic appointment fell victim to his revolutionary views.

Although Strauss' work was generally rejected in his own

day, that of his prolific professor, Ferdinand Christian Baur (1792-1860), gained wide acceptance. On the surface this is surprising, because the Tübingen mentor eventually did more than his pupil to undermine orthodox views of the Bible. Just as Michaelis had seen the Old Testament as a product of Hebrew history, Baur regarded the New Testament as the handiwork of the apostolic and post-apostolic church. Heavily influenced by the Hegelian dialectical system of history as a never-ending sequence of thesis, antithesis, and synthesis, he cast the first two centuries of church history into a framework of bipartisan strife between Petrine and Pauline factions. These two antithetical parties, in Baur's parlance the Jewish-Christian _Gesetzeskirche_ centered in Palestine and the Gentile _Geistkirche_, were reconciled in the second century to become the Catholic Church. But during their period of mutual hostility, they produced two bodies of Christian literature, including books which were eventually canonized as the New Testament. Proceeding from this historiographical scheme, Baur identified each of the twenty-seven books as either Petrine or Pauline. He also questioned the authenticity of several of the epistles attributed to Paul, and concluded that only Galatians, Romans, and First and Second Corinthians were the work of the great apostle. Finally, he differentiated between the Gospel of John and the Synoptics and, like Strauss, insisted that the fourth Gospel was not written by the disciple of the same name, but in fact had been penned at a much later date. Although Baur's conclusions caused a furor during his years at the University of

Tübingen, the so-called "Tübingen school" soon became a highly influential group of Biblical scholars and church historians in Germany.

Subsequent German research in the New Testament was equally irreverent in the eyes of many conservatives. A group of scholars loosely known as the *religionsgeschichtliche Schule*, or history of religions school, agreed with Baur that the New Testament must be read in the context of early church history. They went beyond the Tübingen historian, however, in analyzing in detail Hellenistic ideas and their impact on New Testament theology. Otto Pfleiderer (1836-1900), for example, who is often called "the father of the religio-historical theology in Germany," devoted several decades of his career to investigations of the impact of Greek wisdom on Hellenistic Judaism, particularly the background of Paul's epistles. They stressed probably differences between the original Gospel of Christ and the Hellenized theology which emerged later in the first century. These scholars thought the sacraments were among the elements of early Christianity which underwent a major transition when subjected to Hellenistic culture. They argued that baptism and the Lord's Supper took on meanings originally associated with Eleusinian mysteries when interpreted by Paul and other figures in the Gentile church. Much of this school's scholarship has been subsequently refuted or extensively revised, but men like Pfleiderer opened new fields of research by pointing out that early Christianity did not exist in a cultural vacuum and remain unchanged during the formative period before the Scriptures were canonized and the decisions of ecumenical councils differentiated between orthodox and heretical theology. Their works also challenged traditionally accepted views of the inviolability of New Testament language by arguing that non-Christian cultural factors had made a profound impact on the pre-canonical texts.

The closing decades of the nineteenth century witnessed the climactic assault upon orthodox views of the Old Testament's origins by Julius Wellhausen (1844-1918), the most famous Old Testament scholar of this period and also a German. Wellhausen, whose bailiwick included Semitic languages and Israelite history as well as the Old Testament, popularized the "documentary hypothesis" associated with his name. The hypothesis, set forth in his 1878 Geschichte Israels, a work which was translated into several European languages, was a final major blow to the supposed unity of the Pentateuch. Wellhausen argued that the first five books of the Old Testament had been written over a period of several hundred years, and that practically none of the extant texts of the Pentateuch were composed during the lifetime of Moses. By the 1870's many German and other scholars doubted that all of the Torah was of Mosaic authorship; as we have seen, de Wette had questioned this at the beginning of the century. The works of such men as the Strassburg professor Eduard Reuss and Abraham Kuenen of The Netherlands had also anticipated much of the Wellhausen hypothesis. But the publication of Wellhausen's widely read book renewed the controversy in Germany, from whence it spread to Scandinavia. The furor raged there during the formative years of the Covenants.

Danish churchmen had been exposed to heterodox theology long before the works of these late nineteenth-century German scholars arrived in Denmark. Although traditional Biblicistic and Grundtvigian parties had dominated Danish Christianity during the first half of the century, any clergyman or other individual in the country who wished to read radical theological literature had ready access to it. Heinrich Nicolai Clausen (1793-1877), who joined the theology faculty at the University of Copenhagen in 1821, bridged the theological gap between Germany and Denmark. After studying theology and philosophy in Copenhagen, he undertook a two-year academic journey through Germany to southern Europe. While in Berlin Clausen came under the influence of Schleiermacher, whose ability to be both a pietist and a critical theologian impressed the young Dane. Clausen's experiences in Germany made a life-long impression on him and, indirectly, on many of his countrymen. In 1833 he began to publish *Tidskrift for udenlandsk theologisk Litteratur* [Journal of Foreign Theological Literature], which carried Danish translations of foreign, chiefly German, theological articles and sections of books. During its first year it featured pieces by such famous theologians as Schleiermacher, de Wette, and Neander. Works by Tholuck, Ranke, and Baur joined the list shortly thereafter. In 1836 its Danish readers were introduced to Part II of Strauss' *Leben Jesu*. From its inception *Tidskrift for udenlandsk theologisk*

Litteratur was surprisingly popular. A list of subscribers appended to the first volume reveals that several hundred Danish pastors, divinity students, and other interested readers purchased it, as did several dozen of their Norwegian colleagues.[15]

Despite the popularity of this frequently heterodox literature, radical German Biblical scholarship did not make a deep impression on Danish Christianity until the fourth quarter of the century when the Mission Covenant came into being. There is no evidence that more than a handful of the country's churchmen questioned such traditions as Mosaic authorship of the Pentateuch or the value of the fourth Gospel as a historical source prior to that time. Apparently they were too preoccupied with other battles, including the Grundtvigian question, the rise of the free churches, urban problems, and Kierkegaard to devote much attention to current Biblical research abroad. The major controversies over the Bible were thus postponed until after 1875.

When the battle of the Bible finally began, it was fought primarily at the University of Copenhagen. The hostilities commenced shortly after the appearance of Wellhausen's Geschichte Israels in 1878. At that time Frants Buhl (1850-1932), who had received a theology degree at the university, was pursuing post-graduate studies in Semitic languages in Leipzig. Like many of his contemporaries, he initially rejected the Wellhausen hypothesis.[16] But as it gradually gained acceptance, Buhl changed his mind.[17] After securing a professorship at the University of Copenhagen in 1880, where he taught Old Testament theology for the next decade, Buhl softened his attacks and eventually became an enthusiastic supporter of Wellhausen. In the 1880's he wrote several articles in which he applied both higher and lower criticism to the Old Testament. Peder Madsen (1843-1911), who had joined the faculty shortly after Buhl, was primarily a systematic theologian but also lectured on New Testament exegesis. His theology never became radical in the eyes of many of his colleagues; in fact, Madsen was appointed Bishop of Zealand in 1909. But he defended higher criticism and suggested that Christ's human knowledge was fallible.

Buhl and Madsen awakened the attention of other churchmen in Copenhagen, and the theology faculty, whose conservatism had drawn the fire of Grundtvigians, socialists, and other groups in the 1870's, now suffered attack for undermining the Biblical basis of the Christian faith. Vilhelm Beck of the Inner Mission led the opposition against what he believed was the work of Satan at the university:

> Another demand which the Inner Mission definitely makes of the university is that it train future pastors to be true to the Bible. We belong to the Lutheran sector of the Christian church and it is our chief principle that the Bible be the rule for doctrine and life. For this reason the Inner Mission demands that the university abandon that destructive biblical criticism which crept into our

> university at the beginning of the century. It has already affected a large number of our young students. . . . We know what the devil sought to accomplish at that time by attacking the New Testament with biblical criticism, namely, to deprive our Savior of his divine glory and reduce him to an ordinary human being. This is precisely the goal of the present cunning assault on the Old Testament which makes its statements doubtful or outright false. Our Savior refers repeatedly to and affirms the statements of the Old Testament. But the Bible critics declare that these statements are false. . . . On your knees for the Bible, you professors![18]

Tired of controversy, Buhl left Denmark in 1890 to become Franz Delitzsch's successor at the University of Leipzig. His departure, however, did not end the debate over what his opponents called Bibelkritikken. Buhl's successor was one of his former students, Johannes Jacobsen, who continued the investigation of the Old Testament along the lines which Buhl had drawn. Moreover, Buhl returned from Germany in 1898 and once again became entangled in the debate, which lasted well into the twentieth century.

The controversy over Biblical criticism in Norway also occurred during the years after 1870, a period known as the "breakthrough of modernity" in Scandinavian scholarship generally. Socialism, Darwinism, positivism, the Industrial Revolution, and other challenges of modernity converged to upset the stability of traditionally rural northern Europe. Although these forces arrived later in Norway than in Denmark, the major debates over Biblical scholarship occurred nearly simultaneously in the two countries. While Frants Buhl was polarizing Copenhagen's Lutheran clergymen over the issue of Old Testament research, Fredrik Petersen (1839-1903), a Norwegian systematic theologian, was preparing to take a stand against the orthodox view of Scriptural inspiration in Christiania.

Petersen began his theological studies in 1857. During the 1860's he studied theology and philosophy at the University of Berlin. From 1862 until 1875, when he was named professor of theology at the University of Christiania, Petersen continued to investigate the relationships between theology and secular culture in Germany and his own country.

Petersen foreshadowed the subsequent dispute in his address of 1880, "How Should the Church Confront the Infidelity of Modern Times?" The materialistic view of life was a departure from orthodoxy, he admitted, but nevertheless one which was increasingly gaining acceptance. Hence, the church must appropriate empiricism for its own purposes and restructure the forms of its theology, including its view of the Bible. Petersen devoted his academic career to the fulfillment of these suggestions. Most significantly, he advocated modifying the orthodox Lutheran concept of Biblical inspiration. Petersen insisted that the human element in the writing of the Scriptures, the limits of the writers' knowledge, and their fallibility, be recognized. Like many of his contemporaries elsewhere in Europe and in the United States, he denied that such an admission would undercut the Bible's authority.[19]

Although the position which Petersen represented ultimately dominated much Norwegian Lutheranism, conservatives initially rebuked him and his small circle of supporters. Johan Christian Heuch, who had defended the old ecclesiastical order from polemics by George Brandes and Bjørnstjerne Bjørnson in the 1870's, led the attack. As co-editor of Luthersk Ugeskrift he continued his verbal warfare against what he viewed as another phase of modern infidelity. Another of Petersen's opponents was Knud Krogh-Tonning (1842-1911), who served as pastor of Christiania's Gamle Aker Church until he dramatically began the twentieth century by resigning his pastorate on January 1, 1900 and converting to Roman Catholicism. He upheld the Lutheran view of Scriptural inspiration and Biblical infallibility both before and after abandoning the state church.

Michael Færden (1836-1912), on the other hand, represented a growing moderate school in Scandinavia during the 1880's and 1890's. Realizing, as he admitted in 1887, that theology was in a period of transition, he sought a via media between Petersen and Heuch. Færden had difficulty navigating between the Scylla of what he called "negative Bible criticism" and the Charybdis of the Lutheran doctrine of inspiration, which he was willing to modify, although he did not know what would replace it. In 1887 Færden reviewed a book by Sigurd Odland, then a research scholar and after 1894 a relatively critical professor of New Testament at the University of Christiania, and referred to recent scholarship as "negative Biblical criticism which, like a wild boar, uproots everything."[20] But during the 1890's Færden's conservative side gradually gave way to modern scholarship which, he confessed, was partly defensible.[21] After the turn of the century he wrote several books which helped popularize recent Biblical research in Norway.

The place of the Bible in Sweden after the middle of the nineteenth century was essentially similar to that in Norway. One significant difference, however, was the absence of a strong Grundtvigian tradition in the largest Scandinavian country. As in the other Nordic lands, "new Lutheranism" advanced rapidly in Sweden, seeking to recover orthodoxy's losses to the Enlightenment. The movement placed renewed emphasis on the Scriptures. At the universities and among the clergy the conservative dimensions of German Biblical scholarship found a warm reception. Johan Ternström's journal, Nordisk kyrkotidning, published from 1840 until 1849, brought Hengstenberg's Repristinationstheologie to several thousand readers.[22] Otto Myrberg (1824-99), professor of exegetics at the University of Uppsala after 1866, popularized Beck's Biblicism among theology students at that important training ground for the clergymen of the established church.[23]

Among the lay preachers, to whom many Swedish free churches can be traced, the Bible occupied a central position. These laymen, who in tandem with some of the Lutheran clergy breathed new life into Swedish Christianity through their "new evangelism," perhaps surpassed the pastors in emphasizing the Scriptures as the central authority for Christian life and thought. Although they lacked a systematized doctrine of the Bible, it nevertheless became the touchstone for revivalism's theology.[24] Moreover, lay preachers repeatedly referred to the Scriptures when defending themselves against ordained pastors and the courts which sought to suppress their movements.[25]

As was the case elsewhere in Scandinavia, sincere Christian scholars brought German Biblical criticism to Sweden in the 1880's and 1890's. These men had no intention of weakening the Bible's authority by examining the Scriptures in the light of Wellhausen's hypothesis or the findings of the history of religions school. Erik Stave (1857-1932) serves as a prime example. A professor of exegetics at the University of Uppsala and a pastor in that city, Stave was probably the leading exponent of Old Testament higher criticism during his lifetime. His 1894 study, _Om uppkomsten af Gamla Testamentets kanon_ [The Origin of the Old Testament Canon], reflects a heavy reliance on the works of Wellhausen and Buhl. Yet he refused to label his own research "Biblical criticism." That negative term, Stave believed, did violence to his purpose of making the Old Testament more comprehensible to his students and parishioners. He insisted that Biblical scholarship could make a positive impact on Christian ethics, and stressed this point in a much-publicized address to a student meeting in 1901.[26] Many of Stave's colleagues disagreed, however, and opposition to his position was strong at church conferences during the next few years.

New translations of the Bible which were intended to replace the venerable 1703 version, also occasioned controversies which involved both the state church and leaders of the Swedish Mission Covenant. Esias Tegnér (1843-1928), a leading Semitic philologist, headed the Bible commission from 1884 until 1917 and fought numerous battles against literalists who protested what they believed was his capricious handling of the oldest extant texts of the Scriptures. Paul Peter Waldenström, the leading theologian in the Swedish Mission Covenant, became one of Tegnér's most vocal opponents around the turn of the century.[27]

Thus, when the Swedish Mission Covenant was organized in 1878, radical Biblical criticism had not yet made a great impact there. The research of such scholars as Wellhausen did not gain widespread respectability among Swedish churchmen until the early years of the twentieth century. The Mission Covenant was not initially so concerned with criticism of the Scriptures as it later became, when it perceived threats to its Biblical faith. As we shall see, however, men like Waldenström were committed to Biblical literalism several years before criticism became a central issue in Sweden.

In Norway and Denmark recent German Biblical scholarship was already gaining some acceptance, but also antagonizing more conservative churchmen, when the Covenants of those countries came into being in the 1880's. From their earliest years these two small denominations expressed hostility to Biblical criticism and, moreso than their sister church in Sweden, remained loyal to literalist hermeneutics.

CHAPTER V

BRITISH AND AMERICAN MILLENARIANISM IN SCANDINAVIA

Three of the traits which eventually characterized the Norwegian and Danish Mission Covenants -- Biblicism, emphasis on revivalism and conversion, and attempts to create congregations composed exclusively of born-again Christians -- had begun to play important roles in Scandinavian religion by 1850. Millenarianism, however, which ultimately became equally fundamental in these two denominations, but never characterized the Swedish Mission Covenant, remained a minor current in northern Europe until the 1880's, when successive eschatological waves from Great Britain and the United States crossed the North Sea and the Atlantic.[1] Bearing proclamations of the imminent Second Advent of Christ, they made deep impressions in the cosmologies of both state church Lutherans and adherents of many dissenting communions.

Belief in the imminent return of Christ, although brought to the Nordic countries from abroad during the nineteenth century, was not foreign to Lutheran history. Indeed, the first Lutheran millenarian was the Wittenberg Reformer. In a sermon commemorating the first Advent, Martin Luther professed that the second was at hand:

> I do not wish to force anyone to believe as I do; neither will I permit anyone to deny me the

> right to believe that the last day is near at hand. These words and signs of Christ (Luke 21: 25-36) compel me to believe that such is the case. For the history of the centuries that have passed since the birth of Christ nowhere reveals conditions like those of the present. There has never been such building and planting in the world. There has never been such gluttonous eating and drinking as now. Wearing apparel has reached its limit in costliness. Who has ever heard of such commerce as now encircles the earth? There have arisen all kinds of art and sculpture, embroidery and engraving, the like of which has not been seen during the whole Christian era.[2]

This sentiment that history was on the verge of fulfillment runs throughout Luther's works. Moreover, other Reformers repeatedly expressed it from their pulpits and in print.

Their expectations were hardly an unprecedented chapter in the history of the church. The apostle Paul, of course, had awaited the return of Christ within his own lifetime, as had many other pre-Augustinian Christians. Although Augustine (354-430) placed the Second Advent and the Kingdom of God outside of history, where they remained in most Catholic theology, some medieval sectarians became millenarians and believed that Christ's return in glory was impending. Concomitantly, these dissenters frequently identified the Antichrist of Revelation with specific popes whom they had antagonized. Expectations of the Son of Man's Second Coming flourished on the eve of such years as 1000 and 1033, the latter regarded as a millennium after the Resurrection. Luther was not, however, a direct heir of these medieval beliefs. In contrast to the sectaries, he did not single out one pope and pin the label of the Antichrist on him. Rather, Luther and other Reformers initiated the tradition of regarding the office of the papacy as the Antichrist. Anti-Romanist artists and printers of the Reformation era enthusiastically took up this theme, which they perpetuated in countless woodcuts which juxtaposed the poverty and humility of Christ and the papacy's worldly power and ostentation.

Early Protestant depections of the supposed _Vicarius Filii Dei_ as the archenemy of Christ were the fountainhead of modern historicist millenarianism, the eschatological school which believes that the prophecies in Daniel and Revelation are already being fulfilled in history. The Counterreformation, in defense of the papacy, quickly developed a countervailing theory of the Apocalypse. Seeking to protect their church from adversaries who regarded it as Babylon, Catholic Reformers, most notably the Spanish Jesuit, Francisco Ribera (1537-91), insisted that none of these prophecies had come to pass. According to this school, called futurist millenarianism, the events relating to the Antichrist of the Apocalypse would not begin until an unknown future date.

Despite the central place which the early form of historicist millenarianism occupied in the Lutheran Reformation, this eschatology did not endure as a main current in the Lutheran tradition. Lutheran congregations soon coalesced into highly structured state churches. In an era of ascending nationalism, expectations of the world's demise lost their appeal. Millenarianism survived in some pietistic circles, but it did not resonate with the spirit of the times in Europe. The Enlightenment appeared to deliver millenarianism a lethal blow in the eighteenth century. Rationalists usually viewed history optimistically; their cosmology was one of gradual progress toward man's mastery of his environment. God was in His heaven where, most Enlightenment scholars who did not become atheists or deists seem to have believed, He would remain.

Although many eighteenth-century European Protestant theologians shared this progressive sense of history, not all agreed. One divine who swam against the stream was the Swabian pietist, Johann Bengel, whose Biblicism we have already noted. Working in a historicist framework, he boldly announced that the end of the world would take place in 1836. Although Bengel died in 1752, his influence survived among his followers until 1836 came and went.[3] In Great Britain and the North American colonies millenarianism, although a central tenet of Puritan theology, lost much of its support in the eighteenth century. While some churchmen continued to search the Scriptures for signs of an imminent Second Advent, more seem to have been either amillennial or else optimistic postmillennialists, such as the influential Salisbury rector, Daniel Whitby, or Jonathan Edwards, America's first important post-Puritan theologian.[4]

The anticlericalism of the French Revolution revived historicist millenarianism. During the decade of the 1790's the Roman Catholic Church's hold on France was finally broken. Its property was confiscated and many of its royalist priests fled the country. French armies crossed the Alps, occupied Rome and the Vatican, and banished Pius VI in 1798. To contemporary students of prophecy these events, especially the supposed termination of papal power, were not only spectacular, but illuminating, as well. As one historian of millenarianism has remarked, "the identification of the events of the 1790's with those prophesied in Daniel 7 and Revelation 13 provided biblical commentators with a prophetic Rosetta stone. At last a key had been found with which to crack the code."[5] Employing the "year-day theory," which substituted "year" wherever "day" occurred in Biblical prophecies, these scriptural cryptographers quickly assumed that the 1260 "years" of Revelation 13 (which, they believed, describe the duration of the papacy's tyranny) had ended in 1798. Counting backwards, they calculated that the papacy had become a political power in 538, when Belisarius asserted himself against the Goths in Rome.

The events in France and Italy stimulated millenarian fervor in much of Europe, but perhaps nowhere did the renewed study of prophecy flourish more abundantly than in Great Britain. Clergy and laymen in the Church of England, the Church of Scotland, the Church of Ireland, and the nonconformist denominations joined the millenarian movement, swelling it to great proportions. Societies for proselytizing among Jews and restoring them to Palestine -- both endeavors conducted with the intention of fulfilling Revelation's prophecies -- were organized. Millenarians penned hundreds of interpretive books and pamphlets and also began to publish prophetic journals. In the churches, ministers who had been won for the movement electrified their congregations with eschatological sermons emphasizing the imminent return of Christ.

Edward Irving (1792-1834), until found guilty of heresy and expelled from the Church of Scotland's ministerium, temporarily enjoyed a meteoric career as one of London's most prominent millenarians. A Scotsman by birth and education, he became minister of the city's Caledonian Chapel in 1822. While in this capacity Irving fell under the influence of English millenarians. In 1826 he translated both volumes of _Venida del Mesías en Gloria y Magestad_ /The Coming of the Messiah in Glory and Majesty/, an eschatological study which a Chilean Jesuit, Manuel Lacunza, had completed in the 1790's. Lacunza's study was hardly typical of Romanist millenarian scholarship. Unlike most other Catholics who had probed Biblical prophecy, this Jesuit was a historicist. As a corollary of this starting point, Lacunza regarded the Roman Catholic priesthood and hierarchy as the Antichrist.

Shortly after completing the translation, Irving participated in the first of several series of British prophetic conferences which gave the millenarian movement there much of its structure and continuity. Approximately a score of millenarians convened at the Albury Park estate of Henry Drummond, a well-to-do banker and philanthropist. This group of historicists founded the Catholic Apostolic Church in the early 1830's. Irving, whose Scottish presbytery defrocked him after glossolalia and healings broke out among his followers, died shortly after it was organized. But the new denomination, popularly known as the "Irvingites," continued and became the first British millenarian communion to gather congregations in Scandinavia.[6]

No one was more instrumental in bringing "Irvingism" to northern Europe than Charles Bøhm. Born in Copenhagen in 1812, his mother was an Englishwoman, his father a Danish civil servant. After the elder Bøhm died, Charles accompanied his mother to England in 1834 and found employment in the Hambro banking concern. He came into contact with the Irvingites in Liverpool and John Bates Cardale, then the group's "senior apostle," ordained him an "evangelist" in the summer of 1836.

Bøhm did not, however, immediately return to Denmark. The Catholic Apostolic Church began missionary work in Germany in 1836 and gave the young Anglo-Dane a position in this field. The following year he accompanied one of the Church's "apostles," Henry John King-Church, to Copenhagen, where they attempted without success to begin cooperative work with the Danish state church. Bøhm returned to the more fertile German mission field, where the Irvingite movement eventually included several noted theologians, such as the Marburg professors Heinrich Thiersch and Ernst Rossteuscher.

The constitution of 1849, as we have seen, eased the constraints upon foreign sects operating in Denmark. The freer religious climate seeming more amenable to proselytism, Bøhm returned to Copenhagen five years later and began to work as a millenarian evangelist. For several years his activities bore little visible fruit. Not until 1861 did Bøhm organize a congregation in Copenhagen. Its first pastor was a surveyor and member of parliament, Adolph Frederik Hilarius Fleischer. The Copenhagen Irvingites worshiped on Sundays and on weekday evenings gave lectures dealing with the awaited Second Advent.[7] Their congregation originally reported about forty members.[8] As had been the case with several other Danes who joined dissenting denominations, Søren Kierkegaard's attacks on the state church had made an impression on Fleischer. He became convinced that the Danish church was irredeemably worldly and would have to be replaced by a restored apostolate. The Catholic Apostolic Church claimed to offer precisely this.

But even if Kierkegaard had not unwittingly helped to set the stage for Irvingism, the movement may still have been able to strike a sympathetic note in Denmark at that time. Discontent with the established church's worldliness, inclusiveness, and general unwillingness to take any steps which might threaten its stability and privileged position was widespread in the

1860's. To Lutherans who were disenchanted -- or simply bored -- with their own church's tendency to lull its birthright members into a spiritual somnambulance, the Catholic Apostolic Church presented a genuine and exciting alternative. While the Lutheran pastors tended to ignore millenarianism, which they historically associated with chiliastic excesses such as those at Münster in the 1530's, the Irvingites proclaimed the glorious imminent return of the Lord. Moreover, they offered more pomp than did the state church. In stunning contrast to the somber black robes and white fluted ruffs which had characterized the Scandinavian Lutheran clergy for centuries, the "angel" Fleischer appeared in a white gown appropriately adorned with blue wings. The Eucharist which he administered combined the familiar Lutheran doctrine of the real presence of Christ in the bread and wine with the mystique (if not the theology) of the Roman Catholic Mass. Moreover, the Irvingites' eclectic liturgy borrowed antiphonal chants from Greek Orthodox worship.[9] The sect did not, however, re-baptize converts, nor did it practice adult baptism. This unique combination of familiar and exotic elements probably explains why the Catholic Apostolic Church eventually became one of the largest nonconformist denominations in Denmark. By 1885 the membership had reportedly climbed to over 1,000, which ranked it fifth behind the nation's Baptists, Roman Catholics, Mormons, and Reformed.[10]

Despite the Irvingites' professed ecumenicity and willingness to participate in the state church's worship and sacraments, the initial Lutheran reaction to their appearance was hostile. Almindelig Kirketidende, an Aarhus monthly which supported the Evangelical Alliance's campaign against the spread of Roman Catholicism and devoted a considerable amount of space to the fight against the intrusions of what it called papisme in Denmark, apparently found the denomination's name confusing. It resented all proselytizing among Lutherans, and in the same breath accused both the Catholic Apostolic Church and the Jesuits of "trying to fish in troubled waters."[11]

Dansk Kirketidende, a newspaper which faithfully represented the interests of the state church, charged the sect with legalism and authoritarianism shortly after the Copenhagen congregation was gathered. "Despite the Irvingites' calling on the spirit and the appearance of spirituality in which they clothe themselves as they probe their scriptures," the editor wrote, "they seem bound to a law of their own making. Their insistence on unquestioned obedience to the 'elders' and 'angels' must lead to a clerical tyranny worse than popery." He also challenged the Irvingite claims of ecumenicity. "Disregarding all of their rhetoric about not having separated from the state church . . . they have begun to worship God in a unique way and establish offices which differ from those of the state church."[12]

A year later the same Lutheran newspaper added an allegation of heretical Christology to these accusations of hypocrisy. Its editor quoted approvingly a critical Anglican review of the Irvingite book, The Restoration of Apostles and Prophets in the

Catholic Apostolic Church, which charged that the Irvingites believed Christ's human flesh had been that of fallen man. Bøhm had defended Catholic Apostolic orthodoxy against this charge three years earlier in his Hvad ere de saakaldte Irvingianere for Folk? /What Kind of People are the So-called Irvingites?/ The Danish Lutheran journal was aware of this book but, obviously elated to have found a specific doctrinal Achilles' heel in the sect, ignored it and proceeded to attack an anthology of British Irvingite sermons which Fleischer had translated into Danish for maintaining a progressive view of Christ's divinity. At birth he had not been a revelation of God, but through faith and fulfillment of the law during his lifetime he developed into the God-man. Dansk Kirketidende reminded its readers that this teaching could not be harmonized with the orthodox view that Jesus had been both fully human and fully divine from birth. "Nobody, we can be assured, will wrongly suspect us of having presented an unrepresentative sample of /Irvingite/ exegesis," the writer concluded. "But if their exegesis deviates so far from the heritage of the church fathers, then its heretical and fanatical character is already obvious."[13] Significantly, the review did not attack the Irvingites' millenarianism. Perhaps its writer realized that this historicist eschatology meshed with early Lutheran orthodoxy.

Not all Danish Lutheran clergymen were convinced that the Catholic Apostolic Church was a departure from the faith once delivered to the saints. Julius Thomsen, who had recently taken a theology degree at the University of Copenhagen, demurred. He joined the Catholic Apostolic Church in Copenhagen, where he assisted Fleischer as the congregation's "evangelist." Thomsen's role in proliferating historicist millenarianism, however, was not limited to the Danish capital city. In 1867 the popular Bornholm revivalist, Peter Christian Trandberg, placed a notice in Dansk Kirketidende, requesting that a clergyman come to the Baltic island and assist him in his awakenings.[14] Thomsen was one of several who eventually responded to this call. His cooperation with Trandberg, although short-lived, began a new direction in the latter's theology and homiletics. On subsequent visits to Copenhagen Trandberg repeatedly visited Fleischer, Thomsen, and other Irvingites.[15] His sermons began to reflect a preoccupation with the millenarian theme. Frequently departing from the Biblical texts in the Lutheran lectionary, he preached on such eschatological passages as Revelation 13 and 21 week after week.[16]

Trandberg used the press to publicize the new departure in his thought beyond the bounds of his Bornholm parish. In January, 1872 he placed an announcement in the island's largest newspaper, expressing his "solemn, joyous expectation, that the return of the Lord is at hand." Trandberg announced that the imminence of the Second Advent demanded that he travel about Bornholm to prepare its inhabitants for the cataclysmic event which, he believed, in contrast to the Irvingites, would precede the great tribulation.[17]

Trandberg's return to the Danish state church later that year did not signal an abandonment of his millenarian beliefs. His motives are not clear, but it seems plausible that he did so in order to reach a larger audience with his eschatological message. His diaries and sermon notes reveal that he continued to preach on texts from Revelation more frequently than on the rest of the Bible. He kept in contact with the Irvingites in Copenhagen for several years, and often discussed the Second Coming with his state church colleagues.[18]

It is more difficult, however, to assess the impact of historicist millenarianism on the Danish Lutheran clergy as a whole. The Nordic church council, which convened in Copenhagen in 1871 and discussed "The Irvingites' Understanding of the Last Things," disclosed that Scandinavian state church pastors differed about Irvingite teachings. N. G. Blædel, a leader of the Copenhagen Inner Mission and pastor of the city's Garrison Church, chided the state church for having lost hope of the millennium and suggested that the Catholic Apostolic Church offered a much-needed anecdote. He praised it for having applied a sense of prophecy to Christians' understanding of history. But as a loyal Lutheran, Blædel found fault with the Irvingites' insistence on a restored apostolate and first-century "gifts of grace," by which he apparently meant glossolalia, for which they were known. He furthermore criticized their posttribulationist eschatology which posited the appearance of the Antichrist as a prerequisite to the Second Advent. "They have the hope, if one dare say so, that the Antichrist will come immediately. . . ."

At this point Thomsen sprang up to defend Catholic Apostolic theology on New Testament grounds. He expressed his gratitude for Blædel's well-intended remarks, but claimed that the Lutheran had misunderstood Irvingism.[19] Citing II Thessalonians, Thomsen maintained that Paul had explicitly stated that the Antichrist must come before Jesus could return. He added that this doctrine need not alarm true Christians, who would survive the great tribulation.

To Pastor C. Rothe, the debate between Thomsen and Blædel over the sequence of eschatological events seemed irrelevant. Claiming to represent a majority position, he suggested that Biblical references to the millennium should be interpreted figuratively. Rothe also warned against dabbling in things which mankind is not intended to comprehend. "We should not lift the veil from a future which perhaps does not concern us. All of this prophetic business should be placed into the hands of the Lord."[20]

Perhaps owing to the uneven advance of religious toleration in Scandinavia, the Catholic Apostolic Church became far more popular in Denmark than in the other Nordic lands. While it eventually counted over 4,000 communicants in more than thirty Danish congregations, in Norway the Irvingites never numbered more than a few hundred.[21] The Swedish branch of the sect quickly exceeded 1,000 members, but after 1900 shrunk as rapidly as it had expanded.[22] Moreover, owing to its limited size and centralized polity, the Catholic Apostolic Church never shed its image as a British intrusion in Scandinavia. This is perhaps most clearly revealed in its literature. Although the sect published its own magazines, such as the Danish _Pastorale Meddelelser_ /Pastoral

Reports/, and a small number of books and printed millenarian lectures, it continued to rely on the translated works of John Cardale and other English founders for its systematic theology.

The next wave of foreign historicist millenarianism to strike northern Europe was neither ecumenical nor English. It can be traced to William Miller (1782-1849), a farmer from Low Hampton, New York, who began to probe the Scriptures shortly after joining a Baptist church in 1816. He became obsessed with predicting the date of Christ's return. Perhaps uninfluenced by other millenarian studies, Miller reproduced the main aspects of historicist millenarianism which Englishmen were concurrently developing.[23] In the early 1830's he began a fateful career as an itinerant lay evangelist, proclaiming that Christ would return "about 1843." Aided by Joshua Himes, a social reformer from Boston, he built up a following of more than 50,000 devoted adherents and, according to Winthrop Hudson's estimate, perhaps 1,000,000 people who were "skeptically expectant."[24] In January, 1843 Miller predicted that the Second Advent would occur by March 21, 1844, a date which he eventually changed to October 22 of the same year. The appointed day arrived, but Jesus did not.[25]

Miller, who was subsequently excommunicated from the Baptist church in Low Hampton, faded into oblivion and died in 1849. Many of his disillusioned followers apparently abandoned millenarianism. But others, under the leadership of Ellen White (1827-1915), soon began a new movement which combined historicism with temperance and other health reforms then current. Regarding Saturday as the Sabbath, they assumed the name "Seventh-day Adventists." The visionary prophetess White and her associates established their headquarters at Battle Creek, Michigan, where they also founded a college and structured their movement into a permanent denomination.

The new addition to the increasingly intricate constellation of American denominations soon became known for its missionary zeal. Many Scandinavian congregations on both sides of the Atlantic were incorporated into its worldwide organization before the end of the century. But the rapidity with which proselytism was undertaken in the Nordic countries can be attributed to the efforts of a single convert, John Gottlieb Matteson (1835-96). Born on the Danish island of Langeland, Matteson emigrated with his family to the United States in 1854. They settled near New Denmark, Wisconsin and joined a Lutheran church. Before the decade ended, however, Matteson underwent a spiritual crisis and became a Baptist. He served temporarily as a lay preacher, and was ordained after brief studies at a Baptist theological seminary in Chicago. In 1863, however, Matteson and most of his Baptist parishioners in Wisconsin joined the new Adventist denomination. The Adventists commissioned Matteson as a revivalist, and in this capacity he led awakenings among Scandinavian immigrants throughout the Midwest. In 1872 he began to publish a newspaper for them, Advent Tidende /Advent Tidings/.[26]

Matteson's aggressive proselytism soon aroused the

opposition of the immigrant Lutheran clergy and press. The Norwegian Lutheran organ Lutheraneren /The Lutheran/ termed his newspaper and the Adventist doctrine of annihilationism, according to which the soul of a wicked individual perishes upon his death, "soul-corrupting poison."[27] The Swedish-American Augustana Synod attacked the Adventist organ for Swedish immigrants, Svensk Advent Härold /Swedish Advent Herald/, and the denomination's Sabbatarianism, which it called a judaizing tendency.[28] Erik Norelius, president of the Augustana Synod, agreed that belief in the Second Advent constituted an important part of the Christian faith, but took exception with speculation over the date of its occurrence.[29] Writing from Waupaca, Wisconsin in 1872, the Danish Lutheran pastor Rasmus Andersen complained bitterly to his sponsors in Denmark that the Adventists were competing strongly for the immigrants whose loyalty to their birthright religious tradition he was seeking to preserve.[30]

Danish-American Baptist ministers especially resented Matteson's apostasy and the inroads which Adventism had made in their small flocks. "John Matteson was here last autumn," wrote a pastor from Freeborn, Minnesota early in 1873. "Some members of our congregation joined the Adventists, and many Lutherans were re-baptized, but whether they had been converted Christians previously is questionable." This Baptist accused the Adventists of entangling converts in Old Testament legalism and also excoriated their doctrine of annihilationism.[31] Later that year L. Knudsen, who ministered to the Danish

Baptist church at Neenah, Wisconsin, admitted that conversions to Adventism had neutralized the growth his flock otherwise would have had. Writing in the Baptist periodical in Denmark, he delivered a broadside at the teachings and evangelism of his Adventist rivals.[32]

Undaunted by these verbal assaults, the redoubtable Matteson expanded his efforts to convert other American Scandinavians to the Adventist faith. During the 1870's he wrote several books and tracts in Danish, some of which were translated for Swedish-American readers. He also edited a Danish hymnal. When the denomination's press initially declined to publish some of Matteson's works for immigrants, he raised one thousand dollars to underwrite their publication.[33] He also had a hand in educational work among Nordic newcomers, part of which was conducted at an immigrant department of the denomination's college in Battle Creek.

Some Adventist doctrines arrived in Scandinavia before Matteson returned to northern Europe in the late 1870's. Immigrant readers of _Advent Tidende_ and _Svensk Advent Härold_ appear to have sent copies of these journals to friends and relatives in the Old World. Mogens Abraham Sommer, the former Danish free church leader, began to receive _Advent Tidende_ in 1873. He requested and received permission to reprint some of its articles in his short-lived monthly, _Indøvelse i Christendommen_ [Training in Christianity].[34] In Sweden, Andreas Fernholm (1840-92), a Baptist who had previously been a Lutheran pastor and later joined the Swedish Mission Covenant, began to publish a millenarian newspaper, Tidens Tecken /Signs of the Times/, in 1873. His theology matched that of the Seventh-day Adventists in respect to annihilationism and the Saturday Sabbath. The Roman Catholic Church, he charged, had "introduced a different day of rest from the one which the Lord ordered."[35] But in contrast to the Adventists, Fernholm did not regard this as a vital question.

Responding to the invitations of scattered sympathizers in Scandinavia, Matteson left for Denmark in 1877, where he conducted revival meetings in the northwestern province of Vendsyssel and, the following spring, gathered twenty-three Danes into Scandinavia's first Seventh-day Adventist congregation at Alstrup.[36] The fact that Matteson was no longer a Danish citizen was used as an excuse for denying him permission to sell religious literature in Denmark, however, a move which curbed his effectiveness in that country.

Matteson moved the base of his Scandinavian mission to Christiania in the autumn of 1878, and on October 27 began to give public lectures in a theater in Møllergaten.[37] Even hostile observers conceded that the Danish evangelist was an engaging speaker and talented singer.[38] When his audiences grew progressively larger, Matteson began to preach in the auditorium of a school in nearby Mariboes gate which, he recalled, seated more than 1,000 people.[39] One amazed Lutheran observed that the large hall could not possibly hold all of the Norwegians who wanted to hear Matteson, and commented that he had not seen so much public interest in revivalism for several years.[40] The Adventist preacher also reached seekers through Tidernes Tegn /Signs of the Times/, a periodical which he began to publish in 1879 and quickly reached a circulation of 1,200.[41]

Despite the popularity of Matteson's sermons and magazine, the gathering of Adventist churches proceeded slowly. In Christiania a congregation with eighty members was organized early in 1879 and immediately gained recognition as a legal dissenting denomination.[42] During the 1880's congregations were formed in the southern coastal cities of Moss, Kragerø, Arendal, and Skien. The Adventist movement spread even more slowly in northern Norway, although eighteen adherents on the island of Hadsel formed a congregation in 1889.[43]

The rather slow proliferation of Adventist churches in Norway can probably be attributed in part to the stiff opposition which the Lutheran clergy began to afford shortly after Matteson arrived. Pastor Johan C. H. Storjohann (1832-1914) directed a series of well-attended lectures against Adventist theology, while his colleagues Sven Brun, Julius Riddervold, and Michael Færden attacked Sabbatarianism and annihilationism, and defended infant baptism, which the Adventists rejected.[44] The state church periodical, Luthersk Kirketidende, carried many anti-Adventist diatribes,[45] and pamphlets, such as Appel til Sjælhyrderne i Kristiania /Appeal to the Pastors in Kristiania/, circulated among the Norwegian divines, warning them to defend Lutheran orthodoxy or else accept the results of Matteson's preaching.[46]

As in the United States, leaders of non-Lutheran denominations also resented Adventist competition for Norwegian Christians. One foremost anti-Adventist dissenter was the Christiania Methodist preacher, S. A. Isacsen, who gave a lecture in a labor union hall and wrote a series of related articles and booklets against the new sect.[47] The Norwegian Baptist press commented little on the Seventh-day Adventists, although the editor of Unions-Banneret reported in 1881 that the rival sect was declining in the nation's capital.[48] This virtual silence is surprising in view of the Adventists' successes in proselytizing Baptists. The millenarian denomination's Swedish historian has gone so far as to generalize that the "nuclei of the early Adventist congregations . . . consisted of Baptist converts."[49]

Despite such opposition, the number of Norwegian Adventists climbed steadily to 652 by the end of the century. In 1887 the four congregations (Christiania, Drammen, Moss, and Larvik) organized a national conference at a camp meeting which Ellen White and other prominent Adventists attended. At that time the denomination had approximately 300 members in Norway, 223 of whom belonged to the congregation in Christiania.[50]

From the nation's capital Adventism spread eastward into Sweden. Matteson organized a small school for colporteurs in Christiania which attracted Swedish students. Two of these men were Jonas Pehrson Rosquist, a cobbler from Grythyttehed (now Grythyttan) and Olof Johnson, a farmer from Åmot. Matteson sent both back to their hometowns, where they soon gathered small congregations. Although a Swedish Conference was organized in 1882 and received financial support from the denomination in the United States, it grew slowly. In fact, in none of the Nordic countries did the number of Seventh-day Adventists surpass 1,000 until about 1910.[51] Ecclesiastical persecution can be cited as one factor for the retarded growth in Sweden. Shortly before the Swedish Conference was founded, Rosquist was forbidden to preach in Grythytthed on the grounds that his activity threatened to divide the parish. In defiance of an ecclesiastical court, he continued to do so. Rosquist's recalcitrance cost him eight days in jail.[52] His case, although perhaps an extreme example, reveals the harsh treatment afforded proselytizing dissenters at that time.

Adventism appears to have appealed more to economically disinherited Scandinavians than to the wealthier classes. Matteson admitted in 1881 that he and his colleagues were having considerable difficulty reaching the financially comfortable.[53] After inspecting congregations in Denmark, Norway, and Sweden a few years later, Ellen White stated that "most of our people are poor, and it is very difficult for them to obtain work, even at low prices."[54] She did not, however, indicate whether Nordic Adventists were more indigent than other Scandinavians during that depressed decade when Nordic emigration to North America reached its peak. Nor did White state whether the Adventists' refusal to work on Saturday had excluded some from jobs they might otherwise have had. Poverty did not, in any event, characterize all millenarians in Europe, Great Britain, or the United States. Theories which postulate economic deprivation as a motive stimulating belief in the imminent end of an unjust world have, as we shall see, only limited applicability in Scandinavia.

It is clear, however, that Seventh-day Adventism was largely a movement of the working class in northern Europe. A perusal of selected congregational records in Norway reveals that nearly all of the adult male members were artisans, farmers, or fishermen. The nine male charter members of the congregation on Hadsel Island included four farmers, two fishermen and, curiously, three colporteurs. During the next year, however, a sheriff and a teacher, along with several more working class individuals, joined the church.[55] All of the men admitted to membership in the Adventist church at Arendal between 1892 and 1895 were carpenters, farmers, or artisans.[56] In his survey of the denomination's early history in Norway, Øivind Gjertsen has characterized the members of the large congregation in Christiania as coming "largely . . . from the poorer classes" during the nineteenth century.[57]

The same congregations all included a preponderance of women, an imbalance typical of Scandinavian free churches at that time. In Hadsel, twenty-five of the first fifty-six members (54%) were women, while in Arendal fifteen representatives of the fairer sex constituted 68% of the members received from 1892 until 1895. The large congregation in Christiania had 139 female (62%) and only eighty-four male members in 1887.

Historicist millenarianism remained a strong current in British eschatology throughout the nineteenth century, although it lost some ground there and in the United States as futurist millenarianism gradually gained acceptance among Protestants. Spectacular religious and political events in Europe had revived historicism; further occurrences, such as the decree of papal infallibility in 1870 and the rise of Napoleon III nurtured this school, especially among a coterie of Anglican interpreters of prophecy. Indeed, one historian of eschatological thought has commented that "the mystique of the Napoleonic legend so clouded millenarian eyes that many of them were convinced that he was destined for more than mere mortality; he was usually picked out for the greater role of the Antichrist."[58]

One of the most influential popularizers of this interpretation was an Anglican priest, Michael Baxter. The son of Robert Baxter, who had temporarily affiliated with Irving's congregation in London, he began in the 1860's to pen a long series of books in which he not only identified contemporary events with Biblical prophecies, but also, like a minority of other millenarians, set several dates for the Second Advent. A few of his works, including _Coming Wonders Expected between 1867 and 1875_[59] and _Louis Napoleon, the Destined Monarch of_ the World, and Personal Antichrist,[60] appeared in American editions shortly before or after they were published in London. Another of Baxter's speculative tomes, Forty Coming Wonders, was offered to Norwegian readers in 1887.[61] Its translator, Engvald Hansen, the son of a Lutheran pastor, was a medical doctor in western Norway. A deeply religious man who also participated in workers' health programs and efforts to extend the nation's railway system to remote areas, Hansen described himself as "one of these strongly religiously attuned individuals who regard the next world as their real home, but in their daily lives stand with their feet firmly affixed to the ground."[62] His translation, complete with a "prophetic calendar" which predicted early twentieth-century dates for the "wonders," became sufficiently popular to warrant publication of an abridged version after World War I.[63]

The millenarian works of Henry Grattan Guinness (1835-1910) appear to have enjoyed even greater popularity in Scandinavia. An Irishman by birth and a Catholic-baiter, this Anglican clergyman is generally regarded as the most influential historicist of his time. In harmony with a central tenet of historicism, he argued that the papacy was the Antichrist and that the struggles of the Reformation would soon have to be repeated. Swedish Baptists were introduced to Guinness' interpretations in 1883 when their publishing firm printed a compendium of his works.[64] A different firm, though, published a translation ofGuinness' Light for the Latter Days twelve years later.[65] Engvald Hansen rendered the same book into Norwegian soon after he finished Baxter's Forty Coming Wonders.[66]

But Guinness' most influential Scandinavian popularizer was undoubtedly Paul Wettergreen (1835-89), a pastor who had withdrawn from the Norwegian state church and become a leading figure in the Lutheran Free Church. While preaching a series of sermons on Daniel in the southern coastal city of Arendal during the early 1880's, he received a letter from a sea-going friend in London, who urged him to acquire a copy of Guinness' The Approaching End of the Age. Wettergreen incorporated in his sermons several excerpts from this volume, which he called "one of the most profound and thorough books I have ever read."[67] The periodical which he edited for the Lutheran Free Church, Budbæreren [The Messenger], frequently carried articles which kept its readers informed about developments among British historicist millenarians.[68]

Guinness' works do not appear to have aroused so much interest in Denmark as they did in Sweden or Norway. On the island of Bornholm, however, many of whose inhabitants were still receptive to new religious currents, Light for the Latter Days came out in a Danish translation in 1896.[69]

Twelve years earlier, the Danish Lutheran pastor O. C. Ipsen of the Inner Mission penned a historicist interpretation of Revelation. He relied in part on millenarian works by his fellow Bornholmer, Peter Christian Trandberg, as well as the

German Irvingite Heinrich Thiersch and the Swiss Protestant Frederic Louis Godet. Ipsen carefully avoided historicism's temptation to predict the date of Christ's return.[70]

Egypt's pyramids furnished part of the basis for one curious variety of historicist millenarianism. During the second half of the nineteenth century a small number of people in Great Britain and the United States sought to combine Egyptology with eschatology by correlating various dimensions of the Great Pyramid of Cheops near Gizeh -- which, they believed, was the "altar in the heart of Egypt" referred to in Isaiah 19:19 -- with historical events. C.A.L. Totten's American book on the subject was also published in Sweden in 1893.[71] Hans Guldberg (1843-96), a captain in the Norwegian army and a respected lay leader in the state church,[72] illustrated and wrote the foreword to the Norwegian translation of James Keith's British study in 1887. Guldberg was unswervingly convinced of the pyramid's genius, asserting that

> although it is silent, it speaks through all of its dimensions, corridors, measurements, and location about all of the Lord's great, wonderful laws and ways both for the dead and the living; it confirms the laws regarding the heavenly bodies' motion and distance; it teaches us the plain and simple laws of physics and mathematics; it has solved untold problems to date, yes, even the

> history, sufferings, and redemption of the human race; it relates and confirms all of God's great prophecies and promises to his people; and, remarkably, to date nobody has been able to find any errors in the fulfillment of its calculations.[73]

Some Scandinavian church historians have regarded this kind of speculation as the quintessence of millenarianism and concluded that nineteenth-century expectations of an imminent Second Advent were to be found largely on the sectarian fringe of Christianity. This charge contains some truth if applied only to the three decades immediately after 1850. Yet, however strange some of their calculations appear in retrospect, people like Guldberg disprove this assertion more than they confirm it. The Norwegian captain was neither a madman nor a social outcast, but a well-regarded officer who was active in the "Treider movement," an independent Lutheran laymen's undertaking which conducted missionary and social work in the nation's capital. To supplement his Norwegian education, the independently wealthy Guldberg had studied engineering and mathematics in Göteborg, Aachen, and Zürich, and applied this training to his prophetic studies. Another leader of the Treider movement, Johannes Jørgensen (1850-92), had served as a clergyman in the state church for several years before his sharp criticism of its formalism brought him into conflict with J.C.H. Storjohann, his superior in the chaplaincy of the women's penal institution in Christiania. After Jørgensen left the ordained ministry he joined Guldberg and Otto Treider in their urban mission and also edited its newspaper, Evangelisten, as well as Menneskevennen [The Friend of Man], the organ of the Norwegian Total Abstinence Society.[74] Like his two colleagues in the Treider movement's leadership, Jørgensen was involved in cooperative ventures between Lutherans of the state church and nonconformists in Norway. The leading roles which men like Hansen, Guldberg, and Jørgensen played in popularizing British and American eschatology in Scandinavia suggest that unsubstantiated assertions about their "fanaticism" tell us more about their authors' prejudices than about millenarians' mentalities.[75]

Influenced both by Baxter and the pyramid investigators, Guldberg plotted out in the 1880's the coming half century of the world's history, dividing it into seven dispensations, or "seals" (after Revelation 6-8), which included more than two decades of tribulation. The first, which had ostensibly begun in 1882, was a seven-year time of "great evangelization." In 1889, Guldberg prognosticated, wars would usher in the great tribulation. Famines were to characterize the 1896-1903 period, while between 1903 and 1910 swords, hunger, plagues, and wild animals would kill one quarter of the earth's inhabitants. But during a two-year seal beginning in 1910, a large, innumerable group would be saved. Those who survived -- including the 144,000 recipients of salvation referred to in Revelation

7:4 -- would be "sealed." Guldberg scheduled the final seal, the Battle of Armageddon, for 1916-1920, when Christ would defeat the army of Antichrist and rescue his bride from the tribulation. Satan would be bound for 1,000 years, and the millennium would begin, ironically, in 1933.[76] A fatal fall from a horse at the Gardermoen army base in 1896 spared him from seeing how far afield his interpretations would run.

A related branch of the historicist school searched the heavens for evidence which would corroborate Biblical prophecies. Jabez Bunting Dimbleby, a British writer and self-styled astronomer, popularized this approach, with which he also tried to disprove Darwinism and higher criticism of the Bible. In _The Appointed Time_ Dimbleby "proved" that the Second Advent would occur in 1898¼. O. A. Østby, a pastor in the Hauge Synod, a small, revivalistic Lutheran body, rendered this book into Norwegian and published it in Minnesota in 1896.[77] A Swedish translation appeared in Minneapolis only a year before the predicted event.[78] This urgent appeal does not appear to have been published in Scandinavia, but another of Dimbleby's astronomical-millenarian treatises, which Østby also translated for his fellow Norwegian-Americans, was printed in both Sweden and Norway in the early 1890's.[79]

The Anglo-American tradition of prophetic conferences reached Scandinavia in the 1880's. In February, 1887, for example, millenarians from several Norwegian nonconformist bodies and a smaller number of state church Lutherans staged a four-day convention in Christiania's Evangelical Lutheran Free Church. They modelled their parley after the Second International Prophetic Conference, held in Chicago three months previously.[80] Like the Chicago symposium, it was a poorly organized assembly, but it was very well attended, nevertheless. Several hundred people were reportedly turned away when the sanctuary proved too small to accommodate all those who desired to hear the eschatological speeches.[81] The chaos of the assembly increased when Guldberg announced that a large earthquake had just rocked southern Europe. He explained the cataclysm as a response to prayers for the rapid return of Christ offered at the convention the previous day.[82]

The various and frequently conflicting historicist interpretations helped to bring Scandinavia to its summit of millenarian fervor during the 1880's. But the excitement of that decade was further heightened and expectations of the Second Advent made even more intense when futurism finally came to northern Europe. In contrast to historicist millenarians, futurists argued that none of the prophetic events described in Daniel and Revelation had yet occurred. Their interpretation of the Second Coming eventually became the prevailing millenarian current in the Nordic countries.

Much of the credit for this school's success must be given to John Nelson Darby (1800-92), an Irish Protestant who organized the small Plymouth Brethren sect and developed the prevailing variety of futurist millenarianism, which he proclaimed during several decades of evangelism in Europe, the British Empire, and the United States. Darby was a typical futurist only insofar as he believed that none of the apocalyptic prophecies had been fulfilled. Beyond this point of consensus, he added a number of designs to the futurist fabric. Darby foresaw both second and third comings. The earlier, which he called the pretribulationist "secret rapture," would be perceptible only to the true Christians, both living and dead, who would be united with Christ in heaven. This rapture could occur at any time, Darby felt, a belief which added a sense of immediacy to his message. The prophecies relating to non-Christians would take place at a later time. The spiritual nature of the first step demanded a spiritual church. Darby believed that no denomination could encompass all of the present and past Christians who would be caught up in the secret rapture. He maintained that the true church was an invisible spiritual fellowship, an idea which in Protestant history was perhaps first articulated by Sebastian Frank in the sixteenth century. Finally, like many other nineteenth-century millenarians and non-millenarians, Darby divided history into a series of eras, or "dispensations."[83]

Darby had little direct impact on the Nordic countries. Plymouth Brethren meetings were organized in a few Scandinavian communities beginning in the 1870's, but they remained very small. As in Great Britain and the United States, few accepted everything the Irishman offered. Apparently most rejected his ecclesiology, even if they were won over to the appealing doctrine of Christ's "any-moment coming."

Americans to whom Darby had brought his eschatology were far more important in promoting it in Scandinavia. Dwight L. Moody (1837-99), the nineteenth century's most popular American evangelist, was among the most important. The Chicagoan cooperated with Darby during the latter's visits to the Windy City and gradually accepted his millenarianism. James F. Findlay, the American revivalist's biographer, has concluded that "it is entirely possible that Moody came under Darby's direct influence in 1868, and certainly no later than 1872."[84] Moody frequently preached on the Second Advent and, beginning in 1880, held annual conferences in Northfield, Massachusetts, which many leading American and British millenarians attended and frequently dominated.[85] During his 1873-75 evangelistic tour of the British Isles, which brought world fame to the previously obscure layman, Moody's name also became well known in Scandinavia, although he never visited any of the Nordic countries. His sermons and the songs of his colleague, Ira D. Sankey, were soon translated into all of the Scandinavian languages and enjoyed immense popularity. His plain diction, down-to-earth manners, ecumenicity, use of a gospel singer, and Arminian theology offered alternatives to the main currents in Scandinavian Lutheranism and harmonized well with the period's religious optimism.[86] As we shall see in Chapter VII, Moody quickly became a hero of the Norwegian and Danish Mission

Covenants, whose periodicals brought dozens of his sermons to their readers.

But it was the Swedish-American Fredrik Franson (1852-1908) who played the most important role in bringing Darby's eschatology to Scandinavia. Born on a farm in the southwestern Swedish province of Värmland, Franson emigrated to Nebraska with his family when he was a teenager. Both his mother and stepfather had been active in mid-century Swedish revivals, and lay preachers and colporteurs frequently visited their rural home. Franson's own conversion, however, did not occur until he was twenty and suffered a lengthy illness. After his health returned he joined the Baptist church in Ensteina, Nebraska, and became a regional lay evangelist among Scandinavian immigrants. When Moody returned from the British Isles in 1875, Franson moved to Chicago and joined his new Chicago Avenue Church, which rose from the ashes of that city's devastating fire. William J. Erdman, a leading Presbyterian millenarian, preached at this church from 1875 until 1878. It seems plausible that Franson (and perhaps Moody) became a Darbyite at that time although, unlike Erdman, he believed the Second Coming would precede the great tribulation. He also became proficient in American revival methods, adopting nearly all of Moody's proven techniques. He conducted awakenings in any edifice which would accommodate him, and addressed his hearers as sinners whose salvation depended on their immediate acceptance of Christ. Whenever possible, Franson supplemented his preaching with the songs of a gospel singer. Finally, like Moody, he organized Bible courses to continue the fruits of his revivals. Equipped with these means of winning converts, he proceeded to Minnesota, where he briefly worked as an evangelist before setting off for the lion's den of Utah, where he spent most of 1879 and 1880 trying to reconvert Scandinavians who had thrown in their lot with the Latter-day Saints. Upon returning to Illinois, Franson began a period of fruitful cooperation with another Darbyite, John G. Princell. Princell, himself a Swedish immigrant and a former pastor in the Augustana Synod, taught at Ansgar College, a diminutive institution affiliated with the Ansgar Synod, one of the ancestors of the American Mission Covenant. This fairly well known millenarian later addressed the Second International Prophetic Conference, which met at Chicago in 1886. The two Swedes staged a "nonsectarian convention" in the Windy City in April, 1881 to discuss questions pertaining to the Second Advent. This parley proved to be a much greater success than a millenarian gathering which Franson had called in Denver the previous year but had been forced to cancel when nobody attended. Its proceedings were published in Chicago-Bladet, a newspaper connected with the Ansgar Synod and later with Princell's Swedish Evangelical Free Church.

Shortly after the 1881 conference Franson departed for Scandinavia, where he spent several years proclaiming the imminent Second Coming in controversial revival meetings which frequently surpassed Moody's awakenings in commotion and the intensity of his personal appeals to those in attendance.[87] He continued the prophetic conference tradition with a convention in Sweden in 1882, and also arranged to have the proceedings of his Chicago conference published in that country.[88] Franson expounded his own interpretation of futurist millenarianism in two brief treatises during the 1880's, Kort öfversikt öfver Uppenbarelseboken /A Brief Look at the Book of Revelation/, originally presented as a lecture in Norrköping, and Antikrist, which Chicago-Bladet carried after it was published in Sweden. In 1897 he completed his lengthier study, Himlauret /The Clock of Heaven/, published in Sweden that year and in Chicago in 1898.[89]

Franson's Darbyite futurism challenged the prevailing historicist millenarianism in Scandinavia at several points. He attacked the historicists' exegesis of Biblical prophecies on the grounds that they did not interpret the Scriptures literally. Specifically, he singled out historicism's year-day theory as a departure from literalist hermeneutics. All of the historicists' calculations, he asserted, were wrong, because they rest on the mistaken assumption that a prophetic "day" should be construed as a year. "The Bible represents the literal fulfillment during so many days and not years."[90] Franson also rejected the venerated historicist equation of the papacy and the Antichrist. Indeed, although he shared some of his fellow Scandinavians' distrust and suspicion of

Roman Catholics, he briefly sought the support of the Vatican for his evangelism. On a trip to Rome Franson ascended the Santa Scala on his knees and tried to secure an audience with Pope Leo XIII, but gave up when he learned that visitors were required to kneel before the Holy Father.[91]

"Who the Antichrist will be is difficult to say," Franson admitted in 1882, "and because of this, various guesses have been made. That he is already born is more than likely." Franson acknowledged current interest in the Napoleons as candidates, but declined to commit himself to any of them. "Many believed that Napoleon I, a truly remarkable person, was the Antichrist, and even today there are those who believe that he will rise from the grave to command the armies of Europe once again and make its kings tremble on their thrones." But this was too implausible for Franson. "Without further comment on this rather absurd assumption, it must be mentioned that a large number of Biblical scholars in England and America believe that somebody of that family, or at least of that name, will be the man." Realizing that many millenarians expected the Antichrist to belong to one of the twelve tribes of Israel, Franson broached the theory of Anglo-Israelism to bridge the ethnic gap. "We must therefore say that it is assumed by many, and with fairly good reason, that the ten lost tribes are to be found among the Anglo-Saxon peoples."[92]

In typical Darbyite fashion, Franson told Scandinavians on both sides of the Atlantic that a pretribulationist secret rapture would precede the personal Antichrist's appearance. He also adhered to the Irish mentor's teaching of the any-moment coming. Franson never tired of preaching that Christ could come <u>när som helst</u> -- at any time. To avoid misunderstanding, he carefully defined his use of the phrase:

> The expression "at any time" does not mean that he can come on any day or at any hour, but rather there is a certain day and a certain hour when he will come, and no other day or time. But since we do not know which day or which time this will be, we say that he can come at any time, <u>so far as we know</u>.
>
> By that we mean that there is nothing revealed in God's Word which gives us reason to believe that he could not come at any moment.[93]

Events in the 1890's, however, gave Franson the courage to venture further out on the chronological limb. While "we cannot know the precise day and hour of the Lord's return," he affirmed, "we can know the approximate time."[94] Like many other millenarians, Franson attached great significance to the conversion of Jews to Christianity and their return to Palestine as signs of the imminent Second Advent. The 1897 Zionist congress in Basel fired his hopes to a fever pitch. Furthermore, "a lot of Jews in Russia have begun to study the New Testament because their own prophecies have not been fulfilled," he announced gleefully. "No small number of Jews in Russia, Hungary, England, Germany, America, and even some in Scandinavia have given their hearts to Jesus and await elevation to the heavens and the national reblossoming which will follow." Linking prophecies in Daniel and Revelation, Franson concluded that the Second Advent would occur within seventeen years of the Zionist congress, or by 1914.[95]

Early in the twentieth century a Swedish church historian assessed Franson's impact on millenarian thinking in Sweden. "In the vast majority of free churches in our land the final result of the new apocalyptic pronouncements, both spoken and written, was that Christ's return certainly could not be precisely calculated, but that it is near, and this became a basic tenet of free church faith. It was . . . Franson who created this new apocalyptic spectacle."[96] Like most other generalizations, however, this one must be taken *cum grano salis*. The Seventh-day Adventists, for example, remained loyal to their historicist position, and the translated editions of Baxter's and Guinness' works continued to be read in Scandinavia, as were those of the Tübingen historicist, Johann Bengel. Within the established church, moreover, Otto Myrberg of the University of Uppsala wrote a critical reply to futurist millenarianism in the 1880's. In historicist fashion he identified the harlot of Revelation 17 with the Roman Catholic Church and the Beast of Revelation 13 with the papacy.[97]

Myrberg apparently sought to defend much of Luther's exegesis of Revelation against countervailing interpretations. But as a historian of the Seventh-day Adventists in Sweden has observed, "in rejecting the futurist interpretation, Myrberg unintentionally supported Adventism's method of exegeting the Apocalypse."[98] Despite the persistence of historicism, though, the importance of Franson and his Darbyite futurism in the genesis of a new millenarian wave in Scandinavia seems beyond dispute. He spent much of the 1880's and 1890's preaching the any-moment coming throughout northern Europe, encouraging the formation of the thoroughly millenarian Mission Covenants of Norway and Denmark, organizing prophetic conferences, and writing millenarian works.

The futurist eschatology which Franson brought to Scandinavia made a definite impact on the clergy and laymen of the established churches, as well, although the precise extent to which these Lutherans adopted it is difficult to determine. Beginning in the late 1880's, several of them began to write futurist treatises. In 1887, for example, Haldor Grønsdal of Bergen, then one of Norway's leading pedagogues, penned a short book on _Christi gjenkomst til Tusindårsriget_ /Christ's Return to the Thousand Year Kingdom/. He declared that "Christ's Second Coming will not only be sudden and unexpected, but also perceptible only to them who await him." This concept of the any-moment coming echoed Darby's eschatology, as did Grønsdal's assertion that the great tribulation would begin _after_ the secret rapture had occurred.[99] On the other hand, he used the year-day theory and a "bourgeois year" consisting of 360 days in determining that Christ's thousand-year reign would actually last for 360,000 years.[100]

In a far more detailed and scholarly study, Bishop Lars Dahle (1843-1925), a respected former Norwegian missionary, cautiously accepted futurist millenarianism.[101] An English translation of this work was published in Scotland three years after it appeared in Norwegian in 1893,[102] a rare example of Scandinavian theology influencing the British Isles. The bishop indicated his caution by stating explicitly that the Bible tells us little about the sequence of events pertaining to the Second Advent and does not reveal when the end of time is to be expected. "The great misfortune," he lamented, "is that there has been too much thoughtless venturing upon this last domain."[103] In harmony with many other millenarians, however, Dahle interpreted anti-Semitism, the conversion of Jews to Christianity, and Zionism as signs of the imminence of Christ's return.[104] Like Franson and other futurists, he believed that the Antichrist will be a specific, historic person, not an abstract anti-Christian spirit or the papacy.[105] Moreover, Dahle emphasized that Christ would come unexpectedly but, unlike most other futurists, allowed that "His coming may . . . lie far away in the future, and be prepared through many steps of development in God's kingdom."[106]

At no time, however, did the clergy of the established churches accept uncritically the eschatological currents which were flowing from British and American sources to Scandinavia. One astute observer, Michael Færden (1836-1912) of the conservative Norwegian newspaper, Luthersk Ugeskrift /Lutheran Weekly/, quoted the well known Swiss Protestant, Frederic Louis Godet, in 1884 when he reviewed the Dane O. C. Ipsen's study of Revelation: "The more securely the church pitches its tent on worldly ground, and the more comfortably it adapts itself down here, the more John's Revelation becomes a foreign book which awakens our dislike." He added, however, that "contemporary storms are seriously shaking the church's tent. The poles are creaking and the lines are loosening and snapping, one after the other. . . . For this reason, the Revelation of John has once again become the object of serious study by the church's believing theologians. . . ."[107] Færden correctly perceived the close relationship between this renewed interest in apocalypticism and a more general revival of religion. "At the present time," he wrote in 1888, "a religious storm is passing over the southern mountains of Norway . . . whose equal in intensity we have not experienced since the 1850's. In some respects it reminds one of . . . that movement which took place in Skien and gave rise to separatism there -- also in its rejection of infant baptism and its expectation of the Lord's imminent return."[108] Færden did not indict any specific individuals for bringing this spiritual tempest to his homeland, but it seems more than likely that he was referring to revivalistic millenarians like Franson who were frequently accused of fostering separatism.

Færden's equally conservative colleague, Johan Christian Heuch (1838-1904), who later served as bishop of Kristiansand, used a clerical conference in 1886 to attack millenarianism as a deviation from what he termed the "pure doctrine" (*ren Lære*) of confessional Lutheranism. "Some are thoroughly convinced that the return of Christ will occur before the end of the nineteenth century," he noted. Heuch regarded such a conviction as dangerous to Christianity because, as he put it, it is difficult for a pastor "to continue to work for the progressive edification of his people if he believes that after fourteen years they will no longer exist."[109]

Some Danish and Swedish Lutherans also excoriated aspects of modern eschatology. In a eulogy at O. P. Ipsen's funeral in 1897, Vilhelm Beck of the Danish Inner Mission called his commentary on the Apocalypse "a clear and balanced introduction to John's Revelation, an excellent book, which one today wishes were more widely distributed to counter all the nonsensical calculations about the Lord's return, with which the English are showering us."[110] In Sweden, much of the controversy focused on the missionary Otto With, whom Paul Peter Waldenström, a member of the established church as well as the Swedish Mission Covenant, opposed strongly.[111]

Despite protests against certain speculative tendencies within millenarianism, the movement thrived until well into the twentieth century and, in some of the free churches as well as among some of the older Lutheran pastors, is alive and prospering today. It had not yet crested when the Swedish Mission Covenant was constituted in 1878, but reached its apogee in the 1880's when Fredrik Franson returned to Scandinavia and stimulated the organization of its sister denominations in Norway and Denmark. The Swedish Covenant developed from the strivings of revivalistic Lutherans to create congregations composed exclusively of reborn Christians. It never became a millenarian body. But the Covenants of Norway and Denmark, as we shall see, grew directly out of Franson's revivals in those two countries.

Actually, Anglo-American millenarianism in Scandinavia was even more diverse than described in the present study. But even this brief cross-section of the most influential eschatological schools reveals that some assertions about and interpretations of the subject do not stand up under scrutiny.

One of these is Thorstein Gunnarson's frequently echoed charge that millenarianism went hand-in-hand with "sectarianism and fanaticism."[112] There were, admittedly, a handful of erratic people in the movement whose behavior cast shadows on millenarianism.[113] But their numbers hardly warrant dismissing all who anticipated the imminent Second Advent as fanatics. Nor can the movement be written off simply as a sectarian phenomenon, as the important roles which men like Hans Guldberg, O. C. Ipsen, and Lars Dahle played in it demonstrate. While it is usually easier to analyze a movement's leaders than its followers, there is reason to believe that interest in the millennium spread fairly deeply into the Scandinavian laity. According to both sympathetic and hostile reports, attendance at millenarian revivals outstripped the small number of official dissenters in nineteenth-century Scandinavia. The number and variety of millenarian books, tracts, and newspapers also indicates considerable interest among members of the state churches.

In his study of millenarianism in Norway, Gunnarson sought to analyze "why expectations of the judgment day are especially characteristic of religious minorities."[114] He offered a variety of reasons, including persecution, resentment of the established churches' power, and the like. Yet one must question the assumptions underlying his statement of the problem. Millenarianism cannot be described simply as a minority group phenomenon. Did it appeal especially to dissenters, as Gunnarson suggested? The Seventh-day Adventists, who succeeded in converting many Baptists when they brought historicist millenarianism to Scandinavia in the 1870's, fit his thesis beautifully. But how about the Norwegian and Danish Mission Covenants, which drew their membership largely from the state Lutheran churches? Furthermore, the line separating those who awaited the imminent Second Advent from Scandinavians who were indifferent or hostile to millenarianism did not run between the established and the free churches, but rather cut through both camps. Among Norwegian Baptists, for example, there does not appear to have been much apocalyptic interest after the initial losses to Seventh-day Adventism, and the Norwegian Methodist press frequently carried both millenarian and anti-millenarian articles.

The trans-Atlantic millenarian community whose British and American members Ernest Sandeen has described included many Scandinavians by the 1880's, when the Norwegian and Danish Mission Covenants came into being. Although most of the Christians who brought historicist and futurist millenarianisms to northern Europe after 1850 were dissenters, their eschatological influence soon spread into the established churches. Consequently, none of the Scandinavian religious movements of that period could avoid these pervasive millenarian currents, although they reacted differently to them. The general hostility of the Swedish Mission Covenant to apocalyptic thought, and the enthusiasm of the Norwegian and Danish Mission Covenants for Darbyite futurism were to place these three denominations into two divergent traditions which have endured right down to the present.

CHAPTER VI

CONSERVATISM IN THE SWEDISH MISSION COVENANT

The conservatism of the Swedish Mission Covenant during its formative years reflected that organization's debt to the Lutheran tradition in which it stood and the nineteenth-century pietistic revivalism from which it developed. While returned immigrants who had tasted American revivalism and denominationalism as well as Darbyite millenarianism in the New World shaped the Covenants of Norway and Denmark, that of Sweden was an essentially Swedish product. The men who fashioned it were, for the most part, Swedish Lutherans, few of whom had travelled extensively outside Scandinavia or had close contacts with members of other communions. A small number of the Covenant's early leaders rejected Lutheranism and advocated total separation from their state church and its theology. Its principal founders, however, particularly Paul Waldenström, cherished Sweden's Lutheran heritage. Although these Covenanters did not share Luther's millenarianism, and differed from the established church's theology on such vital points as the nature and meaning of Christ's atonement, they insisted that their missionary society -- not the state church -- was Luther's real heir in Sweden. The ambivalences of the Lutheran tradition on the church and the Bible posed difficulties for the movement during its early years, but Swedish Covenanters on both sides of the Atlantic found solutions which are generally identified with conservative Protestantism.

Both their conviction that the true church congregation was composed exclusively of regenerate Christians and their generally uncritical acceptance of the Bible had countless precedents in the history of Protestantism. English Puritans, for instance, had much in common with nineteenth-century "Mission Friends" on these points. But the Swedes arrived at these positions without significant influences from non-Lutherans. This was an important fact in their history, and often set Swedish and Swedish-American Covenanters apart from Covenanters in Denmark and Norway, as well as from the immigrant forebears of the Evangelical Free Church.

No problem vexed revivalistic Swedish Lutherans in the nineteenth century more than the presence of the unawakened at the communion rail. A law making communion in the state church mandatory for all its birthright members -- and earlier for all citizens -- was not abrogated until 1880. It placed born-again Swedes into a dilemma. Mission Friends had either to participate shoulder-to-shoulder with the ungodly in a ritual which they regarded as too inclusive to be the Lord's Supper or risk legal action by refusing to commune.

Three possible solutions were suggested. The first was to remain members of the established church but celebrate communion in conventicles without a clergyman. A small number of non-separating Swedes took this path. In the 1850's Oscar Ahnfelt (1813-82), a clergyman, organized several small congregations in southern Sweden in which converted laymen administered the Eucharist.[1] Their purpose, according to Ahnfelt, was "to observe communion in the manner of the disciples, but also to be able, through a closer union, to serve each other in love."[2] To traditional Lutherans, however, lay administration of the sacraments was an unsavory novelty which smacked of separatism and violated the principle of <u>rite vocatus</u>, according to which only properly called clergymen conducted services. The initial experiment was short-lived among non-separating Lutherans, although lay administration appeared again in the 1870's.[3]

A second answer was the formation of communion societies. These groups of converted individuals did not have laymen administer the Lord's Supper, but sought the ministrations of sympathetic state church pastors. These were sometimes difficult to obtain. When communion societies in central Sweden petitioned the king for permission to call a state church pastor, the Evangelical National Foundation, which handled much of the home missionary work in the nation, refused to consider their request. State church officials in the Diocese of Karlstad likewise refused to cooperate. They advised the dissatisfied communion societies to secede from the established church and form a separate denomination under the provisions of the newly enacted dissenter law.[4]

Very few of the societies, however, were willing to take the dramatic step of becoming separatist congregations, the third alternative. Many of their members expressed strong opposition to secession. In 1872 C. J. Nyvall, an important lay revivalist in the province of Värmland, lamented in his diary that "the free friends in Örebro have requested the schoolhouse for private communions. God forgive them for their carnal desire in asking too much."[5]

Other Mission Friends, however, believed that the situation had compelled them to adopt the first alternative, and to celebrate communion privately under lay administration. In defiance of a state church warning the Karlskoga Mission Society began to do so in 1872. A few months later its members justified their action in a letter to Rector Hammargren of Karlskoga which is one of the most illuminating documents in the history of the Swedish Mission Friends. "More than two years ago," they wrote, "we awakened to the consciousness of how wrong it is to give communion to obvious enemies of Christ, despisers of the Word, and impudent sinners, as is generally done in our State Churches." By studying the Scriptures, the writers continued, "we came to the conviction that we did not have permission to participate and, in our small way, further promote this distorted view of church order contrary to the Bible." In a specifically Lutheran variation of a theme frequently found in free church and conservative Protestant rhetoric, they asserted that they were part of the true church and not separatists from it:

> We also wish to mention that we do not concede that we have separated from the Evangelical Lutheran Church nor do we think of separation; but we stand by

> the difference between the spiritual and the earthly kingdoms which the twenty-eighth article in the Augsburg Confession, according to the Word of God, declares. We exclude from the church and communion obviously ungodly people according to God's Word without force as the same article according to the Bible decrees. About the church, we believe it is made up of believers, the holy ones, and the sheep that hear the Shepherd's voice.[6]

The Karlskoga Friends' recalcitrance did not soften the position of the established church against lay-administered communion. With few exceptions its clergymen remained hostile to the lay societies within the state church, and regarded their members as *de facto* separatists. The hierarchy admonished its pastors not to administer the Lord's Supper outside state church sanctuaries and also denied the communion societies use of these structures.

At this point Paul Peter Waldenström (1838-1917), a pastor in the established church who eventually became the most creative figure in the Swedish Mission Covenant, spoke out in favor of removing legal restraints from communion. An active Mission Friend, Waldenström had already gained notoriety in Sweden and among Swedish Lutherans in the United States as the instigator of the Uppsala communion case. More than any other event, that case led to the formation of the Mission Covenant. He was clearly the most learned person among the Mission Friends, having graduated from the University of Uppsala where he also earned a doctorate in classical languages. Waldenström's intimate knowledge of the Lutheran tradition and his effective leadership guided the Mission Covenant along a path which rarely deviated from Reformation principles.[7] Probably owing to his vigorously Lutheran theology, the new society maintained the ideal of pure congregations while remaining legally within the state church. His views of the Bible also left their mark on the Mission Covenant.

The Uppsala communion case, in contrast to most previous incidents of cooperation between pastors and mission societies, involved communion outside a church sanctuary. In 1876 the Uppsala Mission Society requested use of the city's prestigious cathedral for a celebration of the Lord's Supper with Waldenström officiating. When permission was denied, the Society turned to the Church of the Trinity in Uppsala, but again the hostility of the bishop to Waldenström prevented an affirmative response. The communion service was consequently held in the Mission Society's chapel, which was not a consecrated sanctuary and thus not legally approved for sacramental purposes. During the next few weeks Waldenström continued to administer communion illegally in Uppsala and his hometown, Gefle.[8] This violation of church law drew sharp rebukes from the Swedish Lutheran hierarchy. These warnings, however, apparently only confirmed Waldenström's belief that the state church had placed unwarranted restrictions on communion. A committee which he chaired sent a petition to the king, demanding "that the observance of Holy Communion be made unrestricted" and "that consequently such regulations in our church law which . . . make it a crime for Lutheran Christians who are forced by their consciences to use this freedom which . . . Christ's and Luther's words grant them, be removed."[9]

Although this petition had little immediate effect, the repercussions of the Uppsala communion case stimulated some Mission Friends to formulate more precisely their doctrine of the church, which few if any of them identified with the state religion. Waldenström and others produced in 1878 a brief statement of their ecclesiology:

1. The Church of Christ (the true congregation) has two meanings in the New Testament:
   a. The communion of saints
   b. The local congregation of believing Christians
2. The Christian congregation in the latter sense comes into existence when believers unite for mutual edification, discipline, and aid, as well as for the work of extending the kingdom of God.
3. The congregation receives as members those who believe in Christ and have been baptized either as children or adults.[10]

This streamlined definition of the church harmonized fairly well with conservative Protestant ecclesiology in general. It was Biblically based, exclusive, and implicitly differentiated between "believing Christians" and birthright members of Swedish parishes. On the other hand, the statement was silent on several matters where conservative Protestants have disagreed. It did not, for example, mention creeds of any sort, and it ignored such matters as millenarianism, a doctrine which had not yet made a strong impact in Scandinavia. The statement was silent on practical aspects of polity and discipline. Moreover, it did not address the central issue of communion, perhaps because the framers assumed they had resolved that matter by retaining the Lutheran doctrine of Christ's "real presence" in the sacrament while removing all legal regulations upon its administration. Nevertheless, as Karl Olsson has observed, "the essence of the definition, thin and ambiguous as it was, did become a working rule for the Swedish Mission Covenant when it was organized a few months later."[11] When in 1885 fellow believers overseas organized the Swedish Evangelical Mission Covenant of America, they proceeded upon a similar doctrine of the church.[12]

The 1878 definition did not satisfy all of Sweden's Mission Friends. For several years the Evangelical National Foundation had been divided into factions. Until his death in 1868 Carl Rosenius, one of the leading laymen in the pietistic revival movement, clung to the inclusive ecclesiology of Swedish Lutheranism and, despite his criticism of the state church, opposed separation from it. Rosenius respected the clergy's role in administering the sacraments. E. J. Ekman, who headed the Mission Covenant from 1886 until 1904, and Andreas Fernholm, a former state church pastor who successively became a Baptist and a leading figure in the Covenant, occupied the opposite flank. Both Ekman, who resigned from the Lutheran ministerium in 1879, and Fernholm were willing in the 1870's to abandon confessional Lutheranism and form congregations on what they regarded as a simple, New Testament basis. Fernholm, in fact, strove for a merger of free Lutherans with Swedish Baptists.[13]

Between these two extremes stood Waldenström and what eventually emerged as the most powerful group in the Mission Covenant. Waldenström had never minced words in criticizing the state church, but he maintained a lifelong membership in it. In Squire Adamsson, the allegory which he wrote in the early 1860's, he lampooned the established church as a "factory" and, in harmony with countless other revivalistic Swedes, accused its pastors of spiritual deadness. After succeeding Rosenius as editor of Pietisten in 1868, Waldenström became even more outspoken in his attacks on the state church. He also resisted efforts to bring mission societies under closer surveillance of the hierarchy.[14]

Waldenström's attitudes toward the formation of the Swedish Mission Covenant reveal much about his ecclesiology. He initially disapproved of its founding and refused to participate in the convention which organized the Covenant in 1878. Apparently

Waldenström still believed that a solution to such problems as the administration of communion could be found within the Evangelical National Foundation. Accordingly, he did not resign from the state church's ministerium until 1882. In the meantime Waldenström had concluded that simultaneous membership in the established church and the Mission Covenant was not self-contradictory. The latter, he argued, was not a dissenting sect, but simply a union of mission societies comprising regenerate Lutherans within the Church of Sweden. Waldenström insisted that the Covenant's member societies fit well Luther's concept of the church as a congregatio fidelium. The inclusive state church, on the other hand, could not be the church of Christ.[15]

Why, then, did Waldenström and most other Covenanters retain membership in it instead of seceding and forming a separate denomination? The stigma of separation may have been one factor. David Nyvall, an important figure in the early Mission Covenant and the son of Waldenström's associate, C. J. Nyvall, apparently believed this. Writing retrospectively in the 1920's, he maintained that among Swedish Covenanters "the denominational idea was never far removed. The thought was there but not the word."[16] More recently, however, Bror Walan has suggested another reason for the Covenanters' remaining at least nominal members of the state church. Around the middle of the nineteenth century the Tübingen theologian Johann Beck began to argue that a state church could be tolerated if it did not claim to be the real church, but rather a paidagogos, or teacher, to prepare Christians for the church of Christ. Professor Otto Myrberg of Uppsala spread Beck's thinking in Sweden during the 1860's. According to Walan, it became a source of the Mission Covenant's prevailing view of the Swedish state church.[17] In 1878 Waldenström acknowledged that he was aware of Myrberg's view of the established church, and three years later he echoed Beck and Myrberg in referring to it as a "state institution."[18]

When Waldenström formally stated his ecclesiology several years after the Mission Covenant was organized, he revealed that he still held this view of the church as well as the twofold definition of Christ's church which his committee had formulated in 1878. In the New Testament, he explained, "the word _ecclesia_ means 'a summoning out' or 'those who are called out' and refers primarily to a gathered people in general. . . ." Waldenström added, however, that _ecclesia_ is also used in the New Testament to designate an individual congregation of the faithful. He pointed out that neither Biblical usage of the term could be applied to state churches. "A state church which encompasses all inhabitants within certain geographical borders without regard to who is faithful or not, holy or not, cannot be a Christian church or congregation according to the New Testament or the Augsburg Confession."[19]

But Waldenström, who was also a member of the Swedish parliament, was not prepared to remove all religion from the civil arena. "To say that religion is exclusively a private matter of each individual, with which the state has nothing to do is unreasonable," he wrote in the same treatise. "The state has not only the right, but also the duty, to employ all means which promote its own security and the people's welfare. The most powerful and indispensable of these means is religion. No state has been able to exist without religion. But a state church is not needed to serve this purpose."[20]

Although Waldenström's ecclesiology became normative for the Swedish Mission Covenant in the 1880's, a few of his colleagues found it contradictory and believed that the Covenant should declare its independence from the established church. Perhaps the most vociferous of these was Andreas Fernholm, who had earlier been a revivalistic pastor in the state church and then a Baptist evangelist. After joining the Mission Covenant in 1880 he taught at its seminary in Kristinehamn. Fernholm called the established church a "poisonous snake" and a "harlot which came from the great mother harlot . . . the papacy."[21] He and the seminary's rector, E. J. Ekman, co-edited the Mission Covenant's monthly newspaper, Förbundet [The Covenant]. During the early 1880's Fernholm used this journal vehemently to attack the Lutheran establishment, identifying it with the Babylon of Revelation which "is recognized by its antipathy to God's real children, who constitute the Lord's real church."[22] Ekman, who adopted a Reformed theology of the Eucharist and regarded infant baptism as unbiblical, demanded that members of the Covenant have nothing to do with the sacraments of the established church. In 1880 he noted with regret that the free churches still had "one or two believers who still can participate in the state church's communion."[23] Later that year Fernholm expressed his surprise that free church members took part in "the world's hypocritical, sham worship services . . . as though that were not a sin."[24] He also suggested that participation in the Covenant's Eucharist be strictly limited to believers who had seceded from the state church and joined the Covenant.[25]

These challenges to Waldenström's toleration of the state church were short-lived. Publication of Förbundet ceased in 1885. Fernholm resigned from the seminary the following year and never again played a leading role in the Covenant. Although Ekman became the Covenant's presiding officer in 1886, a position he held for eighteen years, and continued to strive for a congregational polity, he apparently realized that the stronger sentiment within the Mission Covenant was for maintaining connections with the Church of Sweden. Indeed, although in 1948 the Covenant became a charter member of the International Federation of Free Evangelical Churches, few of its members withdrew from the established church. The ideal of the holy assembly and acceptance of the inclusive state church coexist harmoniously for most of the Covenant's 84,000 members. Mission Friends who emigrated to the United States, of course, did not have to deal with this ecclesiological problem. As we shall see, however, they often clashed with the Church of Sweden's American daughter, the Augustana Synod.

In addition to its search for a pure communion and a believers' community, a second hallmark of the Swedish Covenant in the nineteenth century was its unswerving allegiance to the Scriptures. Both before and after their organization in 1878, the Mission Friends evidenced great reverence for the Bible, although few of them appear to have developed sophisticated doctrines concerning its inspiration or its use as a theological source. Dissatisfied with the state church and many of its clergymen, the revivalistic Lutherans had simply sought a Biblical basis for personal faith. The Swedish Bible Society provided one, and the increasingly literate Swedes used it enthusiastically. As Karl Olsson has observed, "there grew up among the läsare what amounted to almost a Bible cult. . . . In almost every fellowship there seems to have been a small group of men (and women) whose orientation in the Bible was good enough to challenge the pretensions of any lay preacher or even church pastor. . . ."[27] David Nyvall agreed with this assessment and also recalled that as early as 1865 his father, who had no formal theological training, began to read a Swedish translation of Konstantin von Tischendorf's recent study, Wann wurden unsere Evangelien verfasst? [When Were Our Gospels Written?], a seminal work of German textual criticism.[28] "It is not too much," the younger Nyvall wrote, "to say that the question 'Where is it written?' became the liberation and the password of the free church people -- a signal for departure and new movements everywhere."[29]

Waldenström was one of the Mission Friends who began in the early 1870's to demand Biblical authority for every belief and practice by asking this question. Indeed, commitment to the Bible as the final authority on theological questions turned this erudite but relatively obscure editor of Pietisten into one of the most respected and disliked men in Sweden. By 1870 he had begun to doubt the Biblical basis of the so-called "satisfaction theory" of the atonement. According to this doctrine, which had existed in various forms since the age of the Fathers, Christ's death on the cross appeased God's wrath toward fallen man. Waldenström searched the Old and New Testaments without success for the phrases "reconciling of God" and "God reconciled in Christ," both of which occurred repeatedly in explanations of the atonement. In 1872 he published his own interpretation in Pietisten. Waldenström denied that the fall had changed God's heart. Rather, it had changed only human beings, making them sinners removed from God and unwilling to seek an improvement of their relationship with the Lord. Consequently, the purpose of the atonement was not to appease God (who still loved humanity), but rather to make human beings righteous by persuading them to accept salvation. In short, God initiated the atonement, not to appease himself, but to change the hearts of his children.[30]

Waldenström's challenge to the satisfaction theory elicited a storm of protest. To those who accepted the theory, and had stressed God's wrath toward fallen man as a reason for accepting Christ, his interpretation of the atonement seemed to remove the motivation for repentance. They accused him of heresy and departure from the Augsburg Confession, practically synonymous to traditional

Lutherans.[31]

Waldenström was not impressed by his opponents' appeals to historic creeds, which he regarded as dubious touchstones of doctrine. He pointed out inconsistencies between the Latin and German versions of the Augsburg Confession,[32] and declared that his detractors' use of it to counter his Biblical arguments violated"the Lutheran Reformation's basic principle, that the Holy Scriptures are the supreme judge in all spiritual things."[33] He confronted his adversaries at a pastors' conference in 1876 with the question "What is the correct relationship between the Scriptures and the confession?" In the event of differences of opinion on doctrinal matters, he asked, "shall the Biblical word or the Evangelical Lutheran Church's confessional writings be regarded as having higher authority. . . .?"[34] Paraphrasing Luther, Waldenström answered his own question by insisting that "as soon as it is discovered that the confessional books in any way teach differently from what the Scriptures teach, the symbolic books must yield to the Scriptures' plain and clear statements."[35] The subordination of creeds to the Bible became through such arguments a chief characteristic of the Swedish Mission Covenant.

The Mission Friends' early Biblicism did not, however, proceed from conservative doctrines about the Scriptures which men like Hengstenberg and Beck were developing in Germany. These scholars' works were known to some of their colleagues in Sweden, but there is no evidence that they had any perceptible impact on the laymen who were the key leaders of the movement. Even an erudite clergymen like Waldenström professed that he had read neither Beck nor Myrberg before he began to depend on the Bible as the ultimate authority in questions of faith.[36] The "Princeton theology" of Biblical inerrancy, which Benjamin Warfield and Archibald Alexander Hodge of Princeton Theological Seminary developed in the 1880's, was apparently unknown in Sweden during the nineteenth century.

Furthermore, the Mission Friends' devotion to the Scriptures was not a reaction to attacks from "higher" critics, for the works of the latter were little read in Scandinavia until after the Mission Covenant was founded. The Friends had uncritically accepted the Bible as God's Word years before higher criticism became an issue in northern Europe. Fernholm, for instance, claimed to have been preoccupied with the Bible as a boy in the 1840's.[37] Throughout his ministerial career, which began in the 1860's, he evidenced a commitment to the literal truth of the Scriptures. After the Covenant was formed, Waldenström and other leading figures in it responded vigorously to what they regarded as challenges to the Bible's divine origins. But before the 1890's the Covenanters' Biblicism was largely an unsophisticated acceptance of the Old and New Testaments.

Mission Friends also rooted their innovative ecclesiologies in the Bible. As we have seen, in 1878 a pioneering group developed a twofold definition of the church which rested on a New Testament basis. They zealously defended their view against the state church's inclusive interpretation, which they believed was unbiblical. Waldenström maintained this position throughout his life. His most outspoken opponents within the Covenant, Ekman and Fernholm, also based their arguments on the New Testament when they demanded withdrawal from the established church. And when Ekman asserted that the Covenant should declare itself a "denomination," C. J. Nyvall remarked simply that "the Bible does not speak of church denominations."[38] In the United States Mission Friends used similar Biblical arguments when debating whether they should organize a denomination and relied heavily on the Scriptures for answers to most other theological problems.

During the 1890's Waldenström became the Mission Covenant's chief critic of recent departures in Biblical scholarship. In books, articles, and speeches he analyzed lower and higher criticism for Swedish and Swedish-American audiences. This thoroughly Biblical theologian was well acquainted with recent Scandinavian and German research in the Scriptures and labored arduously to promote those findings which he thought sound and to oppose those aspects of scholarship detrimental to Biblical faith. He did not regard textual, or "lower" criticism, which he differentiated from what he alternately termed "Bible criticism" and "so-called higher criticism," as a threat to Christianity. In 1893 he suggested that the Covenant welcome textual criticism as a way of purifying the faulty Swedish translations of the Scriptures.[39] He devoted a great deal of time during the following years to a study of the Greek texts of the New Testament, with which he was intimately acquainted.

In 1898 Waldenström began to express publicly his dissatisfaction with the Swedish Bible Commission's new translation of the Scriptures. He complained that the commission had violated the two central obligations of Biblical translation: "to follow the correct original text, so far as this can be ascertained, irrespective of any exegetical, dogmatic, or other considerations;" and "translate the words of the original text just as they read," ignoring "exegetical, dogmatic, or other considerations."[40]

The commission's breach of the first principle seems beyond dispute. It had allowed the traditional Swedish text to stand, as Waldenström put it, "in places where it contradicts some of the following authorities: the codex sinaiticus, the codex vaticanus, the codex alexandrinus or some of the oldest Syriac translations."[41] Waldenström pointed out, for instance, that certain passages used in the Swedish Lutheran liturgy, such as the doxology of Matthew 6:13, were in neither the codex vaticanus nor the codex sinaiticus, but nevertheless had been retained in the new Swedish Bible.[42] He cited several other examples where modern liturgical tradition had seemingly prevailed over scholarship, and charged that in many other instances the commission had followed "readings whose inaccuracy has been placed beyond doubt by recent textual criticism, especially the work of Tischendorf, Westcott, and Hort."[43]

He then turned to the commission's choice of Swedish words to express crucial New Testament concepts. Waldenström accused it of mistranslating II Corinthians 5:19 to fit the satisfaction theory of the atonement and rendering the term <u>metanoia</u> into Swedish as "improvement" instead of the more literal "change of mind."[44] Both of these matters were of vital importance to the Mission Covenant and set it apart from the main theological currents in the Church of Sweden. Most prominent Covenanters had adopted Waldenström's interpretation of the atonement and also stressed the centrality of conversion, which the apostle Paul had described with the term <u>metanoia</u>. The commission seemed thus to be trying to justify the state church's inclusiveness and position on the atonement. But according to the even more Biblically-oriented Waldenström, his own group was more faithful to the oldest extant texts and left no room for tradition as an authority.

Waldenström also reproached the commission for undermining the Lutheran commitment to casting the Scriptures in popular language, so as to make them accessible to the masses. "Luther reports that during the period of his work on Biblical translation, he and Melanchthon frequently went to the market to hear how the people spoke, so that he could give them the Bible in their own language," he noted. But "in far too many places the present translation reveals that the commission is not following this example. The commission writes the language of the lecture hall, not that of daily life."[45]

Waldenström began to oppose higher criticism shortly after

the works of such scholars as Wellhausen began to gain acceptance in Sweden. In January, 1894 he wrote to the American Congregationalist Frederick Emrich that the new direction in Biblical scholarship would lead to the "ruin" of many believers.[46] Waldenström was especially alarmed when at the end of the century Professors Waldemar Rudin and Erik Stave defended higher criticism. Stave told a Scandinavian student gathering that rather than fearing such scholarship, they should "work and fight for it" and that anyone who opposed it should have a "guilty conscience."[47]

Waldenström replied in a slashing treatise titled Låt oss behålla vår gamla bibel [Let's Keep Our Old Bible], which argued that "behind the guise of science and research and a sham love of the truth" scholars were simply robbing the people of their Bible.[48] Waldenström suggested that Rudin bore much of the responsibility. The Uppsala professor had studied briefly under Beck at Tübingen, but later had begun to separate the literal text of the Scriptures from the message which lay semi-concealed within it and which, Rudin believed, was comprehensible only to the spiritually awakened. Waldenström believed Rudin's postulate violated Luther's insistence upon the Bible's lucidity. Once a wedge had been driven between the Bible's text and its meaning, the Scriptures would lose their decisive authority. He expressed amazement that critics had in fact begun to use heathen sources to test the Bible's veracity, and that

> whenever the Bible contains statements which contradict statements in the works of heathen authors or on the ruins in Babylon or elsewhere, it seldom occurs to scholars to doubt the latter. But when they find something in these records which agrees with the Bible's accounts, they say that "the Bible has gained confirmation." It practically never occurs to anyone that it is the Bible which confirms the accuracy of the former. . . . At least serious Christians understand that.[49]

Waldenström devoted most of his book, however, to a refutation of Stave's arguments which, he believed, were based on this willingness to use external sources to judge the Bible. Waldenström responded by using other Biblical passages to defend those under attack. He regretted, for instance, Stave's belief that "Daniel could not have been written prior to 168 B. C., or 400 years after Daniel's time." Waldenström commented, ironically, "Of course, one cannot heed the fact that Christ regarded Daniel as the author of the Book of Daniel (Matt. 24:15). After all, he had no training in Biblical criticism. He had not read Wellhausen, Personne, or S. A. Fries."[50] Waldenström launched a similar offensive against the Wellhausen hypothesis that the Pentateuch "came into being during the course of several centuries and long after Moses' time. That Christ called them books of Moses

(John 5:47) means nothing."[51]

Waldenström's conclusions about recent Biblical scholarship reveal his Lutheran background and appreciation of the Wittenberg Reformer's devotion to the Scriptures. "It was Luther's great achievement to remove faith from the loose sand of a human foundation and place it on the bedrock of the Scriptures," he wrote. "He who now believes that he is continuing Luther's work by removing faith further 'to the left' and detaching it from the Scriptures' authority betrays himself and others." Waldenström accused Stave of leading a "counterreformation" and requested Biblical critics to admit that they had "completely separated from the Lutheran Reformation's basic principles."[52]

Waldenström view of the New Testament canon also revealed his debt to Luther. He questioned the apostolicity of II Peter, thought little of James, and asserted that II and III John were probably written by someone other than the evangelist of that name. Like Luther, Waldenström doubted that Hebrews and Revelation were the works of apostles. The former, he maintained, contained undeniable mistakes.[53] Waldenström's interpretation of Revelation relied heavily on the famous commentaries which the German New Testament scholar Heinrich Meyer had begun to edit in the 1830's, including the latter's view that the Apocalypse was a product of its times rather than a work inspired by God.[54] Believing that its author had predicted the return of Christ during the reign of Domitian, he could not regard Revelation as infallible, an attribute he reserved for those New Testament books which he believed were unquestionably apostolic.

Waldenström's denigration of Revelation helps explain why the Swedish Mission Covenant never became a millenarian body. While a premillennialist like Fredrik Franson was preoccupied with the Bible's last book, most Swedish Covenanters seldom referred to it.

The essentially Lutheran and European roots of the Swedish Mission Covenant seem clear. Given the facts of its birth within the Church of Sweden and its continuing attachment to the parent body, the Covenant could hardly have avoided taking most of its theology from the Lutheran tradition. Both the ideal of the pure congregation and acceptance of the state church were part of that variegated legacy, as were reliance on the Bible and a willingness to embrace textual criticism in searching for the correct understanding of the Scriptures. Excepting, of course, membership in the established church, the Swedish Mission Covenant bequeathed these characteristics to its adherents who emigrated to the New World. They meshed well with most other aspects of what developed into "evangelicalism" there, although the Swedes' acceptance of infant baptism and rejection of Darbyite millenarianism placed them at odds with many conservatives (including some of their fellow Swedish-Americans) who drew heavily upon non-Lutheran traditions.

CHAPTER VII

THE CONSERVATISM OF THE NORWEGIAN AND DANISH MISSION COVENANTS

When the Norwegian and Danish Mission Covenants were organized in the 1880's, they shared several traits with the Swedish Covenant. All three were to some extent outgrowths of mid-century revivalism and strove for pure congregations. Furthermore, the Danish and Norwegian bodies followed the Swedish one in subordinating systematic theology to Biblical teaching and in opposing the "cultural liberalism" of the late nineteenth century. Beyond these shared characteristics, however, the Norwegian and Danish Covenants had little in common with that of Sweden. In both Denmark and Norway the Covenants were and remain millenarian denominations whose combined membership has never exceeded 10,000.

Ironically, the person most responsible for these variations, Fredrik Franson, was a Swedish-American. Franson brought Darbyite millenarianism to Scandinavia in 1881 and more than any other individual shaped the Norwegian and Danish Covenants. While Waldenström strove with considerable success to preserve the essentially Lutheran theology of the Swedish group, Franson's Anglo-American eschatology and revival methods became determinative in the other two bodies. Owing heavily to his influence, they became members of the trans-Atlantic millenarian community and adopted evangelistic techniques which Franson had learned from

Dwight Moody in the 1870's. The Norwegian and Danish Mission Covenants adoption of Darby's eschatology and Moody's revival methods set them apart from their respective state churches and elicited hostile reactions from their privileged and often nationalistic clergy. The latter regarded Franson and his associates as threats to the stability of the established ecclesiastical order.

The Norwegian Mission Covenant stemmed in part from the separatist movement which Gustav Lammers led in the 1850's. Although Lammers re-entered the state church, more than thirty congregations continued to function on a free church basis. Carl Bernhard Falck, a southern Norwegian teacher and merchant, emerged as a leader in the sporadic conventions which gave these independent congregations some measure of cohesion during their early years. When Franson's millenarian revivals and his prophetic conference of 1882 in Sweden aroused the interest of Norwegian free churchmen, Falck was sent to meet him and invite him to Norway. Franson accepted and arrived in Christiania on January 1, 1883.

During a year and a half of fervid evangelization in Norway, Franson cooperated closely with the independent congregations which had invited him there as well as with the Lutheran Free Church. Paul Wettergreen, the leading figure in the latter group, welcomed him to the Free Church in Arendal, where Franson preached to large audiences in the spring of 1883. The Norwegian pastor had just completed his translation of Guinness' <u>The</u>

Approaching End of the Age. His historicist millenarianism differed from the Darbyite futurism which Franson espoused. The differences in their eschatologies, however, did not stop Wettergreen from giving him a letter of recommendation, with which Franson tried without much success to gain access to state church sanctuaries elsewhere in Norway. Most of his revival meetings were consequently smaller gatherings held in buildings which had no official connection with the established church,[1] except for the occasional use of church prayer chapels.[2] Through Falck, whom Franson persuaded to launch a millenarian newspaper designed to spread his eschatological message and more closely unite scattered congregations, the evangelist remained in close contact with the people who in 1884 formed the Norwegian Mission Covenant.

Unfortunately, dispassionate accounts of Franson's meetings in Norway do not appear to exist. Hostile observers described Franson as an ecstatic and unstable intruder who showed no respect for traditional Norwegian forms of worship. They depicted his revivals as chaotic assemblies where those in attendance were compelled against their will to participate in rowdy procedures. On the other hand, Franson's devotees defended his awakenings as occasions when the Holy Spirit was finally allowed to penetrate the spiritual dormancy of state church formalism which had prevented individuals from accepting Christ. Hence, all contemporary accounts of Franson must be read with these prejudices in mind.

The editor of the conservative journal Luthersk Kirketidende spearheaded the state church's assault, declaring that the meetings had "considerably more in common with Franson's spirit than God's spirit." He charged, further, that the Swedish-American evangelist relied on theatrics because he "does not possess real talent as a preacher, nor is a serious, thorough, and comprehensive proclamation of God's Word his concern. His method, his procedure -- if that is removed, Franson is nothing." The editor described how the evangelist began one revival by separating "God's children" from "the world's children" by having the former raise their hands. "In this way all of the world's children became apparent and were made the objects of intimate questions and common prayer." Then, the report continued, "all who were troubled were called forward to a certain place where they had to kneel, and then people prayed for them in strong, noisy oaths. Occasionally hesitant people were forced forward."[3] More sympathetic accounts also mention Franson's techniques of dividing the congregation, directly addressing individuals, and leading prayers for sinners who came forward. Although Franson had worked with Moody for three years in Chicago, he seems to have learned more from the tradition of Charles Finney than from Moody, if James Findlay is correct that Moody did not use the "anxious bench" or any of the other innovations which Finney had popularized earlier in the century. "Never did Moody make a final plea for converts in one of his large general meetings. . . . Finney's tactics simply were not appropriate."[4] In Scandinavia, however, Franson conducted innumerable small revival meetings in prayer chapels and schoolhouses. He may have believed that under these intimate circumstances more personal methods were appropriate; certainly he used them with considerable effect.

Other aspects of Franson's evangelization program were almost certainly taken from Moody. The first of these was the "after meeting" in which individuals whose interest had been aroused by the preaching were given special counseling. Moody did not invent the after meeting, but began to use it extensively during his tour of the British Isles in the 1870's. Moody participated actively in this spiritual counseling, but found it necessary to train associates, called "gapmen," to handle the volume of inquirers. They needed a solid command of the Scriptures. Moody accordingly began to insist on minimal Biblical training as a prerequisite for service in his evangelistic campaigns. To achieve this, he organized in Chicago the training school which later became the Moody Bible Institute.[5]

In 1885 one critical observer of a Fransonian after meeting described it in derogatory terms. "One had the feeling that it was like setting a machine in motion," he wrote, perhaps unconsciously linking his rhetoric to the term "manufactured faith" which opponents of revivalism had frequently employed on both sides of the Atlantic. "Several distressed individuals assembled before the pulpit . . . while a swarm of workers spread out to all parts of the church and up to the galleries -- a swarm of activity as in an anthill." "Each worker selected a place where he wanted to work," he continued, "and soon there were just as many teachers as listeners." The writer believed that the pressures exerted on inquirers overstepped the line of propriety. "If any of 'God's children' did not do his duty . . . he was shown with many reasons from God's Word that now was the time to 'fish,' that one sins if one does not make the most of one's talents. That was meddling and obtrusiveness, the likes of which I had not previously witnessed."[6]

Franson's estimation of after meetings, of course, was much more positive. He recommended that recent converts be protected from individuals "who go around and speak to those who have recently found peace, with the intention of instilling doubt and anxiety in their souls." "In this way," Franson warned, "these people seek to win the confidence of new converts and then exercise their influence on them in partisan ways."[7] He did not, however, provide any details about this alleged spiritual sabotage.

Franson also recommended house visits as a means of supplementing revivals. This, too, was an evangelistic method taken from Moody. "A few years ago, when Moody and Sankey conducted awakenings for three months in Chicago, every home in that metropolis with its 500,000 inhabitants was visited." Franson urged that this effort be emulated in Norway. With a note of urgency he reminded his followers that "the sinner is dear, the time is costly and short, and the work to be done is spread over the whole world."[8]

Franson designed short Bible courses for training workers to conduct these tasks. He held the first one in Christiania for sixty Norwegians and Swedes in 1884. Franson described the backbone of the course as the "study of 100 to 200 of the simplest and most practical Bible texts, which can be best used as revivalistic arrows against those who are dead in sin and against backsliding. . . ." A second dimension of the curriculum was "discussion about the after meeting, use of the Bible in it, and the best way of leading it."[9]

One of the students in Franson's first Bible course was a woman, Cathrine Juell (1833-1901), an independently wealthy Norwegian from the capital who had traveled extensively in the United States and was briefly affiliated with Moody's church in Chicago. After returning to Norway Juell underwrote the publication of Norwegian versions of several of his books and sermons. She also financed Franson's hymnal, Evangelii-Basun, modelled after the recent book of gospel songs consistently used at Moody's revivals, but adapted largely from a Swedish-American hymnal which E. August Skogsbergh, "the Swedish Moody," had published in 1880, and two of Franson's Norwegian tracts, "Vink og råd til nyomvendte" [Hints and Advice to New Converts] and "Skal du blive tilbage?" [Will You Remain Behind?][10]

Findlay has generalized that owing to the popularity of Moody's singer, Ira D. Sankey, "every professional revivalist from Moody's time on felt it a necessity to have a partner who could sing the gospel."[11] Ludvig Ellingsen, who subsequently became a preacher in the Norwegian Mission Covenant and among both Lutheran and free church Norwegians in the United States, joined Franson in this musical capacity in northern Norway.[12] The two cooperated closely during Franson's crusade in Norway, stimulating one observer to compare their work to everything which he "had heard about Moody's and Sankey's activities and procedures."[13]

Some Norwegian Lutherans and dissenters disagreed with this comparison. The editor of Luthersk Kirketidende quoted approvingly a bitter article in the Methodist organ, Kristelige Tidende, which lamented that Franson had not emulated Moody's ecumenism. "When Franson came to Norway it was said that in his activities he would follow Moody's example," the Methodist newspaper reported. "There was certainly room for this kind of work in Norway." But "it was not long before he began to form mission societies with the goal of gathering all of the new converts into a new kind of church with its own polity and activities."[14] Franson was compelled to ward off such charges of sectarianism throughout his long stay in Scandinavia. The Norwegian and Danish Mission Covenants suffered similar criticism during their early years.

Franson arrived in Denmark in the autumn of 1884 and spent about six months attempting to awaken Danes with his millenarian message. Estimates of his success in Denmark vary, but even his sympathetic Danish biographer agrees that he made few conversions.[15] Hampered by legal difficulties and state church hostility, he was deported before he and his followers could give their evangelism the kind of structure which would have assured its continuation. Nevertheless, Franson and his associates, some of whom were foreigners who remained in Denmark, paved the way for the Danish Mission Covenant, which was constituted in 1888. Consequently, his brief stay in Denmark needs to be examined.

To a small degree, the remnants of Mogens Abraham Sommer's separatist revival movement of the 1850's in Denmark supplied a basis for Franson's evangelism there. N. P. Lang, a school-teacher who briefly worked with Sommer before emigrating to Chicago and joining Moody's church, became acquainted with Franson in the Windy City in the late 1870's. In 1882, the year that Peter Trandberg, who had helped organize what became the Lutheran Mission Society, left Denmark for Chicago, Lang left Chicago for Denmark, where he became a lay revivalist for that organization. After a quarrel with its leaders over his use of American revival methods, Lang withdrew and continued his evangelism independently in Copenhagen. He also formed a "Christian Tract Society" in the Danish capital.[16] In May, 1884, though, Lang once again emigrated to the United States. When the Inner Mission of the Danish state church refused to cooperate with Franson, he began to work with the Christian Tract Society. For several months Franson led revivals in nonconformist churches and various buildings which the society rented in Copenhagen, and also preached in smaller Danish communities.

Sympathetic descriptions of Franson's revivals in Denmark

indicate that he used the same methods there that he had employed in Norway. One teenage observer, Christian Nielsen, described an awakening in the Copenhagen Brethren church:

> The attractive, white sanctuary was full of people. Franson preached with a power and movement which was unequalled. After the sermon there was an after meeting. This part of the revival was not tranquil. On the contrary. In one place a little group assembled and sang a spiritual song; in another place a man kneeled in prayer for troubled people. All of this took place while the preacher and the believers went about the assembly, talking with seekers and whomever wanted to speak with them. . . . My brother, who was bashful about meeting Franson, tried to be at the opposite end of the hall from the preacher. But Franson saw the handsome, tall boy and could probably tell what was wrong. Before I knew what was happening, the two of them were on their knees side by side. . . .[17]

Another Danish observer described Franson's homiletics at an awakening in a smaller community. "His preaching was of the Methodist sort with strong emphasis on the undeserved grace of Christ's atonement. Christ would gather the saints in his eternal kingdom. Not a word about faith healing or great feats.

And no violent language. [Franson was] a person with powerful spiritual gifts and childlike faith."[18]

As in Norway, the state church opposed Franson's methods of conducting revivals. Vilhelm Beck, head of the Danish Lutheran Inner Mission, personally led the attack, while praising his own society's itinerant revivalists, Jeansson and Buchwald, and approving even youth revivals conducted without pastors.[19] Beck was a nationalist and Lutheran zealot, however, who resented any foreign or sectarian intrusions into his country's religious life. Accordingly, shortly after Franson arrived in Copenhagen the Inner Mission denied him use of its Bethesda mission house. In a justification of this refusal, one of Beck's colleagues complained that "often so-called 'missionaries' or 'evangelists' come from Sweden, Norway, and America, who are either sectaries or do not belong to any church at all, because they lack a clear view of the church and sacraments." He pleaded with his Lutheran readers "not to open our houses irresponsibly to factions and schism and strife" but rather to "adhere to our old Lutheran doctrine, which never separates God's Word and the sacraments from each other."[20] Beck accused Franson of posing as a Lutheran to win the confidence of Danish state church members. "Which church Franson belongs to is not known; the Methodists refuse to cooperate with him, but he uses the American Methodist type of preaching while wanting to give the impression that he belongs to the Lutheran state church or accepts the state church's teachings." Beck described Franson's "so-called miracles" as "either fanaticism or conscienceless humbug." "To make a long story short," he concluded, "the only miracle which Franson has been able to perform is making faithful people run after him." In order to rid Denmark of this "nuisance," Beck ordered that "the Inner Mission buildings be closed to him" and its "emissaries may not have anything to do with him."[21]

The legal repercussions of Franson's abortive attempt to heal a woman provided a vulnerable point which Beck exploited. Franson and Cathrine Juell, who had come from Norway to assist him, had anointed and moved the joints of a middle-aged woman whose aggravated rheumatism had kept her bedridden for eighteen years. Her condition worsened shortly thereafter, causing her infuriated husband to report the incident to the police. Franson was jailed and eventually deported. Beck thereupon began to depict him as a rootless, unscrupulous rascal whose revivals were merely a front for fabricated faith healing.

One of Beck's colleagues, Peter Krag of Copenhagen, was less vituperative. In an article titled "Fabrikskristendom" [Factory Christianity], however, he questioned the sincerity of the conversions which Franson had ostensibly effected:

> It is certainly that way at a paper factory, where one can see a soiled cloth go into one end of the machinery and come out at the other end clean white paper, but whether an ungodly man can go into a meeting hall one evening and emerge a few hours

> later a saved person, who has found rest in God because of faith in the forgiving of sins, ought to be doubted seriously.

Like many others, Krag found the after meetings especially repulsive. "They [Franson and his associates] tackle the conversion work with determination. They proceed from one to the other and ask: 'Do you have peace? Are you saved?' If one answers 'no' or gives no answer, he is given special treatment until a confession of sin is extracted. . . ."[22]

Beck accused Cathrine Juell, whom he inaccurately called "an older Swedish woman,"[23] of traveling about Denmark seeking to cause schisms in the established church.[24] Evangelii-Basun also seemed foreign to some Danes. One described it as "a little songbook which contained revival songs of Swedish and American origin, rather poorly translated into faulty Danish."[25]

These attacks on Franson's revivals were counterproductive. Franson had hoped to cooperate with Danish churchmen, but as Emil Larsen has pointed out, their rejection forced him to work with independent groups and organize other mission societies to proclaim the premillennial doctrines which the state church's pastors seldom preached.[26] These local bodies did not coalesce to form the Danish Mission Covenant until 1888. Nevertheless, Franson's influence on the larger organization is unmistakable. It embodied and preserved the Anglo-American revival methods which prominent state churchmen disliked and added another facet to the religious pluralism which they feared. Although he was deported from Denmark, Franson's legacy remained, just as it did in the Norwegian Mission Covenant. Both denominations regard the peripatetic revivalist as their founder, and justifiably so. Both have faithfully maintained his eschatology, Biblical literalism and Bible courses, revival methods, and concept of the church.[27]

In both Norway and Denmark the Covenants were from their inception thoroughly millenarian. Indeed, even before the Norwegian body was officially constituted, the journal which became its organ, Morgenrøden [The Dawn], devoted much of its first issue to one of Moody's millenarian sermons on Christ's Second Coming. Moody had assured his audience that it was "completely safe to take God's Word just as we find it," and quoted extensively from Revelation as well as from the New Testament epistles to stress the imminence of the Second Advent and to describe the "secret rapture" of the saints. "There will be a short period between his meeting the saints in the sky and his arrival with all his saints to exercise judgment over the ungodly, to bind Satan for a thousand years and erect a thousand year reign of power and majesty."[28] These Darbyite words echoed the message which Franson had brought to Norway only a few months before.

The editor of Morgenrøden stated that one of his central purposes was to propagate "the great and significant truth of the Lord's return."[29] He printed many of Franson's shorter millenarian works, often as serials. One series, for instance, taken from Franson's lectures in a workers' auditorium in Christiania, began with a discussion of the Darbyite notion that Christ could return at "any moment." "There has not been a single day or hour since the days of the apostles, when the remarkable occurrence which is discussed in I Corinthians 15:51 and I Thessalonians 4:15-18 or the resurrection of the justified and the transformation of the living believers could not have occurred," Franson declared. "The bride must not wait for a sign, but for the bridegroom."[30] His audience may have been puzzled, therefore, when Franson continued by enumerating "10 of the signs which will not precede his return, but rather the revelation of his return." To Franson, though, there was nothing contradictory about this, because as a Darbyite he distinguished between the secret rapture and the later, revealed Second Coming of Christ. A discussion of the signs was pertinent, he explained, "because there are many circumstances which indicate that the Jews' return [to Palestine], the appearance of Antichrist, the great tribulation, and so on have already begun to be revealed."[31] <u>Morgenrøden</u> also published Franson's meandering, eschatological interpretation of recent world history in several instalments. Franson saw signs of Christ's Second Advent in such diverse phenomena as Jewish gains in civil rights, antisemitism, railroad construction in Palestine, and the popularity of spiritism.[32] His eschatology thus became integral to the Norwegian Mission Covenant's theology right down to the present.

The leaders of the Danish Mission Covenant generally adhered to the Darbyite position. "We have reason to shout 'Alas!' a thousand times at those who have no desire to come along and meet Him in the sky," stated their newspaper, Morgenstjernen [The Morning Star].[33] This journal repeatedly stressed the imminence of Christ's return: "The great communion of the Lord's wedding will soon be held," it announced; "there is still room for many guests."[34] One writer warned that those "who do not come along will find it hard to live on earth during this great, great tribulation."[35] More frequently than its Norwegian counterpart, the Danish Mission Covenant warned its members that participation in worldly pleasures might prevent them from sharing the glory of Christ's return. In one typical jeremiad a preacher asked his congregation: "Do you want Jesus at an entertainment place? At the club, the theater, or a masquerade ball?" He warned that Christ would judge those whose ways have "led down to the boggy swamp of drunkenness and immorality, from which hell is the only exit."[36]

Several forms of historicist millenarianism, however, also made inroads during the 1880's and 1890's. So many types of eschatology came from the United States and Great Britain to Scandinavia that few could sort out the often contradictory messages associated with them. Even Franson was temporarily confused. Although essentially a Darbyite futurist, he briefly recognized the year-day theory usually associated with the historicists. He stated in 1884 that "the 1260 prophetic days or

1260 years" of papal power had ended and that therefore the events related to the Second Advent were already unfolding.[37] The evangelist soon abandoned this argument, however, because he regarded the year-day theory as a violation of literalist hermeneutics. But during the first few years of Franson's evangelistic work in Scandinavia he eclectically reproduced almost any shred of evidence which seemed to point to Christ's imminent return. Morgenrøden published his favorable comments about astronomical speculation in this regard. "It is a noteworthy fact which the astronomers mention, that the star of Bethlehem, or the same star visible at Jesus' birth and which comes into view from our earth every 315th year, will again appear in the year 1887."[38] Franson also defended millenarian interpretations of Cheops' Pyramid. "Many believe it is laughable to ascribe any significance to the great pyramid, but most of these people have neither seen it nor studied descriptions of it." In broad strokes he reproduced several of the parallels which others had drawn between the structure's dimensions and Biblical chronology.[39]

Michael Baxter's prediction that Jesus would return in March, 1896 and that the great tribulation would begin shortly thereafter also found some acceptance in the Mission Covenants. J. Madsen, chairman of the Danish Mission Covenant, translated his "prophetic calendar" for 1890-1901 into Danish and published it in Morgenstjernen.[40] Some readers expressed their dissatisfaction at its publication. Two weeks later the editor explained why it had been printed, but did not explicitly disown historicist millenarianism. "The calendar is simply a translation of Pastor Baxter's explication of the prophecies," he remarked, "and if any of these things does not happen during the time which he calculated, one will have to blame his calculations and not those of Morgenstjernen or its editors." Madsen added that he wished Baxter had avoided setting a date; "we believe it best to emulate those who expect our Lord and Master every day."[41] The Danish Mission Covenant apparently lost interest in Baxter's prognostications, perhaps because the Englishman's prediction of a French conquest of Germany in the 1890's failed to materialize. On the other hand, Morgenstjernen praised the astronomical calculations of J. B. Dimbleby and H. Grattan Guinness.[42] At the beginning of the twentieth century the editors of Missionæren, then the organ of the Norwegian Mission Covenant, published lengthy excerpts from Guinness' works.[43] But the futurism of its heroes, Franson and Moody, became dominant after Franson expunged all traces of historicist millenarianism from his eschatology.

Ernest Sandeen has analyzed the importance of Biblical literalism to nineteenth-century millenarians. Inheriting a view of the Scriptures which antedated higher criticism, "the millenarians assumed that divine inspiration had so controlled the writing of the Bible that the resultant text was free of error or fallibility and that this freedom guaranteed them a divine, not a human source of truth -- an immediate and not a mediated revelation." With such a view of the Bible's inspiration "they were incapable of asking questions about the intention of the author or the character of his literary mode."[44] Any concessions to higher criticism would have undermined the often elaborate explications of the literal texts on which these millenarians based their missions and with which they viewed the world's destiny.

Franson's view of Scripture fit this mold. His eschatology was rooted in thoroughly literalist hermeneutics, a rule which he sometimes accused other millenarians of violating. In his treatise on Antichrist, for example, he challenged historicists' identification of the papacy with this archenemy of Christ. "In Revelation 13:18 he is called a 'person,'" Franson stressed. "If the Antichrist is a person, then this expression cannot refer to the papacy, for that is not a person. . . ." He also pointed out that personal pronouns were repeatedly used in Biblical texts to indicate the Antichrist. Moreover, Franson explicitly denied that "God's temple," in which the Antichrist would place himself, meant a church. "What is meant by 'God's temple?' Answer: Just what it says. . . . To call Christians' meeting places temples is completely foreign to the Bible. Nor is this any figurative language . . . and there is not the slightest hint of allegory."[45]

Franson stressed that the Bible alone should be the foundation of Christian doctrine and discipline,[46] a principle which the Norwegian and Danish Mission Covenants always sought to follow. Their adversaries did not always appreciate their Biblicism. In an article reprinted from a Methodist journal, the Norwegian state church newspaper Luthersk Kirketidende scoffed at the Mission Covenant's assertion that its congregations "have only the Bible as their rule and guide for faith and doctrine."[47] As we have noted, Biblical faith had long been a characteristic of free church movements as well as lay movements in Scandinavia. But Franson's reliance on the Bible reinforced this trait, as was true of his preoccupation with millenarianism. While not all Biblical literalists were millenarians -- one thinks of Waldenström -- nearly all millenarians were literalists. The close relationship of the Danish and Norwegian Mission Covenants to Franson tied them to the trans-Atlantic community of Biblical millenarians. This tie proved invaluable in supplying defenses for their Biblical faith when higher criticism became an issue in Scandinavia. Neither in Norway nor in Denmark did the Mission Covenants have a theologian of Waldenström's stature. They consequently relied heavily on arguments for the inspiration of the Bible written in England or the United States.

Dwight Moody supplied several of these. In the late 1870's the popular American evangelist began to lambast recent works of Biblical scholars, whose motives he failed to comprehend. "When a minister or messenger of Christ begins to change the message because he thinks it is not exactly what it ought to be," Moody asserted in 1879, "God just dismisses that man or woman. . . . We haven't any authority to take out [of the Bible] just what we like, what we think appropriate, and let dark reason be our guide."[48] This and many of Moody's similar comments quickly found their way to Scandinavia. The organ of the Danish Mission Covenant quoted at length Moody's statement that the Bible's inexplicable passages were proof of its divine origins. "I am glad there are heights in the book that I haven't been able to climb," he stated; "I am glad there are depths whose bottom I haven't been able to reach. This is the best proof that the book came from God." In the same article Morgenstjernen printed his advice that "the best way to convert a nonbeliever is to show him the fulfilled prophecies."[49]

The renowned London evangelist Charles Spurgeon also became one of the Mission Covenants' models during their fight for Biblical literalism. His Calvinism was foreign to revivalistic Scandinavians, but not his devotion to the Scriptures. In 1887 Spurgeon resigned from the Baptist Union in protest of the inroads which higher criticism had made into that organization. S. M. Anderson, who published several millenarian books as well as the free church magazine which served the Norwegian Mission Covenant after its original organ ceased in 1888, also printed translations of Spurgeon's books. The latter's popular sermons frequently appeared in Morgenstjernen, as did news of his revivals.[50]

A third foreigner who contributed to the Covenants' verbal arsenal was another American, H. L. Hastings. Morgenstjernen published his lecture of 1883 in which he painted a black and white picture of the Bible's place in Christianity. "Is it the best or the worst book in the world?" Hastings asked. "Is it God's book or man's book?" He based his answer on the Bible's increasing popularity, pointing out that whereas only four to six million copies of the Scriptures had appeared prior to 1800, Bible societies alone had distributed 165,000,000 volumes during the nineteenth century. In an indirect and weak response to research in the origins of the Pentateuch and to a certain man, possibly the American infidel Robert Ingersoll, "who declares himself able to reveal the mistakes of Moses," Hastings asserted that "if Moses were alive and could reply, he would be a dangerous man to tackle."[51]

Clearly, the detailed arguments of men like Wellhausen did not seem relevant to the Norwegian and Danish Mission Covenants in the nineteenth century. Their publications did not even refer to higher critics in their own countries, such as Frants Buhl and Fredrik Petersen. In nineteenth-century Scandinavia recent Biblical scholarship was, for all practical purposes, known only within academic circles. These included a handful of Swedish Covenanters like Waldenström and Ekman, who had received the rigorous training demanded of Lutheran pastors in Sweden, but did not encompass any Covenanters in Denmark or Norway. The latter were vaguely aware that Biblical literalism was under attack, and they sought to protect traditional lay acceptance of the Scriptures by popularizing arguments, however irrelevant, which like-minded conservatives had produced abroad.

Franson's concept of the church was the third major element of his legacy which the Norwegian and Danish Mission Covenants inherited. His ecclesiology revealed the influence of both Darby and Moody. To the former, the church was the invisible company of saints whom Christ would take up in the secret rapture. The visible churches of the world played no positive role in his theology. Franson seems to have accepted the notion of the church as an eschatological community whose members were often unknown to one another. But his understanding of this was tempered by the practicality which he gained from Moody. As the American evangelist's biographer has observed, "in a strict sense he did not possess a doctrine of the church. . . . Rather, he simply paid little attention to it in a formal way, for his concern was to achieve conversions and to work with individual believers."[52] This seems true of Franson, as well. Like his Chicago mentor, he was prepared to cooperate with any church -- including that of Rome -- and hold revivals in any available sanctuary. His purpose, however, was to gather sinners into the spiritual church which anticipated the secret rapture. He initially advised converts in Norway not to secede from the established church. Rather, those "who cannot [conscienciously] commune with the unregenerate" should "let them, if they think fit, exclude you." He maintained that "the dissenters in Norway have committed an error by seceding from the state church. It would have been better if they had all stayed there, even if some had been imprisoned like Hans Nielsen Hauge."

Christians hamper evangelization when they leave the established church, "for the moment they do that, they lose their influence on the state church's members."[53]

Franson's ecclesiology, which evolved during his stay in Norway, directly shaped the Norwegian Mission Covenant. To this revivalist, the inclusive state church meant little. The independent congregations, or "mission societies," which he helped gather, were the visible manifestation of Christ's true church in Norway. Franson suggested modelling them after the Swedish Mission Covenant. The Swedish mission societies, he said, did not allow nonessential matters to prevent various kinds of converts from uniting. Swedish Covenanters, Franson related, were tired of being told by some denominations that "you cannot be one of us because our confessions and statutes forbid us to accept those who do not believe this and that regarding baptism, communion, the state church, Luther, and so on." He added, however, that the Swedes were "very particular about not allowing anyone who did not have life in God to become a member."[54]

The Norwegian Mission Covenant adopted these principles at its organizing convention in 1884. According to its third rule, admission of either societies or congregations to the Covenant could occur "without regard to varying perceptions of these things which are less important for salvation [and] which do not conflict with life in God."[55] The Covenant's constitution did not specify these adiaphora, which Franson seems to have construed to include nearly all religious matters save futurist millenarianism and Biblical literalism, but given his key role in its founding, they almost certainly included the sacraments and membership in the established church, for these two matters have never determined membership in either the Norwegian or the Danish Mission Covenant. To millenarians, they are of little importance compared to the urgent task of proclaiming Christ's imminent return. Even the form of baptism, crucial in many free churches, is a matter of considerable personal freedom in these two Covenants. It was recently reported, for instance, that in Norway "fifty per cent of the members have their children baptized, many of them in the state church."[56]

The Danish Mission Covenant adopted similar views. Like its Norwegian counterpart, it was initially a very loose confederation of the independent mission societies which Franson had helped organize and not all of these approved the formation of a closer union. The reasons for their opposition are not recorded. In any case, only five societies sent representatives to the organizational meeting at Ålborg in 1888, and the new denomination initially numbered only 695 members.[57] Although documents for the early years are sparse, it seems clear that the body followed Franson's guidance along a similar path as the Norwegian Mission Covenant. His friend, F. Johanson, came to Denmark in 1884, and shortly after Franson was expelled he sent to Copenhagen another Swedish associate, Carl Wiktor Gillén.[58] The handful of lay revivalists who formed the Danish Mission Covenant expressed the wish "that all partisan walls, which the devil has built, may fall" and that all true Christians could unite.[59] Jens Jensen-Maar, the fisherman who came into contact with Juell and Gillén in the mid-1880's and later served as the Covenant's chairman, expressed a view of the church which already characterized Covenant ecclesiology throughout Scandinavia and in an abridged form became the motto of the International Federation of Free Evangelical Churches. "The church which opens its doors to unconverted people cannot be God's church, but neither can one which excludes any of them whom God has accepted as his children." He added that "any congregation which consists of truly faithful and broad-minded people can become a member of this Covenant, regardless of its views on sacramental questions and minor matters."[60]

During the 1880's the Norwegian and Danish Mission Covenants thus emerged as members of the trans-Atlantic millenarian community. Through Fredrik Franson, to whom they were heavily indebted, both denominations felt an affinity with like-minded evangelicals abroad, such as Charles Spurgeon and Dwight Moody. They also owed their continuing stress on revivalism to Franson and the American methods which he brought to Scandinavia. Most of the early Norwegian and Danish Covenanters were men and women of humble origins; few if any had formal training in theology. Perhaps because of this, systematic theology (except millenarianism) seemed irrelevant to them. Theirs was a simple Biblical faith which left no room for the radical currents which were beginning to flow in Scandinavian intellectual life. In terms of eschatology, ecclesiology, and polity they identified with the apostolic community of the New Testament, and did not believe they were making concessions either to historical tradition or modernity.

Much of this can be said of the Swedish Mission Covenant as well, but there were significant differences. Darbyite eschatology and the American revival methods of the Danes and Norwegians set them apart from their Swedish counterparts. The ties of the latter to their Old World Lutheran heritage remained quite strong, while in Norway and Denmark Covenanters tolerated Lutheran ideas and institutions but refused to be limited by them. The latter realized that they had more in common with British and American millenarians than with most Lutherans in Scandinavia or North America. When Norwegian and Danish Covenanters emigrated to the United States, they naturally brought this affinity with them, where it influenced their relations with the Swedish immigrants who affiliated with the Evangelical Mission Covenant Church and with Franson's Swedish-American allies who opposed formation of this quasi-Lutheran denomination.

CHAPTER VIII

THE MISSION COVENANT AND FREE CHURCHES IN AMERICA TO ABOUT 1885

The religious currents which led to the formation of the Mission Covenants in Sweden, Norway, and Denmark influenced Scandinavian-American Christians, as well. In the 1870's and 1880's Nordic immigrants formed several small denominations which eventually developed into the Evangelical Covenant Church and the Evangelical Free Church. Members of these diminutive antecedents were revivalistic and strove for pure congregations; moreover, many were millenarians. These characteristics place them into the conservative trans-Atlantic context and reveal their links with the Mission Covenants in Scandinavia. The ties are even more obvious when one examines the immigrant pastors and discovers that many had been involved in free church movements before coming to the New World. The millenarian and revivalistic strains among these newcomers often set them apart from the larger immigrant Lutheran denominations, whose membership policies were relatively inclusive and had little interest in either revivalism or millenarianism.

The position of Swedish immigrant free churchmen cannot be understood without reference to the ethnic group's main religious current in the United States. The Augustana Synod was the largest Swedish-American body from its birth in 1860 until 1962, when it merged with other Lutheran denominations to form the Lutheran

Church in America.[1] It emerged when Scandinavians seceded from the Synod of Northern Illinois, a subsidiary of the General Synod, because they opposed the liberalizing tendencies of "American Lutheranism." Members of this party, most notably Samuel Schmucker of Gettysburg, advocated a "continuing Reformation" rather than rigid adherence to sixteenth and seventeenth-century Lutheran orthodoxy. Schmucker implored his denominational fellows not to insist on unity in unessential matters, among which he included all Lutheran symbola except the Augsburg Confession, the real presence of Christ in the Eucharist, and baptismal regeneration.[2] By 1855, when he published anonymously his Definite Synodical Platform, Schmucker was prepared to dispense with those articles of the Augustana which he felt were unessential to Christianity and unacceptable to the modern American mind, and presented his "American Recension of the Augsburg Confession."[3] The Scandinavian immigrants' withdrawal from the Synod of Northern Illinois was part of a broad confessional reaction to such tampering with the venerated theological statements of the Lutheran tradition, and the name of their new body reflected their loyalty to the Augustana.

The new synod, although it briefly included many Norwegians, felt a close affinity to the Church of Sweden. Its early pastors, liturgy, and theology all came from the Old World, and even in the twentieth century it maintained ties with the mother church. During its early years the Augustana Synod bore the stamp of revivalism which was sweeping through Sweden. The American body never wholly adopted the ideal of pure congregations, but in the New World tried to steer a *via media* between this aspiration and the inclusive parish system of state church Lutheranism. President Peter Sjöblom opposed the position that the Augustana Synod "should receive into the church all the Swedes in the community without regard to their faith or behavior."[4] Another early president of the Synod admitted that "we do not expect or hope that the visible church here on earth will be identical with the communion of saints," but insisted that while "our congregations are not pure . . . neither are they a Babylon from which one must flee."[5] Immigrants who had been members of the established church in Sweden were generally admitted after making a brief statement of faith in which they professed an undefined belief in Biblical infallibility and acceptance of Luther's Shorter Catechism and the Augsburg Confession. Converts from other denominations were accepted on a similar basis.[6] Attendance at theater, drunkenness, dancing, cardplaying, and membership in the Free Masons were among the most frequent grounds for denying admission.[7]

During its first fifteen years Augustana's Swedish immigrant pastors gradually moved away from revivalism while placing more weight on the Lutheran confessions. Two of the most prominent figures, Lars Esbjörn and Tuve Hasselquist, had been revivalists in the Church of Sweden. In Illinois, however, they extended their ministries to all Swedish immigrants and abandoned their previous ideal of a pure visible church. By 1870

Hasselquist, then president of the Synod, vigorously opposed lay ministries and revivalism on both sides of the Atlantic.[8] Indeed, after inspecting dozens of Augustana and free church congregations in the United States during the winter of 1875-76 the Swedish Mission Friend C. J. Nyvall lamented that the Synod's press criticized "nearly all revival meetings," including those of Dwight Moody.[9]

During the 1860's separatism was still very weak in Sweden, and many Mission Friends who emigrated to the United States naturally joined congregations of the Augustana Synod. Waldenström had not begun his attack on the Lutheran symbola, so Augustana's confessionalism posed no barrier to their membership. Its Biblicism meshed well with Mission Friends' views of the Scriptures, and revivalism had not yet disappeared. Hence, the presence of Mission Friends in the Synod did not seem incongruous. In fact, in the early 1860's the body tried to recruit Waldenström to teach at its new seminary in Chicago. He almost accepted the position, but remained in Sweden to care for his aging father.[10]

As in Sweden, however, the questions of lay preaching and communion conducted outside consecrated church sanctuaries upset this relationship. In the late 1860's lay Friends in Chicago organized a society within the Augustana Synod and called a colporteur from Sweden to minister to them. But the congregation with which this society was associated denied him access to its pulpit and altar. The society subsequently arranged to have an ordained Augustana pastor administer communion to its members, thereby duplicating one stop-gap solution to the communion problem which was to lead to the formation of the Mission Covenant in Sweden a few years later. The Chicago group separated from Augustana and became an independent congregation in 1870.[11]

Equally important to the birth of the American Covenant was the organization of an independent Mission Friend congregation in Iowa. Carl Björk, an immigrant cobbler who later headed the Mission Covenant, emigrated to that state in 1864 and settled in the hamlet of Swede Bend. Not long after arriving there, he joined the Augustana church in nearby Ridgeport, but also continued to assist in the organization of conventicles, an activity in which he had been involved in Sweden. In 1867 this layman began to preach, thereby violating the Lutheran _rite vocatus_, which defended ministerial prerogatives. His extemperaneous sermons triggered a revival in Swede Bend and the founding of the Evangelical Lutheran Mission Society there on July 4, 1868.

The Augustana Synod naturally opposed this kind of independent lay activity and separatism. Three weeks before Björk's Swede Bend congregation was organized, Hasselquist warned the Synod that "some Christians from Sweden, especially among those who call themselves 'evangelicals,' i. e. Rosenians, have lately tried to be by themselves. . . ."[12] Seven months later the Western Mississippi Conference of the Augustana Synod reproved unspecified revival activities in the region, probably referring to Björk's separatist awakenings."[13] This polemicizing against revivalism and separatism among immigrants was no more effective than the Church of Sweden's concurrent effort to check the laicizing of the sacraments in the mother country.

During the late 1860's and early 1870's independent Mission Friend congregations emerged in the United States at an accelerated pace. Some resulted from secessions from Augustana churches, while others developed from conventicles of immigrants who had little or no connection with the Synod. One key secession occurred in Galesburg, Illinois in 1868. Members of that city's Augustana congregation presented to the Synod a resolution demanding that lay delegates be allowed to attend its meetings and opposing clerical vestments which, they believed, distracted attention from preaching. Hasselquist and two of his colleagues responded by travelling to Galesburg to admonish the congregation to remain loyal to traditional Lutheran practices. After he had spoken, however, one member requested those who would be loyal to the Scriptures to stand up. Several dozen responded and thereafter united to found the Second Lutheran Church of Galesburg. They called a Danish immigrant, Charles Anderson, to be their pastor and seceded from the Augustana Synod.

In newspaper articles justifying the withdrawal, Anderson criticized the Synod's opposition to the American public school system and lay activity in the congregations. He also lambasted Augustana's relatively inclusive membership policies.[14] Although theologically conservative, he identified himself with American Lutheranism and advocated rapid assimilation of Scandinavians in the United States. Second Lutheran Church of Galesburg began to conduct evening worship services in English in 1869, very early for a Nordic immigrant congregation. This apparent willingness to begin the process of assimilation -- which came somewhat later in the Augustana Synod -- was probably due to Anderson's personal influence. He had already been in the United States for several years and spoke English fluently. Although Anderson also spoke Swedish, there is no reason to believe that he shared Swedish immigrant pastors' love of their language and attachment to the rituals of the state church in which they had been ordained. Karl Olsson has pointed out that a more pragmatic reason for the congregation's readiness to assimilate was its financial dependence on the General Synod, which gave it a large sum of money.[15]

In Minneapolis, on the other hand, Mission Friends did not form a secessionist congregation, but one independent of the Augustana Synod. Three lay preachers in the city, two of whom had also been school teachers in Sweden, began to organize conventicles in various locations. In 1874 they chartered a congregation, "The Swedish Evangelical Lutheran Mission Church." Its birth signalled the beginning of "spontaneous generation" of mission societies -- a development which had characterized certain lay movements in Sweden -- and was repeated in San Francisco, Chicago, and several other communities.[16] Like the Mission Friends who seceded from the Augustana Synod, however, these bodies generally retained the "Lutheran" label and, like the communion societies in Sweden, regarded themselves as the real heirs of Luther.

These and many of the other autonomous congregations of Swedish-American Lutherans allied in three synods during the 1870's. Charles Anderson organized the first of these, the Scandinavian Evangelical Lutheran Mission in the United States, at Keokuk, Iowa, in 1872. In his newspaper, Zions Banér, which he began to publish a year earlier, Anderson had argued for such a Synod, intending that it would ultimately merge with native American Lutheran bodies. The new denomination stressed adherence to the historic Lutheran confessions and the importance of an educated ministry. To ensure the latter, Anderson opened a "Swedish Lutheran Mission Institute" in Keokuk a year after he formed the little synod. Despite his exertion of great personal energy, however, the new organization appealed to only a small minority of Mission Friends in the United States. Its stress on an educated, ordained clergy ran counter to the main currents affecting the group on both sides of the Atlantic in the 1870's.

For reasons which have never been clarified, Anderson reorganized the Scandinavian Evangelical Lutheran Mission in 1874 and rechristened it the Swedish Evangelical Lutheran Ansgar Synod. Like its forerunner, the Ansgar Synod was confessionally oriented and stressed the necessity of a trained clergy. Anderson moved his school from Keokuk, Iowa to Galesburg, Illinois and renamed it Ansgar College. The little synod, which in 1877 embraced twenty congregations, admitted that not all of its 1,300 members were regenerate Christians. All of these characteristics led one church historian to dub it "a small and poor imitation of the Augustana Synod."[17]

The Mission Synod, founded in 1873 and having its greatest strength in the Chicago vicinity, was the third proto-denomination which Mission Friends organized in the United States. Thoroughly pietistic and low church, it placed no emphasis on formal ministerial education, and demanded that its congregations comprise exclusively regenerate Christians. It adopted the Augsburg Confession as well as the three great creeds of early Christianity, but nevertheless felt a close affinity to Mission Friends in Sweden, who were becoming less confessional as Waldenström's influence there increased. The Mission Synod began to publish a monthly newspaper, Missions-Vännen [The Mission Friend], which resembled Waldenström's Pietisten and rivalled Anderson's Zions Banér.

Both of the synods helped spread Waldenström's controversial view of the atonement among Swedish-Americans. Anderson commented favorably on his pamphlet "Om forsoningens betydelse" [On the Meaning of the Atonement] in 1874.[18] Members of the Mission Synod did not speak with one voice on this issue; indeed, Missions-Vännen opposed Waldenström's atonement theory for several years.[19] The Augustana Synod, on the other hand, like the Swedish state church, now expressed unmitigated hostility to the man whom it had tried to hire as a theology teacher a decade earlier. When Waldenström's associate, C. J. Nyvall, came to the United States in 1875, he observed that some people in the Augustana Synod regarded Waldenström "as the herald of Anti-Christ," and remarked that "a bitter and sad conflict" had erupted between the Mission and Augustana Synods.[20]

Events of the late 1870's brought the Mission and Ansgar Synods closer together. In 1878 Anderson resigned from Ansgar College and ceased to play an important role in the synod he had founded. He later became a Congregationalist minister. Karl Erixon, an organist and teacher who had just emigrated from Sweden, was named president of both the college and the seminary, and succeeded Anderson as editor of Zions Banér. The newspaper soon merged with another Swedish journal, Chicago-Bladet, which later became the organ of the Evangelical Free Church. More importantly, Erixon began to press the principle of regenerate membership on the Ansgar Synod and advocated union with the Mission Synod. In December, 1878 the Ansgar Synod proposed such a merger, but it was rejected. Carl Björk, the preaching cobbler who had moved from Iowa to Chicago and become head of the Mission Synod, opposed a union because he regarded the Ansgar Synod's membership policy as too inclusive and thought its emphasis on theological education unnecessary. Björk insisted that any merger between the two bodies would have to be concluded on terms which his own synod would dictate.[21]

Before the two synods united, however, Ansgar tore itself asunder. Much of the responsibility for its fracture must be attributed to John G. Princell (1845-1915), who is generally regarded as the father of the Evangelical Free Church.[22] Pastor of Gustav Adolf Church in New York City from 1873 until 1879, Princell was suspended from the Augustana Synod's ministerium in 1878 because he accepted Waldenström's view of the atonement and demanded that his congregation exclude the unregenerate. Two years later the Ansgar Synod named him president of its struggling Ansgar College. The stormy Princell, however, proved to be more than the small communion could handle. By 1883 he and like-minded confederates were convinced that the Ansgar Synod was a worldly denomination and that all denominational organization was inherently unchristian. Princell accordingly suggested that the Synod dissolve itself and, perhaps to emphasize his argument, resigned from it. In August, 1884 the synod did in fact vote to dissolve the following May and ceded its college to the city of Knoxville, Illinois.

Two months later Princell and twenty other anti-sectarian pastors convened in Boone, Iowa and formed the Evangelical Free Church. The ecclesiology of the new group -- which its founders repeatedly maintained was not a denomination -- was simple and revivalistic. A statement issued at Boone asserted that "the Church of God on earth consists of the entire multitude of converted, born-again and Christ-baptized persons, wherever they as such may dwell."[23]

This position reflected the Darbyite view of the church as a spiritual community which had gained acceptance among Princell's followers during the early 1880's. Franson met Princell in 1881 and the two, along with John Martenson, who edited Chicago-Bladet, held a millenarian conference at Moody's church that spring. This parley, which E. August Skogsbergh and other Swedish free church immigrants of various affiliations attended and which Chicago-Bladet publicized during the following months, infused the Evangelical Free Church with the futurist millenarianism which persisted as one of its chief characteristics.

Franson was one of the featured speakers at this millenarian conference. He explicated Revelation 20 with the aid of a standard dispensationalist diagram which also appeared in 1897 at the end of his treatise, Himlauret. The lecture was thoroughly Darbyite, emphasizing a pretribulationist secret rapture followed by a revealed Second Advent, Christ's thousand-year reign, and a final judgment.[24] Franson also expressed on that occasion an openness to the year-day theory, which he later rejected. In a discussion of "the signs of the times," he broached the venerated historicist argument that the papacy had existed for 1260 years and remarked that "a day in Scripture is often equated with a year."[25] But the conference concluded that "the Bible must be read and understood according to its simple, literal text,[26] a position which, Franson subsequently admitted, clashed with the historicists' year-day theory.

Princell addressed this and other millenarian conferences in both Swedish and English. At the Chicago gathering he implored his fellow Swedish-Americans to emulate apostolic Christians, who "lived a watching and waiting life. They believed that Jesus would come and erect a kingdom, that he would rule over this earth."[27] At the Second International Prophetic Conference in Chicago five years later, he stressed the doctrine of the any-moment coming. He insisted that there was no point in looking for signs of the Second Advent, such as natural catastrophes, Zionism, or political upheavals. He warned especially that Christians should not wait for the tribulation as a sign, because the secret rapture of the saints would precede it. All of this was pure Darbyism. "He whose coming, at its first stage, will not be with outward pomp and manifestation, visible to the whole world; but silently as a thief comes," Princell declared, "will catch up His people, snatching them away from coming disasters and judgments; after that 'every eye shall see Him.'"[28]

Princell pursued these millenarian themes also in Frihet och Frid [Freedom and Peace], the short-lived journal which he began to publish in 1888. By this time, however, he had succombed to the temptation to look for signs of the Second Advent and the other events which historicist millenarians associated with it. In an article about the Antichrist, Princell declared that such phenomena as Zionism, persecution of Christians, the secularization of the church, and increasing distrust of governments were indications that the archenemy's appearance was at hand.[29] Curiously, although he remained a Darbyite, Princell lauded the historicist immigrant millenarian, Peter Christian Trandberg.[30]

When, therefore, Darbyites seceded from the Ansgar Synod in the early 1880's, that body was free to merge with the Mission

Synod on terms which the latter denomination stipulated. The union took place in February, 1885 when leaders of the two groups met in Chicago to form the Swedish Evangelical Mission Covenant of America. Carl Björk was named its first president, a position he held until 1910.

Princell opposed the formation of the Mission Covenant. In a series of articles published in Chicago-Bladet in late 1884 and early 1885, he discussed "The Question of the Union of Christian Congregations with Each Other for Common Activity." Not surprisingly, he concluded that anything more highly structured than a loose confederation of local bodies was "organized hypocrisy."[31] He sought admission to the constituting convention, but was turned away on the grounds that he was no longer a member of either the Ansgar or the Mission Synod.[32] His hostility to the Mission Covenant persisted for several years, although he and the new denomination eventually issued constrained apologies to each other.[33] But the Evangelical Free and the Covenant have never healed the breach between them, although both are members of the International Federation of Free Evangelical Churches.

Lay evangelists from the Danish and Norwegian free church movements also emigrated to North America. They joined lay preachers in the United States in renewing the trans-Atlantic millenarian awakening which Franson and his associates had begun in the United States and Scandinavia a few years before. Severin Didriksen, for example, who preached at Bethlehem Church in

Christiania during the early 1880's, left Norway soon after the Norwegian Mission Covenant was founded to join his older brother in Boston. Ludvig Ellingsen, Franson's answer to Ira D. Sankey, followed shortly thereafter and in the late 1880's took pastorates in Boston and Providence. N. P. Lang, the Dane who had been associated with Moody's church in Chicago from 1864 until 1882, returned to the Windy City in 1884 where he resumed his career as a revivalist.

In a letter to Missionæren, Ellingsen described his revivalism among Swedes and Norwegians in Rhode Island in 1890. "We have had blessed meetings here and there," he remarked. "In one place God saved more than 20 children from 12 to 20 years of age, mostly boys."[34] Lang reported that he spent seven months in 1889-90 travelling "over 2,000 miles in 3 states, holding revivals nearly every evening and often 3 times on Sunday." He had also made "countless home visits in all of the communities which I have visited [and] where Scandinavians live." Lang had preached in the forest of Wisconsin's Door Peninsula as well as in the cavernous Swedish Tabernacle in Minneapolis, where he briefly worked with Franson.[35]

As in Denmark and Norway, then, millenarianism furnished much of the impetus for immigrant revivalism. Correspondence from the 1880's reveals that even in rural Midwestern settlements many Scandinavian newcomers shared the trans-Atlantic eschatological community. Writing from Alta, Iowa in 1884, Christian Corneliussen disclosed that Darbyite millenarianism dominated his view of the world's destiny. "The times are bad," he wrote, "but the Lord will come soon to fetch His own and protect them in His abode until the tribulation is over." Corneliussen had been in the New World for at least a decade and appears to have been unaware that a series of millenarian waves had arrived in Norway since his departure. During his youth, he complained, "this glorious hope had been lost or buried in form Christianity and explained away. . . . I never heard a word or received a writing by any pastor or teacher about this matter."[36] Meanwhile, in Rhode Island, Ellingsen, like Franson, pointed to signs of Christ's imminent return, as did the Dane J. C. J. Klim in Iowa.[37]

Echoing another of Franson's concerns, these immigrant evangelists stressed the need for Christian unity and pleaded for tolerance in what they regarded as less important theological matters. Ellingsen urged that Norwegian-American free churches cooperate more closely with Free Lutherans of Norwegian origin, but acknowledged that any closer relations between the two groups would be impossible if the Lutherans refused to abandon their narrow confessionalism."[38] Seven years later he lamented the lack of ecumenism among the various free church parties in Norway.[39] Evangelisten, the unofficial organ of these Danish and Norwegian immigrant congregations, printed one of Waldenström's frequent calls for greater unity among Christians.[40]

The churches which men like Ellingsen and Didriksen gathered remained relatively isolated for several years. They did not have a newspaper until American Congregationalists began to publish one for them in 1890. Shortly thereafter, members of that Yankee denomination assisted them in forming the Eastern and Western Evangelical Free Church Associations, their first inclusive organizations. These facts, as well as their futurist millenarianism which seems to have discouraged preservation of church records, make it difficult to analyze the origins of the earliest congregations. Consequently, the historian is often forced to rely on contemporary observations by native Americans.

One Congregationalist described the genesis of a Danish free church in New Haven, Connecticut. In 1882 a group of about fifteen Danes there began to hold occasional meetings. They arranged for a Lutheran pastor to visit them monthly, but his inclusive ecclesiology clashed with their ideal of a pure congregation. A lay member of the group, a watchmaker named L. C. H. Haubroe, then assumed the pastoral duties. His ministry apparently sparked the little congregation, which began to hold several meetings each week. Haubroe began to preach in Bridgeport, Hartford, and other communities in Connecticut. He claimed to draw approximately one-third of New Haven's Danes and half of those in Bridgeport to his worship services, but admitted that attendance in Hartford was much lower. "Only about ten are yet converted there."[41]

In Boston, David Didriksen and Olai Johansen were the prime movers in founding a Norwegian free congregation. They first attended a Norwegian Lutheran church in that city, but were disenchanted with the failure of its pastor to stress the need for conversion. When Didriksen's brother, Severin, emigrated to Boston, the three began to hold meetings in a Congregationalist church on Sunday afternoons. In 1885 they and four other immigrants from Norway organized the Norwegian Evangelical Free Congregational Church in Roxbury. The small congregation soon encompassed several Swedish-Americans, as well.[42]

The Scandinavian Evangelical Church of Tacoma, Washington was also the product of lay initiative. In 1884 sixteen Norwegian-Americans in that harbor city began to worship together in a private home. They called as their pastor L. P. Paulson, a Norwegian immigrant Lutheran. The congregation soon affiliated with the Washington Congregationalist General Association. Lack of funds almost forced the group to disband, but a grant of $500 from the American Congregational Union allowed it to build a chapel and call a pastor.[43] In 1890 Paulson claimed that there were "many small brother congregations in the area. . . ."[44]

These scattered Danish and Norwegian congregations, which probably did not number more than two dozen before the 1890's, emulated their counterparts in Scandinavia in striving to rise above sectarianism. Like Franson and Princell, they had little use for denominations and professed to abhor sectarian bickering. A Danish immigrant churchman complained that in the United States "one says: 'I am a Lutheran,' the other: 'Methodist' or 'Baptist' and so on."[45] One of his countrymen in Iowa lamented to the editor of the Danish Mission Covenant's newspaper that whenever he spoke about Christ, he was immediately asked, "What denomination do you belong to? What is the name of the church, the society of Christians, to which you belong?'" When he answered "'I belong to the same one as Paul, Peter, James, and John,'" his inquirer expressed "doubt, astonishment, and scorn, as though such an answer were one of the stupidest which a person could give."[46]

In line with their opposition to denominational zealotry, these immigrant preachers changed their affiliation from one communion to another with surprising frequency. John Hanson Meyer, for example, studied at the Baptists' Morgan Park Theological Seminary in Chicago before his ordination at the Bridgeport Scandinavian Mission in Bridgeport, Connecticut. He subsequently organized Norwegian Congregationalist churches in Jersey City and Hoboken and held several Lutheran pastorates.[47] Another Norwegian immigrant, L. P. Paulson, was ordained a Lutheran pastor before taking the pulpit of the Scandinavian Evangelical Church of Tacoma. In the 1890's he served a Norwegian Presbyterian congregation in Minneapolis.[48]

By the mid-1880's, then, when the immigrants of free church leanings began to interact more closely with Yankee Protestants, crucial distinctions were already perceptible among them. Although all shared the background of nineteenth-century Scandinavian revivalism, they differed strongly on ecclesiology and eschatology. The Swedish Evangelical Free Church which Princell formed was rapidly becoming thoroughly millenarian and consistently opposed denominationalism. The Mission Covenant, on the other hand, paid little attention to the Darbyite fervor which gripped many Swedish-American churchmen, especially in Chicago. Moreover, the Covenant, while denying that it was a denomination, developed a *de facto* denominational organization. The free churches organized among Danish and Norwegian immigrants were so few and scattered in the 1880's as to defy precise generalizations. Nevertheless, one can find in their sparse records clear hints of allegiance to the futurist millenarianism which Franson was popularizing among Scandinavians on both sides of the Atlantic as well as attempts to form churches comprising only born-again Christians.

The lineaments of these Scandinavian-Americans' theological conservatism were beginning to emerge. Whether millenarian or not, they were clearly headed in a different direction theologically from that which was changing Congregationalism, the American denomination with which they began to cooperate in 1885.

CHAPTER IX

CONGREGATIONALISM AND THE SCANDINAVIAN FREE CHURCHES

During the last thirty years of the nineteenth century American Congregationalists cooperated in several ways with Scandinavian free church immigrants. They supplied these newcomers of both the Mission Covenant and Evangelical Free Church traditions with sanctuaries, ministerial and vocational education, and money. These endeavors began on a small scale shortly after the Civil War when the American denomination was beginning to reveal the impact which men like Horace Bushnell were making on it, but well before Congregationalism reached its liberal apogee. They increased considerably during the 1880's when these Yankees were alarmed at the rising tide of southern and eastern European immigrants and consequently sought like-minded Protestant allies in their campaign to preserve traditional America. During that decade many American Congregationalists became intensely nationalistic and conscious of their seventeenth-century heritage. Both of these traits distorted their perception of the immigrants in question and prompted them to increase their contacts with Nordic free church newcomers, whom they tended to regard as _de facto_ Congregationalists. Although the anti-immigrant bias manifest in Josiah Strong's _Our Country_ and other nativist books of the Gilded Age was widespread among Congregationalists, some members of the denomination welcomed Scandinavians into the fold. For several years, until about 1890, these immigrants gratefully accepted aid from the Yankees.

It should be said at the outset, however, that their temporary alliance with the Congregationalists was never very secure and eventually fell victim to their rejection of the American denomination's increasingly liberal image and tendency to combine nationalism with religion.

Congregationalist contacts with Scandinavian immigrants in the 1860's grew out of a new missionary strategy designed to supplement older forms of revivalism. In 1865 the denomination's first National Council recommended that every local body develop a program of "home evangelization" to reach the unchurched through house-to-house visitation. This corollary of revivalism also encompassed religious education for non-members and various kinds of social work conducted through voluntary societies within the congregations. Home evangelization was neither a new nor a uniquely Congregationalist approach to domestic missionary work. The American branch of the Evangelical Alliance and the American Sunday School Union advocated it, as did many other denominations. Dwight Moody and Ira Sankey used home evangelization on both sides of the Atlantic in the 1870's, and in the early 1880's their former associate, Fredrik Franson, urged that Moody's attempt to carry the gospel to every home in Chicago be emulated in Norway.[1] In 1867 the Congregationalists' Chicago Association discussed "how to reach our foreign population with the gospel" and, foreshadowing developments of the 1880's and 1890's, concluded that "the aim should be to nationalize them and gather then into our churches, rather than to establish churches exclusively of foreign elements."[2]

In Minnesota, where the majority of the immigrants were at least nominally Protestant, the denomination did relatively little for them before the 1880's. Some of the state's Congregationalist ministers pleaded repeatedly for large-scale efforts to evangelize newcomers. In 1868 Americus Fuller, secretary of the Congregational General Association of Minnesota, regarded prospective missionary work among the state's foreign-born inhabitants as an integral aspect of the denomination's efforts to build a Christian civilization on the frontier. He remarked that "we must not feel that our duty is done till we have gathered up and united all the Christian influence that comes to us, and brought it effectively to the work of Christianizing the land."[3] Fuller's early plea, however, did not produce immediate results. Richard Hall, the American Home Missionary Society's superintendent in Minnesota, and his successor, Levi Cobb, apparently did not pursue an aggressive missionary policy among immigrants. Cobb was aware of their presence, though, and wrote a letter to his superiors in New York City requesting that more work be undertaken among them:

> Our churches contribute, annually, to send the gospel to "nominally Christian lands." And yet here are tens of thousands from some of the very countries to which we are sending our missionaries. To us nothing is plainer than this: -- that God has sent these people to our very doors for us to Christianize.

We must do it, or they will make Europeans of us.[4]

During the 1870's Minnesota Congregationalists moved slowly to develop contacts with Scandinavian-Americans in the state. At the 1874 meeting of the General Association J. A. Towle, minister of the Congregationalist church in Northfield, had been directed to "prepare a paper to be read at the next Conference, upon the Lutheran Church -- its Theology, and relation to our Christian Work among our Scandinavian population."[5] The following year, however, Towle was no longer a member of the Minnesota Congregationalist ministerium, and no report was made. The General Association transferred the responsibility of preparing the report to its Business Committee,[6] but the 1876 Minutes do not reveal that it was presented.

On the local level, however, some individual churches adopted home evangelization as a means of reaching Nordic immigrants. Under the leadership of Henry A. Stimson, this new direction became a bridge between Plymouth Congregational Church in Minneapolis and that city's Scandinavian immigrants. An alumnus of Yale College and Andover Theological Seminary, Stimson was called to Plymouth in 1869 and soon initiated programs for the newcomers which lasted long after his tenure at the church ended in 1880. This work focused on efforts to reach Scandinavian youth. To that end a "Scandinavian Sabbath School" was conducted, but it was too small to include all of the Nordic young people who did not have spiritual homes in other denominations. When he resigned his pastorate Stimson warned the congregation to "do something, and that promptly and swiftly, to reach these young Scandinavians."[7] The congregation responded by expanding its work among the city's Nordic immigrant population in the 1880's. Members conducted vocational courses for newcomers, and the church's women ran a baby-sitting program. A kindergarten eventually enrolled the children of more than 100 families.[8]

After becoming the minister of a Congregationalist church in Worcester, Massachusetts, Stimson undertook similar work among that city's many Scandinavian immigrants. He became acquainted with George Wiberg, a Swede who was associated with the Ansgar Synod and who organized in Worcester the first Swedish Congregationalist church in the United States. Stimson assisted his and John Hagström's efforts to raise funds for the Synod's Ansgar College in two ways. He contributed twenty-five dollars and also wrote a letter to "the brethren of the American Congregational Churches" in which he endorsed the work of the Mission and Ansgar Synods which, Stimson mistakenly asserted, were "entirely separated from the Lutheran body in doctrine and polity. . . . They are practically Congregationalists."[9]

Other New England Congregationalists also developed contacts with Nordic immigrants. In New Britain, Connecticut, for example, a Mrs. Lyon conducted a Sunday school for Scandinavian children, especially girls, for several years. Her interest in these young people awakened widespread attention among the city's Congregationalists, who helped a group of seventy-two Swedes organize

Bethany Congregational Church in the 1880's. This body received financial support from its Yankee benefactors until well into the twentieth century.[10]

In Chicago, meanwhile, the minister of the Congregationalist Tabernacle Church, Frederick Emrich, attracted a large, polyglot following, including many Nordic immigrants, in the early 1880's. Emrich, an American-born son of German immigrants, acquired a command of both Swedish and Danish and tried to minister to a congregation comprising members from nearly a dozen European countries.[11] When the Danish revivalist Peter Christian Trandberg emigrated to Chicago in 1882, Emrich allowed him to preach at Tabernacle Church on Sunday afternoons, and his millenarian sermons soon attracted a large flock of Danish-Americans.

The receptive attitudes of individuals like Stimson and Emrich toward immigrants, however, did not represent the denomination's feelings as a whole. A strong anti-immigrant bias pervaded Congregationalism in the early 1880's. Eastern Congregationalists were especially vigorous in denouncing the hyphenated Americans. William M. Taylor, the Scottish-born pastor of Broadway Tabernacle Church in New York City, employed a fable to warn the delegates attending the 1881 AHMS convention of the threat posed by the immigrants:

> We must not forget that many of these are bringing with them seeds which, unless we pre-occupy the soil with truth, will take root in it, and spread to the

> peril of our own Republicanism. Weeds sow themselves, but wheat has to be cultivated continuously from year to year. A romantic Scotchman, with perhaps more sentiment than sense, took in a flower-pot a thistle, the emblem of his nationality, from his native land to one of the districts in Australia. Other Scotchmen came to him and got seeds from it, as a matter of curiosity, and now the farmers in the whole region around complain that the thistle is the most pernicious weed with which they have to deal. Now, these immigrants for the most part bring, in some sense or other, a thistle with them. The Russian brings his Nihilism; the German his Socialism or infidelity; the Frenchman his Communism; other nationalities their Romanism; and those are the fewest in number who, like the disciples of Mr. Hughes, bring with them a Christian pastor, and rear among the first of their edifices a Protestant church. All these isms seed of themselves, and scatter themselves.[12]

This hostility, which preceded the swarming of millions of southern and eastern Europeans to the New World, was perhaps one factor which prevented Congregationalist work among immigrants from becoming systematized and expanding beyond scattered local bodies until the mid-1880's.

The arrival of Marcus Whitman Montgomery (1839-94) in the Twin Cities in 1881 began a new chapter in the history of relations between American Congregationalists and Scandinavian immigrants. Shortly after coming to Minnesota, he took an interest in the Nordic peoples there and vigorously pressed for increased evangelism among them. Owing largely to Montgomery's energy, within four years the Scandinavian work became one of the largest projects which the AHMS conducted.

Montgomery's background influenced the nature of Congregationalist activities among Scandinavian-Americans. He was born in Steuben County, New York, the son of New Englanders who had joined the Yankee migration across the Hudson River at the beginning of the nineteenth century. When Marcus was still in his infancy, his family moved to eastern Indiana where he spent most of his childhood. From an early age he displayed the spirit of entrepreneurship. While still a teenager Montgomery supported his family by teaching school and assisting a relative in the construction of a county jail. At age eighteen he briefly attended a business college in Cincinnati, and in 1858 became the official stenographer of the Missouri Legislature. Montgomery soon relinquished this position, however, and returned to Portland, Indiana, where he began to publish a newspaper, The Jay Torch Light. In its pages the young editor declared his loyalty to the recently founded Republican party and the Union cause in the Civil War.[13] Montgomery sold his newspaper for $1,200 in 1862 and began his higher education at Wheaton College near Chicago. To finance his studies he organized a commercial department at the young institution. This was another in a long series of small business ventures which honed Montgomery's abilities as an ambitious administrator.[14] After three years at Wheaton, the more plentiful educational opportunities of the East drew him to Amherst College, where he took a Bachelor of Arts in 1869.[15] Although this institution contributed an average of 17.5 graduates to the Congregationalist ministry annually,[16] Montgomery chose a career in business. For six years he worked as a real estate broker in Cleveland. During this period he is said to have earned more than $25,000 and to have lost most of it, perhaps due to the depression of 1873.[17] In the autumn of 1875 he matriculated at Yale Divinity School, from which he graduated three years later.[18] The AHMS commissioned Montgomery to a debt-ridden Congregationalist church in Fort Scott, Kansas, which he soon led back to solvency.[19] Owing to his wife's poor health, Montgomery resigned his pastorate in January, 1880. Later that year he again exercised his talents as a fund raiser when he was named financial agent of Washburn College, a young Congregationalist institution in Topeka, Kansas. Working primarily in New England, Montgomery secured $8,000 for the struggling college. He was then called to succeed Levi Cobb as the supervisor of AHMS operations in Minnesota.[20]

Montgomery's theology was formed before liberalism began to characterize his denomination. Educated at Wheaton, Amherst, and Yale, he was Biblically oriented and temporarily regarded modern science as a threat to what he imprecisely termed "orthodoxy."[21]

Speaking before the Minnesota Congregational Club in 1886, he demanded a return to more Biblical preaching.[22] Two months later Montgomery suggested that the denomination conduct "a Biblical Institute or Conference, to promote Bible study" among the state's Congregationalists.[23] His conservatism, however, was inconsistent. Montgomery accepted the notion of a postmillennial Kingdom of God on earth and, three years after warning of the threat which science posed to Christianity, he urged readers of his Minneapolis newspaper to read Henry Ward Beecher's volume on the harmony of evolution and the Christian faith.[24]

With characteristic vigor Montgomery plunged into his new task. In 1882 he presented to the Minnesota General Association the report which had been assigned to Towle and the Business Committee several years earlier. It bore the title "The Religious Condition of Our Foreign Population."[25] A summary was printed in _The Pilgrim_, the Minnesota Congregationalist monthly which he edited. Montgomery expressed his gratitude that most of the state's immigrants were either German or Scandinavian, because people from these nations make "excellent citizens." He also described Lutheran, Mennonite, and Baptist efforts to assist newcomers, and concluded by making suggestions for analogous Congregationalist work.[26] The General Association responded by appointing an _ad hoc_ committee to consider Montgomery's proposals, and the following day a groundbreaking resolution was adopted:

> We heartily endorse the sentiments of that paper

> as to the importance of this portion of our population, and the duty of our ministers to evince toward them a warm, Christian interest and sympathy. We recommend that pastors and church members seek the acquaintances of these people, and invite them into congregations and Sabbath-schools, and give them a share in the work. . . .
>
> As to the Scandinavians: that wherever they are sufficiently numerous, Sabbath-schools be organized among them, to be conducted in English; and that as a denomination we send official representatives to their synods, both to assure them of our interest and fellowship, and that we may thus better know them ourselves, and have a warm and intelligent interest in their progress.[27]

The Pilgrim also carried an article titled "Work Among Foreigners" in which Montgomery briefly described Methodist and Baptist churches among the Scandinavians in Minneapolis and chided his fellow Congregationalists for failing to demonstrate "any push and spirit of aggressiveness" in trying to reach even the native born population dwelling in our midst."[28]

During the next several months Montgomery undertook an ambitious campaign to fulfill the General Association's resolutions. At his invitation Sven Oftedal, a brother of the Norwegian Evangelical Free Church organizer Lars Oftedal and a professor at Augsburg

Seminary in Minneapolis addressed the 1883 General Association on "Congregationalism and the Lutheran Free Church."[29] Early in 1884 the Congregational Club of Minnesota held a "Scandinavian Symposium" with the topic "Norwegians, Swedes, and Their Denominations." The two featured speakers were Sven Oftedal, who spoke about revivalism and pietism in Norway, and Stimson's acquaintance, who described his Congregationalist ministry among Swedish immigrants in Massachusetts and Minnesota. Both Oftedal and Wiberg anticipated subsequent conflicts between their ethnic groups and Congregationalists by warning that some Scandinavians were already questioning the doctrinal soundness of the American denomination.[30]

Undaunted by this negative note, Montgomery continued his efforts to promote Congregationalist work among Minnesota's Nordic immigrants. Before he could accomplish much, though, he suffered from nervous exhaustion. A wealthy friend, Judge E. S. Jones of Minneapolis, offered to finance a recuperative trip to Europe. Montgomery accepted and began to make preparations to combine the health voyage with investigations of Scandinavian free church movements. He conferred with Oftedal and the prominent Mission Friend evangelist, E. August Skogsbergh, in Minneapolis, and received from the latter a letter of introduction to expedite contacts with leaders of the Swedish Mission Covenant.[31] Montgomery arrived in Sweden in March, 1884. His first meeting was in Stockholm with N. P. Ollén, secretary of the Mission Covenant. Their interpreter, however, proved unsatisfactory, and conversations with Ollén yielded little more than a breakfast invitation to his home in a suburb of Stockholm.[32] A few days later, though, Paul Waldenström came to Stockholm from his residence in Gefle. Discussions with him in the Swedish capital and on a train *en route* to Uppsala were more fruitful and increased Montgomery's respect for the Swedish churchman. Nevertheless, some doubts lingered in his estimation of the Mission Covenant. "It was provoking bitter opposition from the Lutheran State Church," he noted, but

> its adherents were accounted on all sides excellent Christians. On the other hand, I had often heard it charged by their opponents that they were loose in polity, lacked organization, and were unsound in doctrine. My interviews with Dr. Waldenstrom [sic] and Mr. Ollen [sic] had been too imperfectly interpreted to sufficiently clear up these difficulties. I began to think that perhaps the movement had not yet clearly defined itself and that it was probably too early for Congregationalists to offer their fellowship.[33]

Montgomery's uncertainty abated during his lengthy stay at the Mission Theological School in Kristinehamn, Sweden. While a guest of its faculty, he became convinced that he had made a fateful discovery, "that the Lord was indeed repeating, in Sweden and in

Norway, the historic providences by which, three centuries ago, he led forth his people from the national church of England to plant churches on the New Testament plan, both in old England and in the New World."[34] With these words Montgomery initiated a rhetorical tradition which constantly accompanied and influenced Congregationalist efforts to assist Scandinavian free church immigrants. As we shall see, Montgomery and other Congregationalists who were active in this work repeatedly asserted that the nineteenth-century Nordic free church movements were analogous to English separatism. They ignored the differences in both theology and polity which differentiated the Scandinavian dissenters from those of Elizabethan England. No less damaging was their failure to recognize and admit that by the 1880's American Congregationalists had little in common with the faith of their colonial forebears. On the contrary, Gilded Age Congregationalists repeatedly stressed their identity with their spiritual forefathers.

Montgomery felt an affinity with the Covenant leaders in Kristinehamn. Although he praised the Lutheran Waldenström,[35] Montgomery realized that he had more in common with Ekman and Fernholm, both of whom had been influenced by Reformed Protestantism. Ekman spoke little English, but Fernholm was fluent in the language and, according to Montgomery, was "so strikingly like an American in personal appearance that he would pass even in Boston for a Beacon Street full-blood."[36] They discussed theology at length with their American visitor. Montgomery also commented favorably on their students' reverence for the Bible and observed that "no more pious or consecrated young men are to be found in any theological school, and in readiness to find or cite almost any passage of Scripture, they are not often equaled."[37] He noted that both Ekman and Fernholm, in contrast to Waldenström, advocated believers' baptism.[38] This did not, however, alarm Montgomery, who had repeatedly suggested that closer ties be made between his own denomination and Baptists in the United States.[39] In fact, both adult and infant baptism were widely practiced among Congregationalists and members of the Swedish Mission Covenant. In 1884 slightly more than half of the people baptized in American Congregationalist churches were adults.[40]

On the basis of his discussions with Fernholm and Ekman, Montgomery assured his fellow Congregationalists that the Swedish Covenanters were "orthodox," and carefully defined his use of the term. Among Swedes, he explained, "he is 'orthodox' who adheres in all particulars to the Lutheran Augsburg Confession of Faith." The Covenanters did not fit this definition, Montgomery admitted; rather, they were "soundly 'orthodox' in the American sense of that word." He suggested that the Covenanters could aptly be called "Scriptural." Montgomery also remarked that "there is, happily, much liberty among them on doctrinal questions" but "no more varieties of belief or divergences than among Congregationalists."[41]

From those halcyon days in Kristinehamn until he returned to the United States, Montgomery perceived Congregationalism in almost all facets of the Swedish Mission Covenant and the free churches in

Norway which were about to become the Norwegian Mission Covenant. At a rural church near Kristinehamn he was pleasantly surprised to learn that admission to communion was strictly controlled. Montgomery may have thought this a parallel to the exclusive practices of seventeenth and eighteenth-century New England Congregationalism, although he did not mention that by 1884 few of his denomination's churches demanded more than a brief statement of faith from prospective communicants. The reception of new members was also familiar to him:

> They then kneeled and the ministers present put each hand upon the head of one of them, while the deacons came forward and put their hands upon others until all new members received "the laying on of hands;" then prayers of consecration followed. When they had risen the Lord's Supper was administered, the service being in every respect as in the Congregational churches in our own country. In only two respects did any of these public services differ from similar occasions in the United States. One was the kneeling of incoming members, instead of standing, as with us; the other was in the response of the Swedish congregation during the prayers.[42]

Even the sermon, which Montgomery could not understand, reminded him of a pulpit oration which he had heard in Lawrence, Kansas in 1878.

From Kristinehamn Montgomery went by rail to Christiania to investigate the Norwegian free churches. In the Norwegian capital he met Franson's associates, Severin Didriksen, Cathrine Juell, and M. Hanson. He realized that in Norway the revival momement had been largely contained within the established church and that separatism was not strong. Nonetheless, although his stay in the Norwegian capital lasted only a few days, the free churches which were about to form the Norwegian Mission Covenant made a strong impression on him. Montgomery was again astounded by the similarities which he perceived between these congregations and those of his own denomination. Indeed, one of his first activities in Christiania was to relate the history of Congregationalism in England and North America to a free church congregation. According to the pleased Montgomery, his narrative elicited "many expressions of sympathy . . . from the audience."[43] The Norwegian free church organ Morgenrøden agreed with his comparison of the origins of the Congregationalists and the Swedish and Norwegian Covenanters.[44]

The Norwegian bededag, or prayer day, which occurred the day after his arrival, also delighted him. In the United States Protestants had been striving with limited success during the nineteenth century for similar religious holidays.[45] The fact that the Norwegian Storting, or parliament, had adjourned for bededag particularly impressed Montgomery, as did the attire of the multitudes who filled the churches on that holiday: "There was very little in the personal appearance, dress, or behavior of either ladies or gentlemen in that throng of people which would distinguish them from a similar outpouring of Americans in any of our cities."[46] A final familiarity which he observed was in the church music. One of the hymns sung at the bededag service which he attended was a Norwegian version of "Wonderful Words of Life."

In Christiania Niels A. S. Eie served as Montgomery's interpreter and received lavish praise from the American. He gave Montgomery a copy of a small volume by an English clergyman, A. H. Darling, who had been active as an itinerant revivalist in Norway. Like other British dissenters who visited northern Europe during the nineteenth century, Darling held the Norwegian state church in low regard. He unveiled his prejudices in this book of 1874, An Account of the Spiritual State of Norway, in which he attacked the "semi-popish" established church and probably reinforced Montgomery's preconceived notions about the Norwegian free church movements. In the space of a few pages Darling painted a dismal picture of Norwegian Lutheranism, especially the popular piety of state church members. He repeatedly compared it to that of Roman Catholicism, which Montgomery and many other Congregationalists despised. "A British Christian on entering a Lutheran home," Darling wrote, "would have the impression, unless undeceived, that he had just entered a Roman Catholic's dwelling on account of the Catholic-like pictures, and sometimes a candle on each side of an image of Christ."[47] He also pointed out parallels between Norwegian Lutheran and Catholic cemeteries, funeral practices, catechisms, and vestments. He translated the Dano-Norwegian word præst, the standard term for a state church clergyman, as "priest."[48] Darling then contrasted these targets of his wrath with the Haugean lay movement and the separatism of Lammers' followers, and briefly mentioned the persecutions which they had endured.

Writing ten years after this Englishman, Montgomery also drew a sharp line of demarcation between Scandinavian state churches and revival movements. This is perhaps most clearly revealed in his comments about communion in the Swedish Mission Covenant. Impressed by procedural similarities, he hastily concluded that it was "in every respect as in the Congregational churches in our own country." This was simply not true. Had Montgomery been willing to explore the theology of the Mission Friends, he would have discovered that many held the Lutheran doctrine of the real presence of Christ in the Eucharistic elements. But this he was neither emotionally nor linguistically prepared to do. Montgomery was more concerned with nationalism, ethnicity, and Congregationalist status in a rapidly changing America than with theological nuances. Rather than carefully analyzing the Mission Covenants, he projected his own religious heritage to them and jubilantly pronounced them Congregationalist. Montgomery's comments also reveal the narrowness of his concept of what was American. When he announced that there was practically no difference in the personal appearance of Norwegians and Americans, he was obviously neglecting millions of his fellow citizens who did not in any way resemble the Nordic peoples. But again, Montgomery was more interested in developing contacts with people who bore at least superficial resemblance to the members of his own denomination than in considering factors which would upset the near equation of Congregationalist and American in his thinking.

Upon returning to the United States Montgomery attended the annual AHMS convention in Saratoga, New York, where he informed the delegates that in Sweden he had discovered "a remarkable case of spontaneous Congregationalism."[49] In a lengthy article published that autumn in The Andover Review, Montgomery described the Swedish Mission Covenant and flatly insisted that "these Swedish free churches are purely Congregational. In polity, doctrines, liberty, and variety in unity, in general methods, and in the leading features of their history, they are Congregational to the core."[50] Montgomery expanded his account to include the Norwegian Mission Covenant, and reiterated his conviction that the free denominations were essentially Congregationalist, in a book, A Wind from the Holy Spirit in Sweden and Norway, which the AHMS published in 1885.

The supposed parallels between the origins of Congregationalism and the Mission Covenants in Norway and Sweden constituted the main theme of Montgomery's volume. "The Swedish Free churches are purely Congregational," he repeated. "In polity, doctrines, liberty, and variety in unity, they are Congregational to the core." That the free churches had developed a congregational polity without previous contacts with other Congregationalists Montgomery regarded as providential and "instructive to students of church history."

He tried to bolster his assertion by quoting at length a letter which Waldenström had sent him. The Swede agreed that "these Free churches are, in foundation and ground, Congregational, as you yourself know by your visit in our land."[51]

On the following page, however, Montgomery qualified his generalization. He admitted that "in regard to the Lord's Supper and baptism Dr. Waldenstrom [sic] yet holds, in some minor points only, the Lutheran view."[52] Montgomery either failed to recognize or was not prepared to admit that the legacy of Lutheranism pervaded much of the Swedish Mission Covenant, however similar its superficial appearance to many Anglo-American Protestant communions may have been. Nothing in his published works or his extant papers indicates that he was aware of the Covenant's largely Lutheran theology. Moreover, although Montgomery realized that some members of the Mission Covenants were millenarians, he failed to comprehend the chasm between millenarianism and the nationalistic postmillennialism which had gained much headway among Congregationalists.

Indeed, in only one respect did Montgomery reveal any hesitancy about establishing further contacts with the Mission Friends. In a letter to him, which Montgomery included in his book, Fredrik Franson described faith healing among his Norwegian and Swedish converts. Congregationalists had never espoused faith healing, and it probably seemed ridiculous to them in the 1880's when many were rapidly accommodating modern science. But Montgomery chose to regard Franson as an atypical Mission Friend. He cryptically concluded that "the peculiarities of this earnest worker are manifest."[53]

Montgomery finished his report by outlining a strategy for assisting those Scandinavian free churches, both in Europe and in the United States, which were not already receiving aid from other American denominations. First, the financial resources of the AHMS should be made available "to help support Swedish, Norwegian, and Danish missionaries to preach the gospel among their countrymen in this land." Secondly, he suggested that "two Scandinavian professorships, one Swedish and one Norwegian or Danish," be established at Chicago Theological Seminary. For a quarter of a century Anglo-American Protestants had been training immigrant clergymen at their divinity schools. Northern Baptists, for example, began a German department at their Rochester seminary in 1858, and had established similar facilities for Scandinavian immigrants at the seminary in Morgan Park, Illinois in 1871. Chicago Theological Seminary already had a German department when Montgomery pleaded for an expansion of its work to include educating Nordic-American ministers. Methodists, Presbyterians, and other denominations had also turned their seminaries into polyglot training grounds for the pulpit, or did so before the end of the century. Aaron Abell assessed the extent of these programs. "So ample were the facilities that by 1900 a body of clergymen ready to meet all calls for independent or assistant pastorates had come into existence."[54] Thirdly, Montgomery asked for financial aid to help support the Swedish Mission Covenant seminaries at

Kristinehamn and Winslöf, and finally, he suggested that a similar school be opened in Norway or Denmark, because "the very interesting Free Mission movement now fairly started in Norway cannot have permanent and safe growth without trained pastors and teachers."[55]

Montgomery's travels, book, and articles established him as the closest thing Congregationalism had to an authority on the Scandinavian free churches. He consequently relinquished his Minnesota superintendency and on September 1, 1884 was commissioned the first AHMS "Scandinavian Superintendent." The AHMS opened the headquarters of its new Scandinavian Department in downtown Minneapolis, although Montgomery spent much of his time traveling to many regions of the United States to develop closer ties between his office and Nordic free church immigrants. He and other Congregationalists also arranged to have a small Scandinavian department opened at Chicago Theological Seminary for the 1884-85 academic year as a temporary solution until a more extensive program of ministerial education for immigrants could be arranged there.

The Congregationalists' motives for establishing Scandinavian departments at their Chicago seminary and within the AHMS have often been misunderstood. Swedish-Americans in the Mission Covenant tradition have made several attempts to analyze them. In one of the earliest histories of the denomination, C. V. Bowman attributed the Scandinavian departments to Congregationalism's desire to "extend its influence among the new-comers."[56] He did not, however, explain his laconic statement.

Karl Olsson was more analytical in his commendable By One Spirit, the standard history of the Evangelical Covenant Church. He did not doubt the sincerity of the Congregationalists who offered free theological education to the Mission Covenant. "Their motives need not be questioned. They were there to render a service, perhaps to perform a charity. They offered the denomination not yet born but about to be born what amounted to gratis education for ministerial candidates."[57] But Olsson also suggested that denominational aggrandizement may have been an ulterior motive. The Congregationalists, he wrote, were "engaging in a full-scale propaganda effort to bring all Covenant churches into the Congregational fold."[58] This campaign, according to Olsson, proceeded from the Congregationalists' "happy fiction" that the two denominations were virtually identical and their mistaken belief "that the Mission Friends in Sweden and America were merely waiting to be invited into the American fellowship."[59]

At least two of Olsson's students uncritically incorporated his views in their studies of relations between the Congregationalists and the Mission Covenant. In 1960 Robert M. Anderson wrote that "there is a sense in which one can say the Congregationalists were motivated by denominational aspirations. . . . There is no doubt in my mind that the leaders of Congregationalism would like to have absorbed all of the Mission Covenant and Free churches into their denomination."[60] Six years later P. Richard Lindstrom combined the denominational aggrandizement motive with another reason for aiding Scandinavian immigrants in his study of the Chicago Theological Seminary Swedish Department. "(1) They [the Congregationalists] first of all wanted to Americanize the immigrants. (2) Then they would like to Congregationalize them."[61] Lindstrom did not, however, adequately analyze the Congregationalists' desire to Americanize these newcomers, nor did he explain why this found expression in the creation of Scandinavian departments at their seminary in Chicago.

None of these explanations is satisfactory. Olsson's assertion that the Congregationalists were seeking to swell their own ranks through a "full-scale propaganda effort" is chronologically erroneous and conceals their real motive, which was to create an alliance with these immigrants. There is a wealth of evidence that in the mid-1880's Montgomery and his colleagues were not interested in absorbing Scandinavian-American free churches. Conversely, nothing supports Olsson's hyperbole that the Congregationalists in question were so naive as to believe that "the Mission Friends . . . were merely waiting to be invited into the American fellowship. . . ." As early as January, 1885, a month before the offer of a Swedish department was extended to the Mission Covenant, Montgomery assured readers of The Pilgrim that "Congregationalists certainly do not wish the Free Mission churches to change their name and become 'Congregational.' These words 'Free' and 'Mission' are historic, significant, precious. . . . Then why should not each respect the independence of the other, exchange hearty Christian greetings, and extend to each other Christian fellowship?" A year later he added that there was no need for Congregationalists to proselytize among Scandinavian immigrants, because they were already evangelical Protestants.[62] Writing editorially in The Pilgrim in October, 1886, Montgomery insisted that "organic unity between Congregationalists and Mission Swedes is not desired by either party, but Christian fellowship between them grows with mutual acquaintance."

It seems clear that in the mid-1880's, when this work among Nordic immigrants was being organized, Congregationalists had little desire to force or even persuade them to adopt their language, polity, or name. The Yankees were, however, deeply interested in establishing firm relations with Scandinavian-Americans, because they regarded them as valuable potential allies in the fight for an embattled Protestant America. Montgomery could hardly have been more lucid in expressing his belief that Nordic immigrants could be ideal comrades in this campaign: "They who love liberty and religion will make the best citizens for this republic. Just such are the Scandinavians. . . . They ardently love the principles upon which our republic rests, and hence are intensely loyal. In politics they are generally Republican." He differentiated the Scandinavian-Americans from Italians, Jews, Irish, and other immigrants whom he regarded as less desirable:

> They are not peddlars nor organ grinders, nor beggars; they do not sell ready-made clothing nor keep pawnshops; their religion is not hostile to free institutions; they do not come here temporarily, and, while

> seeking for gain, live a foreign life, praying all the while that their bones may yet lie in the lands from which they came; they do not seek to break down (what there is left of) the American Sabbath; they do not make the United States the plotting-ground against the Government of their native land. . . .[63]

It was in this spirit that Montgomery and other Congregationalists sought like-minded Protestant immigrants who, they believed, would participate in an evangelical coalition to counter the incursions of Roman Catholic and Jewish newcomers.

This does not mean, however, that there was never a campaign to bring Nordic free churches completely into the Congregationalist orbit. In a later chapter I shall discuss heavy-handed Yankee tactics to do precisely that. But contrary to the impression one might gain from the accounts of Olsson and others, the initial impetus to merge came from the Scandinavian side. As we have observed, George Wiberg and Waldenström exaggerated the oneness of the Swedish Mission Friends and the American Congregationalists. Their utterances were only the beginning. With surprising frequency other Scandinavians both in Europe and the United States echoed this sentiment. It is difficult to determine whether they were being completely ingenuous, or whether the indigence of the immigrant churches motivated them to solicit AHMS funds by exaggerating their similarity to the Yankee religious tradition.

In 1885, for example, The Pilgrim reported that John S. Anderson, a Norwegian pastor in the Twin Cities, and B. Johanson, a Norwegian missionary in Forest City, Iowa, had assured the Minnesota Congregational General Association that they were "in perfect harmony with the doctrines and polity of the Congregational churches."[64] Twelve months later the same newspaper optimistically claimed that one segment of the Norwegian Lutheran population (presumably the so-called "anti-Missourians" who opposed a continuation of cooperation with the Missouri Synod) in an unspecified "Northwestern State" was leaning toward affiliation with the Congregationalists following a dispute with other Lutherans over the doctrine of predestination.[65] In a letter which in retrospect looks suspiciously ingratiating, a Scandinavian pastor in Iowa wrote: "I remember the Pilgrim Fathers from England when I look over my Norwegian-Dano church."[66]

Waldenström was only one of several Old World Scandinavians who reinforced American Congregationalists' beliefs that the free churches desired closer ties with them. In Norway, where the movement remained weak for several decades, this hope often found expression. In a letter which was printed in The Pilgrim, a Norwegian wrote to a relative in the United States that

> we "free church" people desire nothing so much as this, that we may become united with the Congregationalists, because their principals [sic] are the same as ours as you also confirm. The circumstances

> in Norway are such that a really free religious movement can hardly be kept up without a connection with a kindred organization older and stronger, to help the young and weak one forward. . . . Could you come to Norway, and remain here, and help us into fellowship with the Congregational churches? Then, we believe, by the grace of God, the free church life will have success in our land.[67]

With this kind of feedback from Scandinavians on both sides of the Atlantic, it was hardly necessary for the Congregationalists to engage in a propaganda effort to lure Nordic immigrants into their ranks.

But there was a second reason for desiring closer relations with these newcomers. Before Montgomery and his American associates became better acquainted with them, they were convinced that beneath a linguistic veneer, the Scandinavian free churches were already *de facto* Congregationalist. Montgomery made this point explicitly in *A Wind from the Holy Spirit in Sweden and Norway*. During the next several years he elaborated his argument and sought to elicit the support of his denomination for the Scandinavians by drawing parallels between the revered Pilgrim fathers and the genesis of the Swedish Mission Covenant. In doing so, however, Montgomery revealed that his perception of both movements was shallow and oversimplified. He began by tracing the origins of his own denomination:

> Three hundred years ago there was in England only a national church. The ruling monarch, king or queen, was the head of the church. It was grounded on a false idea of a true church of Christ. Some of the errors of popery clung to it. Spiritual death and ecclesiastical corruptions prevailed. The Holy Spirit came. His brooding power was at work in many hearts. Some began to cry unto God. The question arose: what is the New Testament idea of a Christian church? Men began to search the Scriptures for more light on this question. The spirit lead [sic] them; light came; the truth became clear. A state church is not a true church. A New Testament church is a company of believers in Christ, in a certain place, united for the worship of God and mutual edification, and for co-working for the spread of His kingdom. Such a church has a right to be self-governing, and no outside ecclesiastical power may have dominion over it. . . . Separation from the national church of England followed.[68]

Montgomery's superficial consideration of early Congregationalism reflected historiographical misperceptions then current. His generation of Congregationalists denied that their denomination's roots were embedded in mainstream Puritanism which, they generally believed, was the father of Presbyterianism. They venerated the

Separatist radicals, especially the Pilgrims who founded Plymouth Plantation, as their spiritual ancestors. Until well into the twentieth century Congregationalists insisted that this small band of come-outers had planted congregational polity in New England and had converted the supposedly non-separating settlers of Massachusetts Bay to their form of ecclesiastical government. Even the erudite church historian Williston Walker maintained this view in his The Creeds and Platforms of Congregationalism, published in 1893. Perry Miller did not provide the needed corrective until the 1930's. Relying on the investigations of the English church historian Champlin Burrage, he demonstrated that although mainstream Puritans did not choose to separate from the established church in England during the early years of the seventeenth century, their polity was nevertheless congregational, and developed accordingly in the New World. The Plymouth Separatists, concomitantly, played a relatively insignificant role in the emergence of American Congregationalism.[69] Montgomery's perception of his denomination's early history, therefore, did not seem so far afield in the 1880's as it does today.

Less excusable, however, is Montgomery's failure to comprehend the distinction between polity and ecclesiology. He realized that the Scandinavian Covenants generally favored congregational polity and, largely on this basis, declared them to be identical to his own denomination. But this simplistic equation papers over two crucial distinctions. First, the Covenants restricted membership to converted individuals, an exclusivist practice characteristic of Congregationalism in the seventeenth century but certainly not in 1885. Secondly, to Congregationalists "church" had always meant the local body of communicant members. But many Scandinavian Mission Friends, as we have seen, held a twofold notion of the church as both the universal and the local communion of believers. Waldenström, who consistently adhered to this double definition, apparently confused Montgomery when he wrote that the Mission Covenant churches in Sweden were "in foundation and ground, Congregational."

The nature of these early contacts between American Congregationalists and Scandinavian immigrants provided a weak foundation for the expanded cooperation in which they engaged beginning in the mid-1880's. Unquestionably, the Yankees were sincerely trying to help indigent newcomers as part of their home missionary strategy in a rapidly changing America. But denominational zealotry tempered this beneficence and prevented them from seeing important differences between themselves and the Scandinavians whom they were seeking to assist. The tempo in which Montgomery made contacts with churchmen whose native languages he did not understand did not allow him and his denominational fellows to examine the Scandinavian free churches carefully before they plunged ahead and created departments within the AHMS and at Chicago Theological Seminary. Had they inspected the situation more carefully, they would have discovered that Lutheran theology was strong in the Swedish Mission Covenant, and that the Covenant of Norway was thoroughly millenarian. They also would have learned that these immigrants were not so unconditionally enthusiastic about assimilating as they hoped. These cultural and religious differences did not become apparent until the 1890's, when they fractured the feeble alliance between Yankee Congregationalists and many of the Scandinavians whom they had regarded as denominational brothers.

CHAPTER X

CHALLENGES TO COOPERATION WITH THE CONGREGATIONALISTS

The period of harmonious relations between the Congregationalists and these Nordic immigrants whom they regarded as their denominational fellows lasted less than a decade. The Yankees continued to give Scandinavian-American free churchmen financial and educational assistance until well into the twentieth century, but many of the Swedes and a smaller number of the Danes and Norwegians who received their help became disenchanted with Anglo-American culture and religion and asserted their denominational independence. These Scandinavians began to believe that the Congregationalists were undermining the orthodoxy of their future ministers, attempting to impose the English language on them, and coercing them to join the American denomination. Other Nordic free churchmen disagreed, however, and urged their brethren to maintain contacts with the Congregationalists. The debate over cooperation with the Yankees crested in the early 1890's and continued until the turn of the century. The arguments of those newcomers who opposed the continuation of close ties reveal that their conservatism was both cultural and theological. Indeed, for the Mission Covenant, which traced its roots to Swedish pietism, Old World culture and nineteenth-century religious conservatism were virtually inseparable.

During the 1889-90 academic year the diverging perceptions which Congregationalists and Scandinavian free church immigrants held of their joint ventures at Chicago Theological Seminary became manifest. Peter Christian Trandberg was dismissed from his position in the Dano-Norwegian Department, while the Mission Covenant withdrew its support from the Swedish Department and employed David Nyvall, who resigned his position there, to teach at its school in Minneapolis. Both of the departments continued to function, educating for the ministry immigrants who in many instances became pastors of groups affiliated with Congregationalist associations as well as of congregations which remained independent or affiliated with the Covenant or other denominations. The events of 1889 and 1890 were crucial to the separate development of the Mission Covenant, which never again cooperated closely with its Yankee benefactors, as well as to the internal life of the various "Free" groups which either declared themselves "Congregational" or at least continued to receive financial and educational assistance from the American denomination.

The difficulties in the Dano-Norwegian Department appeared with seeming suddenness. In 1888 Montgomery wrote jubilantly of the independent Norwegian and Danish immigrant congregations which had united with Congregationalist associations. The American Home Missionary Society and the American Congregational Union had contributed bountifully to these congregations, he declared.[1] Montgomery, however, was not satisfied with these sporadic accessions and urged his denomination to circulate a newspaper among Danish and Norwegian free church newcomers explaining to them that they too were Congregationalists.[2] In a visit to the seminary the following year he informed a meeting of all the Scandinavian students that he was about to return to Europe to learn Swedish and asked the Danes and Norwegians to participate in the publication of his proposed periodical.[3]

To the Lutheran Trandberg, who admitted that his relationship with the seminary rested on expediency, Montgomery's visit and other Congregationalist moves seemed gratuitous intrusions into the ecclesiastical affairs of the Nordic student body. In the 1880's Trandberg had participated in the founding of a few Danish congregations which had declared themselves Congregationalist and, in some instances, joined state associations of that denomination. He had also helped to ordain some of his students as their ministers. But, as Trandberg explained to Montgomery after the latter's address to the students, the accelerated efforts of Congregationalists to lead Danish and Norwegian Christians into their communion was making impossible his dream of an independent, revivalistic Lutheran free church in the United States. Trandberg also announced that he would have nothing to do with Montgomery's proposed newspaper.[4] On June 30, 1889, the determined professor ordained one of his former students as pastor of a Danish congregation in Racine, Wisconsin, which he described as "the first Scandinavian evangelical free church among Lutherans in North America with Biblical, apostolic principles,"[5] and shortly thereafter left the seminary. The records of his departure are contradictory. In a short book which he wrote in 1890 Trandberg stated that Montgomery had requested him to remain in the Dano-Norwegian Department, but he had rejected this plea because his conscience would not allow him to cooperate further with the Congregationalists.[6] Documents in the archives of the seminary, however, suggest that the administration had become disenchanted with his independence and his Lutheran loyalties at least by October, 1889 and forced him off the faculty. An unidentified seminary official wrote Montgomery that month, "The affair of Prof. Trandberg's salary is not arranged as it ought to be. The [unintelligible word] which might avail in your mind for the reduction to $200 might be sufficient for the S[eminary] to dispense with Prof. Trandberg's services." The writer feared, however, that this action "would be equivalent to giving up the Dano-Norwegian department," since no suitable replacement was immediately available.[7] Although this apparent plan to squeeze Trandberg out was not implemented, Professor Samuel Curtiss gave him a virtual ultimatum to become a Congregationalist or resign. "Now if after the reflection that you have given this matter you feel as we do that your usefulness and influence would be increased by forming a closer bond with us and by working entirely in sympathy + coop. with Congregational churches," Curtiss wrote him, "I think the way would be open for the continuance of your labors with us."[8] Refusing at first to bow to this pressure, Trandberg tried to counter the influence of the Congregationalists' new Dano-Norwegian monthly, <u>Evangelisten</u> [The Evangelist], by launching his own newspaper, <u>Vor</u> <u>Talsmand</u> [Our Spokesman]. In March, 1889 he helped to organize a "Scandinavian Evangelical free church" in Chicago, calling it "the first among Lutherans in this city."[9]

Realizing that such implementation of his dream of forming a chain of independent Lutheran churches was incompatible with the plan of Montgomery and other Congregationalists to bring Nordic immigrants into closer affiliation with themselves, Trandberg shortly thereafter resigned his seminary position.

In Afskeden og dens Grunde [The Departure and Its Reasons], written to explain why he had left the school, Trandberg revealed that his Danish nationalism was as important as his Lutheran predilections in the controversy. He lamented that in recent years "Baptists, Methodists, Adventists, Irvingites, the Salvation Army, et al." had brought "Santa Claus Christianity and theater Christianity" to Scandinavia. He further accused Nordic immigrants who assimilated rapidly in the New World of "ethnic suicide." By adopting foreign ways they had "murdered their own peculiar ethnic culture which the Creator gave them."[10]

Trandberg's revolt against what he regarded as Congregationalist efforts to dominate the spiritual and temporal life of Scandinavian free churches in the United States had little direct bearing on the future course of these bodies, but his story is nevertheless significant for two reasons. First, his successor in the Dano-Norwegian Department, a young immigrant from Norway who had studied at Yale, disliked Lutheranism and favored rapid assimilation. An ordained Congregationalist minister, Reinert Jernberg thus fit the American denomination's plans for closer work with immigrants splendidly. Secondly, the Congregationalists' endeavors to bring Norwegian and Danish free churches into their orbit foreshadowed a similar controversy between them and the Mission Covenant.

Meeting at Worcester, Massachusetts in the autumn of 1889, the triennial Congregational National Council passed an ambiguous resolution regarding its future relations with the Covenant.[11] This document, which was sent to the Covenant and published in Missions-Vännen, read in part:

> We believe it would be more pleasing to the Lord Jesus and better promote the spread of His kingdom if the Swedish Mission Friends and the Congregationalists, being thus alike in history and faith, should each declare to the world that they both belong to the same branch of Christ's church on the earth; that they are the same denomination, and do not wish to maintain a division which would be unnatural, sectarian, and merely external; and that they will henceforth co-operate in mutual strengthening and fellowship in the work of the Lord. . . .
>
> We see no reason why the Swedish Mission Friends, if they should accept this fraternal overture, should not retain their present name and organization, and carry on the work in their own language and methods, and send delegates to this National Council (which in the words of its constitution "shall

> never exercise any control over the churches")
> upon the same basis of representation as Congregational Associations.[12]

Perhaps anticipating certain Covenanters' objections, those who drafted the resolution added the assurance that "when our national missionary societies aid Swedish mission churches and ministers to have the Gospel preached, or to build houses of worship or parsonages, or aid Swedish students to attend school, this aid is not given for the purpose of making Congregationalists of them."[13] For nearly a decade, however, Stimson, Montgomery, and other Congregationalists, along with Waldenström and several Swedish immigrant recipients of AHMS support, had argued that the two bodies were virtually identical. This rhetorical tradition had apparently made its mark on the Yankee denomination.

The Mission Covenant's response to the proposal was a swift and unambiguous "No." David Nyvall, then in his second year on the Chicago Theological Seminary faculty, led the attack in _Missions-Vännen_. The suggested merger was irrelevant, he began, because "in the National Council questions are discussed which are foreign to the people among whom God gave us a mission in this land." Indeed, Nyvall continued, joining forces with the Congregationalists would mean that "we would be compelled to surrender our _Swedishness_, that _social independence_ which constitutes a major part of our power." His conclusion was succinct: "I believe of all my heart that the Americanization and Congregationalization of the individual Swedish congregations is a loss of living force in the mission among the Swedes."[14] During the winter of 1889-90 Nyvall continued to argue against the merger and for the preservation of the Covenant's Old World legacy. "We shall not be assimilated because we shall not be Americanized," he declared; there was no contradiction between being good Swedes and loyal Americans. "By making the best use of what we now are, we can best educate the nation in America. . . . In a certain sense one can say that if one wants to serve all, one ought to serve one's self. . . . If we are good Swedes (in an apolitical sense), we are good Americans."[15]

Nyvall apparently did not at that time regard the Congregationalists' theology as a threat to the conservative beliefs of the Mission Covenant. If he was aware of the incipient liberalism among his English-speaking colleagues at the seminary, he did not mention it in his published attacks on the proposed merger. Indeed, at the height of the debate he wrote an article praising the Congregationalists' American Board of Commissioners for Foreign Missions.[16] His opposition to the union was thus primarily cultural, not theological.

On the other hand, Axel Mellander, a Covenant pastor in Iron Mountain, Michigan who later became a professor at North Park College, stressed religious differences in the long campaign waged to preserve Covenant autonomy.[17] Replying to the National Council's proposal in Missions-Vännen, Mellander urged free churches not to join the Congregational denomination. Those which had already done so "would act most correctly and intelligently," he wrote, "by cutting their ties . . . as soon as possible."[18] Mellander alleged, quite incorrectly, that each congregation in the Yankee denomination must accept responsibility for its condition as a whole. "The Congregationalists practice the unbiblical principle of having believers and infidels together in their churches," he continued, whereas the Covenanters' ideal was a pure visible church. Mellander's assertion that "the Calvinist doctrine of election . . . is widely (if not to say universally) acknowledged by the Congregationalists" was anachronistic, of course; Calvinism had long since largely disappeared from the denomination. It was also ironic, because a similar teaching of predestination had sometimes appeared in his own Lutheran tradition. Mellander argued further that many Congregationalist clergymen and seminarians were "quite removed from life in God" and the denomination was doing "nothing to change the situation." His only proof of the last charge, though, was that "a Swedish servant girl . . . worked for a Congregationalist minister's family whose children attended a _dancing school_."[19] Mellander concluded with the warning that "jingling gold is not always a sound motive, at least not in spiritual matters. . . . Our freedom constitutes our most precious heritage from our motherland, and cannot be sold either for Congregational favors or American bribes."[20]

Montgomery replied quickly in _Missions-Vännen_ to these and other objections to the proposed merger, denying particularly that Congregationalist churches tolerated ungodly members.

"If members fall into sin," he wrote, "they are handled according to Matt. 18: 15-17. Churches which tolerate unbiblical teachings or unworthy members, are handled according to the same rule." Montgomery defended his denomination's reverence for the Bible by quoting from the constitution of the National Council, which affirmed a belief in the Holy Scriptures as the sufficient and only touchstone of Christian doctrine.[21]

This response, however, did not convince the Mission Covenant's leaders. By the time that denomination's Executive Board met with a Congregationalist delegation at the Pacific Hotel in Chicago on February 5 and 6, 1890, their rejection of the proposal was a foregone conclusion. The rejection embittered Joseph B. Clark, secretary of the AHMS and a member of the Congregationalist delegation. In a letter to Montgomery he declared:

> I did not intend to threaten the [Covenant] brethren that their rather qualified opinion of our faith and practice might make a difference in the matter of appointments and yet it would make a decided difference if the sentiments expressed by one or two of the Scandinavian brethren were widely published and it were shown that they represent the general feeling. . . . All right, if your interpretation is a correct one, let the Forbundet [sic] go to grass or to the grave. I guess it doesn't matter much which.[22]

Rebuffed by the Mission Covenant's leaders, Montgomery tried to bring individual Covenant and independent Swedish immigrant congregations into the Congregationalist orbit. In 1890 he edited for the AHMS a booklet containing statements by Swedish-American churchmen who extolled the beneficence of the Congregationalists and expressed satisfaction. Titled Frukterna [The Fruits], it was designed to ease Swedish-American fears of Yankee religious domination. "Both I and the congregation are in union with the Congregationalists," wrote a pastor in Willimantic, Connecticut. "I have had the joy of seeing blasphemers, drinkers, card players, and dance-crazy youth fall down at the foot of the cross confessing and receiving grace and forgiveness." He expressed his gratitude "for the help God gave them through the American Congregationalists. . . ."[23] David Magnus, a Swedish immigrant who had become a Congregationalist minister after graduating from Oberlin College, admitted that the denomination had unspecified weaknesses. "But at the same time," he added, "I have found so much genuine, deep Christianity, a certain inner living faith and warm sense of mission, that I am frequently ashamed. . . ."[24]

A central theme of Frukterna was the freedom guaranteed immigrant congregations which had affiliated with the Congregationalists. Montgomery printed the testimonies of several Swedish pastors that they had bartered away neither their liberty nor their ethnic heritage in becoming Congregationalists. Ironically, one of the most enthusiastic accounts came from E. J. Hjerpe, secretary of the Mission Covenant and minister of a Swedish Congregationalist church in New Britain, Connecticut. "I cannot say what the situation was before the church affiliated with the Congregationalists," he wrote, "but I can inform you that in no respect are there obligations on us. . . ."[25] One of Hjerpe's colleagues in Wisconsin stated that while "some Congregationalists expressed the wish that we would unite with them," there had been no pressure to do so, because "we received help from them for three years without having to join them."[26]

Professor Fridolf Risberg, Nyvall's colleague in Chicago Theological Seminary's Swedish Department, took exception to his junior partner's resistance to assimilation. Writing in Frukterna, Risberg insisted that "every European who makes this country his home must think from the beginning that he will become a good American. English must eventually become our mother tongue. In the future our sermons must be preached in English." Risberg, in short, thought Nyvall's determination to retain the distinctively Swedish character of the Mission Covenant naive. In fact, he predicted, "our churches will melt together with the American churches." To prepare for this inevitable fusion, Risberg suggested that the Swedish students at Chicago Theological Seminary "have less Swedish instruction and somewhat more English than we now have there."[27]

Waldenström agreed that the Americanization of the Mission Covenant was inevitable. The Swedish church leader, who was touring the United States while the proposed merger was being debated, observed "how one mission congregation after the other affiliated directly with the American Congregationalist denomination. Nearly all of the mission churches in the East have done that, and also some in the West." He acknowledged the pecuniary reasons for this action, but also believed that the beliefs and polity of the two denominations were virtually the same.[28] Yet Waldenström was never enthusiastic about Americanization. He accused his countrymen of being "too receptive of all kinds of spiritual movements. If someone ever comes from America or England and proclaims that God is four-cornered, he will surely find people who will thank God for this new revelation."[29] Waldenström specifically criticized the "secularization" of the Anglo-American churches, claiming that many of their "ministers preach anything but the simple gospel of Christ, the crucified and risen savior." The Scandinavian immigrant churches, he hastened to add, were generally more fervently Christian than their Yankee counterparts, and assured his Swedish readers that the American Mission Friends were adhering to the ideal of pure congregations.[30]

Waldenström also made it clear that his acceptance of the Covenant's Americanization did not reflect a lack of nationalism on his part. The preacher-politician frequently expressed annoyance that Swedish-Americans boasted about their new land's greatness and was irritated by their readiness to criticize the old country. In one humorous episode Waldenström and an immigrant carpenter inspected a device for moving a wooden shed. "One can't do that in Sweden," needled the expatriate. Certainly not, Waldenström countered. "In Sweden four guys simply take the shed on their shoulders and carry it wherever they wish."[31] In another light-hearted moment he remarked that the Covenant revivalist, E. August Skogsbergh, had become "an enthusiast for America. When he speaks about it, he attains a state of ecstasy." Knowing that Skogsbergh had initially regarded the United States as the abode of Satan, Waldenström admitted that he "couldn't help chuckling inside" whenever the evangelist praised American society.[32]

Waldenström's moderate position notwithstanding, the majority of the Mission Covenant's leading pastors remained hostile to the proposed merger. After the debate of 1889-90 had subsided, the Swede wrote to Montgomery and gave the disappointed Congregationalist his analysis of the Covenanters' refusal to accept merger. The immigrants, he generalized, feared that a formal union would "split the Mission Covenant asunder" because "some congregations would refuse to participate." They were also "afraid of losing some of the independence which a Swedish Mission Covenant now allows," Waldenström explained, although he personally believed this fear was ungrounded. Finally, influential Covenanters thought that because of the allegedly large amount of "worldliness" in Congregationalism the merger would mean stepping back into an ecclesiastical environment not much better than the one they had known in Sweden. Waldenström did not presume to pass judgment on Congregationalists in general, but he assured Montgomery that all whom he had met were sincere Christians who had given him a positive impression of the denomination.[33]

Although the Mission Covenant thereafter rejected Congregationalist aid, other Scandinavian free church leaders in the United States continued to cooperate with the Yankees and occasionally accused the Covenanters of biting the hand which had fed them. An apparent error by the editors of Missions-Vännen in 1891 gave their rivals at Chicago-Bladet an opportunity to criticize the Covenant on that ground. The former newspaper printed a letter allegedly written by "L. Gullander," a Swedish student at Chicago Theological Seminary. The writer asserted that the AHMS had ignorantly sent him to a community in the American East where no Swedish-speaking people resided. His account gave the impression that the Congregationalists were mismanaging their evangelism among Nordic immigrants. Enraged by what seemed to be a spurious account, Montgomery wrote to Gullander, who disavowed any knowledge of the letter bearing his name and affirmed his confidence in the AHMS. This incident, reported at length in Chicago-Bladet, called into question the integrity of the Mission Covenant's journalists and made the Congregationalists look like innocent victims of Covenant vindictiveness.[34]

Montgomery's death in 1894 provided the editors of Chicago-Bladet further opportunity to argue that some members of the Mission Covenant had "first sought the Americans' aid and help and then 'bit them in the back.'" "Montgomery himself," they noted, "had been affiliated with the Covenant for some years, but left it two or three years ago after being libelled several times in

Missions-Vännen."[35]

Owing to Reinert Jernberg's position on the faculty of Chicago Theological Seminary, the educational tie between the Congregationalists and the Danish and Norwegian free church groups continued until well into the twentieth century. Jernberg, a Norwegian immigrant, used the newspaper, Evangelisten, which he edited from 1890 until 1899, to defend Congregationalism and promote AHMS work among Nordic immigrants. Like most of his Yankee colleagues, Jernberg became a fervent American nationalist, and advocated Protestant unity as a means of checking the Roman Catholic threat to traditional, evangelical America. He warned his Danish and Norwegian readers that literacy rates were low in Catholic countries, that "ignorance and fanaticism" were the Catholic church's chief defenses, and that Pope Leo XIII had sent a vice-pope to the United States.[36]

Jernberg was thus annoyed when one of his former Norwegian students, John Hetland, criticized Scandinavian cooperation with the Congregationalists and became a Lutheran pastor. Hetland charged that Congregationalist and free church missionary work among Nordic immigrants amounted to proselytism which divided Lutheran congregations. He also challenged the orthodoxy of the syncretistic theory of the atonement which Jernberg taught, and asserted that limits should be imposed on doctrinal freedom.[37] Jernberg printed these criticisms in detail and tried to refute them point by point. The editor reminded his readers that Norwegian Lutherans in the United States had never been united, and maintained that Congregationalist missionary work among them had not divided a single congregation. He denied that Scandinavian Congregationalists were merely bilingual agents of the Yankees, but did suggest that Nordic immigrants should assimilate more rapidly. Jernberg also defended his theory of the atonement, calling it one which both Lutherans and Reformed Protestants could accept. Finally, he rejected Hetland's argument that the Scandinavian free churches were theologically too heterogeneous to survive. Jernberg countered that Congregationalism was theologically more diverse than any Scandinavian communion, yet had endured for three centuries.[38]

After 1890 Congregationalists made sporadic attempts to convince the Mission Covenant of the benefits of a merger, but immigrant pastors like Axel Mellander continued to resist their invitations as the blandishments of a liberalizing denomination. Events at Chicago Theological Seminary made the Congregationalists' task more difficult and precluded a firm alliance between the two denominations.

An emerging liberal image of the seminary provided the Swedes with added rhetorical ammunition. The professor who personified this trend and bore the brunt of their attacks was George Holley Gilbert. After graduating from Dartmouth College and Union Theological Seminary, Gilbert had pursued advanced studies for two years at the University of Leipzig, where he received a doctorate in 1885. Upon returning to the United States he was ordained a Congregationalist minister and appointed professor of New Testament at Chicago Theological Seminary, joining two other recipients of Leipzig doctorates, Samuel Curtiss and Hugh Scott. Curtiss, like Gilbert, had studied under Franz Delitzsch in Leipzig.

Gilbert appears to have been a relatively conservative theologian in the 1880's who became more liberal in the following decade. In 1886 he affirmed the divinity, humanity, and virgin birth of Christ and stated that the Bible was a book written by men whom the Holy Spirit guided and according to which "the teaching and conduct of men as moral and religious beings are to be regulated and judged." Gilbert also acknowledged that all men would be judged when Christ returns. Most Congregationalists would probably have agreed with these elements of Gilbert's theology in the 1880's as well as with his belief that Christians were constructing the Kingdom of God on earth.[39] A major shift in Gilbert's approach to the Bible, however, became evident in 1895. Like several other scholars on both sides of the Atlantic, he began to insist that the Scriptures be interpreted in the context of the times during which they emerged. Writing in The Biblical World, Gilbert defined Biblical theology as "the historical presentation of the moral and religious teachings of the Bible -- historical in contrast to dogmatic or systematic." He added that "historical implies the recognition of development, if there is development, and the differences of individual types, if there are such differences."[40] Waldenström and other conservatives had affirmed the primacy of the Bible before systematic theology, but Gilbert's approach was different. Unlike these Scandinavian conservatives who tended to regard the Scriptures as the Word of God not influenced by the worldly situation in which they emerged, Gilbert viewed the Bible as the culturally conditioned vehicle of that Word. He became, in short, an exponent of higher criticism.

Gilbert revealed his willingness to dispense with confessional orthodoxy in 1898 when he published an attack on the Apostles' Creed. Many other nineteenth-century churchmen, including most of the Scandinavians discussed in the present study, had insisted upon subjecting traditional statements of faith to the touchstone of Biblical authority. Few if any, though, had dared to temper with this venerated confession. Gilbert felt no such trepidation. In "The Apostles' Creed Revised According to the Teachings of Jesus" he argued that Christ had not taught anything about his own conception and birth, his returning to judge the quick and the dead, or the resurrection of the body. Hence, these phrases should be deleted.[41]

Conservative Congregationalists in Chicago began to oppose Gilbert when in a speech before the Chicago Congregational Ministers' Union the following year he dissented from traditional doctrines of Christ. Gilbert asserted that Christians are saved by Christ's entire ministry, not merely by his death and resurrection.[42] President Charles Blanchard of Wheaton College leaped to his feet and asked the professor how his Christology differed from that of the Unitarians. Another minister who attended the meeting wrote an anonymous article in the Congregationalist newspaper <u>Advance</u>

challenging the views which Gilbert had presented in his address and in his recent book, A Student's Life of Jesus.[43] James Adams, who edited Advance, and conservative members of the seminary's Executive Committee conducted a campaign to oust Gilbert during the 1899-1900 academic year. The professor refused to recant and, after a year's leave of absence to allow him opportunity to rethink his theology, submitted his resignation.

During the controversy a few prominent Congregationalists declared their support for Gilbert. Their defenses of him probably contributed to the increasingly liberal image of the denomination. Lyman Abbott, editor of The Outlook, argued in favor of Gilbert, and the seminary's Board of Examiners concluded that however unsatisfactory his exegesis of the New Testament had been, he was not a threat to the doctrinal soundness of his students.[44]

The Gilbert affair captured the attention of Scandinavian-American free church leaders, who reacted with hostility to this evidence of heresy among the Congregationalists. The newly founded Swedish Congregationalist Ministers' Association of the Northwest, which encompassed a group of free church pastors associated with Princell's millenarian group, complained in October, 1899 that "one or possibly two (2) professors at C.T.S. had shown that they harbor 'rationalist ways of thinking,'" but added that "we have confidence in our Swedish professors at the named place of learning, who adhere to God's Word." These ministers acknowledged that "it is highly improper to condemn an entire school on the basis of a few persons."[45] A Swedish pastor in Pelican Rapids, Minnesota, however, disagreed. In a letter to The Northwestern Congregationalist, H. A. Sahlström asked "whether it is consonant with the interests of Christ's kingdom, in so far as those interests are affected by the teaching of the seminary, to have any part of the students inoculated with doctrines respecting Christ's essential character and work that Professor Gilbert plainly and unequivocally teaches."[46]

The Gilbert affair helped finally to terminate the Congregationalists' cooperative ventures with the Mission Covenant. At the latter's annual convention in 1899, Axel Mellander raised the question of the Covenant's relationship to the Congregationalists and to the Swedish Department of Chicago Theological Seminary. At the same time he wrote several articles in such Swedish newspapers as Missions-Vännen, Minneapolis Veckoblad, and Nya Österns Veckoblad sharply criticizing the American denomination. These articles and a short book, Betänkande i Kongregationalistfrågan [Thoughts on the Congregationalist Question], echoed the themes about which Mellander had written for a decade, but now Gilbert was a visible target. "Professors Curtis [sic] and Gilbert, especially the latter, have made themselves advocates of so-called 'higher criticism,'" Mellander lamented. He asserted that the fruits of Gilbert's exegesis were a denial of Christ's virgin birth, a denigration of his atoning death, and a recognition of contradictions within the New Testament. The Covenanter then pointed out that Samuel Curtiss had taken a similar approach to the Old Testament as Gilbert to the New, and argued that the increasing amount of liberalism at the seminary would inevitably influence the immigrant students there.

"Who knows," he asked, "whether the Swedish Department will become the gate through which rationalist tendencies will infiltrate our people?" Mellander chided Risberg, whose Swedish students were taking a growing number of courses from the seminary's English-speaking professors, for not protesting against higher criticism. He also contended that the Congregationalists and the Covenanters were ultimately incompatible because the former belonged to the Reformed wing and accepted the Calvinist doctrine of predestination, whereas the Covenant was essentially Lutheran in its theology. In making this erroneous assertion about the Congregationalists Mellander committed the common European fallacy of dividing Protestant denominations into only two camps, an oversimplification which even in the sixteenth century (when Martin Luther taught predestination) was inaccurate.[47]

Several Swedish Congregationalists on the East Coast and in the Midwest disagreed with Mellander's negative assessment. A. L. Anderson of Worcester, Massachusetts suggested that "the free churches in the West should realize what we here in the East have known for a long time, namely that it is a major advantage to belong to the Congregationalists."[48] The Swedish Congregationalist Ministers' Association of the Northwest rejected Mellander's oft-repeated warnings against Congregationalist aggrandizement. In a resolution adopted late in 1899 the immigrant pastors stated that they had never been able to understand allegations that their English-speaking denominational fellows were about to swallow them.[49]

Within the Mission Covenant, though, Mellander's view of the

Congregationalists and their seminary in Chicago prevailed. Enrollment in the Swedish Department, which at one time numbered more than forty students and in 1898 still had thirty-four, plummeted to twenty-one by 1900 and dropped to eighteen two years later.[50] The Mission Covenant had ended its official relationship with Chicago Theological Seminary in 1890; after the turn of the century the seminary ceased to train Covenant pastors as North Park College assumed nearly all of that task. This final, de facto severing of relations may have been a crucial event in the theological development of the Covenant.

However distorted Mellander's perception of the Congregationalists' theology may have been, it seems clear that the liberalizing trend at Chicago Theological Seminary accelerated after 1900. Despite strong opposition, Samuel Curtiss remained professor of Old Testament and the dominant member of the faculty. Shailer Mathews, whose liberalism later stimulated controversy at the University of Chicago, came to the seminary to teach some of the courses which Gilbert had previously taught. A few years after Gilbert was compelled to resign, one of his former colleagues, W. D. Mackenzie, informed him that the seminary's theological climate had changed so markedly that had he then expressed the Christology which he espoused in 1899, there would not have been a controversy.[51]

In 1902 David Nyvall, then president of North Park College, requested the seminary to transfer the Swedish Department and its chairman, Fridolf Risberg, to his own institution. The seminary refused. In a lengthy reply, Scott and Curtiss delineated several reasons for keeping Risberg and the department at the Congregationalist school. Two of these were mundane: Chicago Theological Seminary already had a well-developed program for training immigrant clergymen and was not prepared to halt its efforts to supply Swedish Congregationalist churches with educated pastors. Secondly, Scott and Curtiss doubted that the Covenant could raise the $200,000 needed to open a theological seminary to support the department. The other reasons reveal the Congregationalists' continuing concern with the assimilation of free church immigrants. The two American professors were aware that some Covenanters opposed rapid assimilation, and feared that this process would be further impeded if the Covenant were given a larger voice in the education and placement of immigrant seminarians. "From the beginning we have received Swedish students from all the free churches, never asking whence they came," they stated. "We think your students, who have been here, will bear witness that they were never asked to go here or there, but were left perfectly free to accept churches anywhere among the Swedish brethren." They informed Nyvall that their seminary still advocated assimilation through education:

> We feel that our Swedish students should be educated in contact with American students, and should, as far as they can profit from it, receive help from all of the fourteen professors and other lecturers

> in the Seminary. The tendency, as he have observed it, in the foreign Seminaries in America, German, Norwegian, Swedish -- Lutheran and Reformed, has been to keep them as foreign as possible, and to oppose affiliation and assimilation with American life and English language.

Scott and Curtiss then suggested that one solution to what they regarded as a serious cultural problem would be a new "Union Theological Seminary" under Congregationalist auspices. Its purpose would be to educate bilingual clergyman for the Mission Covenant, the Swedish-American Congregationalist churches, and independent Swedish immigrant congregations. Under this plan North Park College would provide undergraduate training for prospective seminarians.[52] But the Covenant, which now had a growing school of its own and had heard Mellander's warnings of the Congregationalists' liberalism, rejected the proposal. Scott made a similar offer in 1907, but again it fell victim to the Covenanters' fears of Yankee domination and liberal theology.[53]

These controversies over Congregationalist control in the 1890's and at the beginning of the twentieth century reveal something of the complexity of Scandinavian free church conservatism in the United States. To many of the immigrant pastors, especially those who belonged to the Mission Covenant, a desire to retain their Swedish ways was interlocked with a reverence for Old World Lutheranism and pride in their new and growing denomination.

Cultural, theological, and sectarian factors made up the conservatism of the Mission Covenant.

To the immigrant congregations which eventually became the Evangelical Free Church of America, these factors were either not so important, or not important in the same ways. Although men like Princell and Jernberg were proud of their Scandinavian heritage, they did not see northern Europe as the fountainhead of theological wisdom or the only root of their culture. Many of them, including Franson, Jernberg, and Princell, had emigrated to the United States as children or young men and had assimilated American ways and the English language more thoroughly than their counterparts in the Mission Covenant. Moreover, their millenarian theology drew heavily from sources in Breat Britain and North America. It is not surprising, therefore, that they frequently praised Anglo-American culture and religion and found it easier to cooperate with the Congregationalists, despite the growing liberalism at that denomination's seminaries. While David Nyvall was urging his fellow Covenanters to preserve their "Swedishness" in the New World, Princell was proclaiming his patriotism in his Chicago church and Jernberg was defending the United States in Christiania.[54]

When such matters as Biblical scholarship and millenarianism became issues among these Nordic immigrants near the close of the century, their churches stood in varying relationships to American Congregationalism. The Mission Covenant had cut its ties with that denomination. The Danes and Norwegians in the Eastern and Western

Evangelical Free Church Associations, on the other hand, continued to receive aid from the AHMS (after 1893 known as the Congregational Home Missionary Society), ordained as their pastors men who had studied at Chicago Theological Seminary, and frequently adopted the label "Congregational." The Swedish millenarians associated with Princell stood somewhere between these two groups. They cooperated loosely with the Congregationalists and occasionally called graduates of Chicago Theological Seminary, but Princell also trained pastors in Minneapolis for the congregations in his Swedish Evangelical Free Church. Whatever their formal relations with Yankee religion were, however, these Nordic free church immigrants were compelled to deal with the same late nineteenth-century theological problems which their counterparts in Scandinavia were confronting. As we shall see, the new Americans reacted in ways which parallelled those of their cousins who remained in Europe.

CHAPTER XI

THE ZENITH OF MILLENARIANISM AND BIBLICAL LITERALISM

During the 1890's the Mission Covenant in the United States as well as the various Scandinavian immigrant "Free" groups became preoccupied with recent Biblical scholarship and millenarian thought. As we have noted earlier, members of these communions had relied heavily on the Bible for answers to theological questions in Europe and brought their reverence for the Scriptures to the New World. Moreover, the Swedish-Americans who affiliated with Princell and Franson, and those immigrants who felt an affinity with the Darbyite Mission Covenants in Norway and Denmark, were emphatically millenarian by 1885. But during the last decade of the nineteenth century Nordic dissenters on both sides of the Atlantic became concerned about radical directions in Biblical scholarship which were making an impact in Scandinavia. Nonemigrating churchmen like Waldenström had almost unanimously rejected higher criticism of the Scriptures. Furthermore, those Scandinavians who remained in Europe reacted in different ways to the eschatological currents which flowed from the British Isles and North America to their homelands. The Swedish Mission Covenant eventually rejected millenarianism, while Darbyite futurism became the normative eschatology of the Norwegian and Danish Covenants. Members of the latter two denominations, however, occasionally showed an openness to historicist millenarianism. In the United States both Covenanters and free churchmen overwhelmingly rejected higher criticism. But they did not speak with one voice on millenarian questions. Franson, Princell, and their Swedish associated remained enthusiastic Darbyites, as did men like Severin Didriksen in the Eastern and Western Evangelical Free Church Associations. Within the Mission Covenant, on the other hand, hostility to millenarianism was strong, although a few anticipated the imminent return of Christ. The eschatological question remained one of the chief factors which separated the Mission Covenant from those Scandinavian-American free church groups which traced their roots to the revivals of Fredrik Franson.

In 1884 the leaders of these immigrant communions began to comment editorially on the attacks which were being launched on traditional Biblicism, a few years before higher criticism became a major issue in Scandinavia. In a series of articles that year Otto Högfeldt and his colleagues who edited Missions-Vännen claimed that a review of the press in Sweden revealed innumerable "denials of the Bible, especially the five books of Moses and the doctrine of Christ's divinity." Moreover, they lamented, "if we examine the fruits of our own land's pens, we discover that they surpass those of old Sweden in diabolical protests against the truths of Scripture." The editors did not at that time develop detailed arguments in defense of these truths, but simply insisted that natural science and Christianity were compatible and quoted such scientists as Liebig, Brahe, Copernicus, and Keppler to corroborate this assertion.[1] Early in 1885, however, they put forth both internal and external evidence in an article titled

"Some Proofs of the Bible's Credibility and Authenticity." In this essay the editors asserted that the works of Josephus, Suetonius, and Tacitus corroborated the testimonies of the four evangelists by their references to "John the Baptist, Jesus, his mother Mary, his brother James, and many of his disciples, along with his execution under Pontius Pilate. . . ." In an attempt to refute the Wellhausen hypothesis of the origins of the Pentateuch, they reminded their readers that "the last four books of Moses make it clear that their authors were eyewitnesses to the events which they report." The editors also asserted that "all the remaining books of the Old Testament show that the books of Moses were written earlier." They sought to bolster their defense of this view of the Old Testament by quoting II Timothy 3:16: "For all Scripture is inspired by God and is useful for teaching the truth, rebuking error, correcting faults, and giving instruction for right living. . . ."[2]

John Martenson and John Princell, the millenarian editors of <u>Chicago-Bladet</u>, the unofficial organ of the Swedish Evangelical Free Church of America, whose eschatology was predicated on a literal interpretation of the Bible, defended the veracity of Scripture with equal vigor. Like their Darbyite counterparts in Scandinavia, they relied heavily on British and American arguments against higher criticism. They published in 1884 a translation of an address by H. L. Hastings on Biblical inspiration, for example, which the newspapers of the Norwegian and Danish Mission Covenants carried later in the decade.[3] The prophetic conference which Princell, Franson, and Martenson had held in Chicago three years previously[4] had concluded that "the Bible must be read and understood according to its simple, literal text,"[5] but this admonition appears to have been a response to allegorizing tendencies of other millenarians and not to higher criticism.

Despite their concern about challenges to the authenticity and veracity of the Bible, these new Americans wrote little about liberal Biblical scholarship for several years. Their preoccupation with the more pragmatic tasks of administering new denominations and assisting infant congregations may partly account for this. The Mission Covenant was organized in February, 1885; Princell and his millenarian friends had formed the Swedish Evangelical Free Church of America only a few months earlier. During the 1880's such practical matters as ministerial education and fund raising were among their chief concerns. Princell and the others who wrote for Chicago-Bladet, moreover, spent a great deal of time organizing millenarian conferences and haranguing against the Mission Covenant. At that time these Swedish-Americans were more concerned with controversies within their immigrant community than with German or Yankee scholarship. Finally, in both Scandinavia and the United States the controversies over higher criticism were mainly within theological faculties for several years. Such European scholars as Frants Buhl of the University of Copenhagen and Fredrik Petersen of the University of Oslo were accused of undermining the Biblical faith of their students, as was Charles Briggs of Union Theological Seminary in New York City. But during the 1880's few if any Scandinavian-American seminarians of either free church or Lutheran leanings were exposed to professors who advocated higher criticism. As we have seen, most of the Nordic students who attended Chicago Theological Seminary during that decade studied almost exclusively under Fridolf Risberg and Peter Trandberg, whose views of Scripture had been formed in Sweden and Denmark before higher criticism came to those countries. Consequently, before the 1890's Scandinavian free church leaders in the United States had little reason to fear that the scholarship of Wellhausen and other critics was influencing their future ministers.

After 1890, however, higher criticism gained more notoriety in the United States and aroused the opposition of many Christians to whom it had previously seemed only a distant threat. Such events as the heresy trial of Charles Briggs, the liberal Presbyterian professor of Old Testament at Union Theological Seminary, made it seem to some Scandinavians on both sides of the Atlantic that radical Biblical scholarship was widespread among Yankee Protestants.

The editors of Chicago-Bladet opened their battle against higher criticism in 1893 by charging that this new direction threatened to "lessen the worth of the Bible's content and reduce it to a common good book written only through and by people, without the help of inspiration. . . ." But at the same time, one of the editors defended the tendency of many millenarians to focus on a relatively small number of Scriptural passages.

He asserted that "we do not reduce the Bible's content when we select one section and shove another aside. It is not unusual for one to prefer to read and explicate the letters of Paul, for example, but seldom take a text from James."[6]

Like their counterparts in Denmark and Norway, the immigrant Darbyites relied heavily on British and American defenses of the Bible. They published in July, 1895 a long account of T. De Witt Talmage's fight against higher criticism, and a week later tried to discredit Darwinian evolution by quoting the views of an unidentified minister from Kentucky.[7] At the close of the century Chicago-Bladet carried another of H. L. Hastings' lectures which had also been published in Scandinavia. The Yankee minister stated that in a recent year the British and Foreign Bible Society had printed 900,000 copies of the New Testament, while the works of such free thinkers as Robert Ingersoll had not sold well. "If the Bible had not been God's book," the editors concluded, "people would have destroyed it years ago. Emperors and popes, kings and priests, princes and lords have all tried to put it down. They are dead, but the Bible still lives."[8]

The Swedes at Chicago-Bladet also reproduced an argument which had been used previously to defend the tradition that Moses was the author of Genesis. They stated that "no uninspired mortal can describe the Creation, because not any people witnessed it. . . ." These literalists scorned attempts to steer a via media between conservative Biblicism and modern science. "A person can perhaps save face among educated infidels and scientific doubters by declaring himself a 'theistic evolutionist,'" they admitted, "but this can occur only at the expense of faith. While it may be hard to believe that God created man from the earth, it is a thousand times more difficult to believe that God created a clump of jelly and that this, over an incalculable period of time, produced men and women with all their wonderful qualities and talents. . . ."[9]

Despite these concerns, it seems likely that many of the millenarians in Princell's Evangelical Free Church shared P. S. Henson's temperate assessment of the threat which higher criticism posed. Writing in Chicago-Bladet in 1901, this pastor, who stressed that he had no sympathy for radical Biblical scholarship, maintained that "it is not higher criticism which is destroying the church's influence . . . but rather Christians' low position in spiritual respects." Henson asserted that "the fog of higher criticism is not dispersed by shooting at it with big cannons. That only adds gunsmoke to the fog." Christians could more effectively counter the negative effects of higher criticism, he suggested, by carrying their faith out of the pews and not forgetting their pastor's sermons ten minutes after he had finished preaching them.[10]

The Mission Covenant in America strove to preserve its traditional view of the Bible. While Princell and other Nordic Darbyites on both sides of the Atlantic marshalled British and American verbal defenses against higher criticism, the Swedish Covenanters in the United States relied on Waldenström's quite different use of Biblical scholarship to ward off the advances of higher criticism. Before the turn of the century the American Covenant did not have a theologian of his stature and, perhaps owing to its general distrust of Yankee religion, was less willing than the Chicago-Bladet party to print articles by non-Scandinavian churchmen. Consequently, Missions-Vännen published Waldenström's slashing attacks on both higher criticism and on the traditional creedalism which distorted the Swedish Bible Commission's new translation of the Scriptures.

The American Covenant's leaders revealed how closely they adhered to Waldenström's Biblicism in 1889 when the Swede made his first visit to the United States and recorded his distress with the number of female preachers in this country. "If only we had the Word of God as clearly in all other matters as in this," Waldenström wrote in Missions-Vännen; "Paul obviously knew what he was talking about when he said women should not speak in church."[11] Shortly thereafter the editors of Missions-Vännen carried without comment Waldenström's article, "Om qvinnans predikande" [Regarding Preaching by Women], in which he stated his Pauline argument in briefer form.[12] The Swedish Covenant leader, true to his Lutheran heritage, revered the epistles of Paul and frequently used them as touchstones in theological questions. His Swedish followers in the United States, who also believed they were spiritual heirs of Luther, agreed with Waldenström in this matter and for several decades opposed the ordination of women.

Beginning in the 1890's the American Covenant followed closely Waldenström's use of textual criticism as well as his response to higher critics in Europe. This dimension of Biblical scholarship sought to determine the precise nature of the original Hebrew and Greek texts and to improve translations of them into modern languages. Textual critics, unlike some higher critics, neither questioned the divine origins of the Scriptures nor attributed them to the ancient cultures in which they were written. Late in the decade Waldenström used the findings of such nineteenth-century textual critics as Konstantin von Tischendorf to attack sharply the new Swedish translation of the Bible. He claimed that the Bible Commission had allowed the traditional Swedish text to stand in places where it contradicted the oldest extant Greek texts of the New Testament. In doing so, it had allowed liturgical tradition to prevail over scholarship.[13]

The editors of Missions-Vännen soon carried Waldenström's protests *verbatim* in several issues, as did the Swedish Mission Covenant's newspaper.[14] Both non-emigrating and American Covenanters were thereby exposed to the Biblical controversy then raging in Sweden. The great interest which Chicago Swedes expressed in their homeland's new Bibles reveals something of their continuing attachment to the spiritual life of Sweden. The American Covenant did not begin to use the English language in its worship services until legally required to do so during World War I. Fridolf Risberg's prediction that its pastors would eventually make the transition to English was fulfilled, of course, but at the turn of the century Swedish was still the almost exclusive mode of communication within the Covenant. The Bibles which these immigrants used in the 1890's were usually older versions of the Swedish text, as Waldenström had not yet completed his translation of the New Testament.[15]

Swedish Covenanters in America also watched closely Waldenström's assault on the Uppsala professor Erik Stave's espousal of higher criticism. Missions-Vännen carried lengthy excerpts from Waldenström's Låt oss behålla vår gamla bibel! [Let's Keep Our Old Bible!][16] Its editors also quoted the praise which the Swedish newspaper, Svenska Morgonbladet, gave to Waldenstrom's sharp reply to Stave, calling it a book which should "find its way into every home in our country." The editors of Missions-Vännen agreed with Waldenström "that this Biblical criticism will in reality take our old Bible from us. . . . This seems especially clear in this country, where this criticism is older and more developed that at home in Sweden."[17] The image of higher criticism which they set before American Covenanters was little more than a caricature. Rather than describing its view that the Bible is a series of books which were historically conditioned by the cultures from which they emerged, editor Otto Högfeldt and his colleagues ridiculed higher criticism for its ostensible denial of Christ's divinity. In doing so, they ignored several of the recent currents which were undermining their view of Scripture, such as the contention of Otto Pfleiderer,

Adolf Harnack, and other scholars that Hellenistic culture had profoundly influenced New Testament theology. In all likelihood they were not aware of these radical approaches to the Bible. Although English and Scandinavian translations of Julius Wellhausen's _Geschichte Israels_ were widely available before the close of the century, the works of many other late nineteenth-century German scholars were not translated into Swedish until well into the twentieth century, if ever. Few Swedish Covenanters, therefore, had an extensive, first-hand knowledge of radical Biblical scholarship. Most of them gained their impression of higher criticism by reading the warnings which Waldenström issued against it during the early years of the twentieth century.

Reinert Jernberg, the Norwegian Congregationalist who taught at Chicago Theological Seminary and edited _Evangelisten_, tried to accommodate recent Biblical scholarship. He began to comment editorially on the subject in 1893, the year the Presbyterian General Assembly suspended from its ministerium Charles Briggs, Professor of Old Testament at Union Theological Seminary. Jernberg had been educated at Yale and Chicago Theological Seminary in the 1880's. Unlike most of his fellow Scandinavian students at the latter institution, he studied under Samuel Curtiss who, like Briggs, had earned a doctorate in Old Testament at the University of Leipzig. His training and acquaintance with Curtiss made Jernberg a unique Nordic free church leader. When other immigrant churchmen were severely criticizing Briggs, Jernberg boldly asserted that Christianity needed scholars like him, "men who do not lose their heads whenever they confront an unusual idea, men whose faith in the power of God and Christ is grounded in personal rather than dry, pedantic, literalistic faith." Jernberg was convinced that Briggs' view of Scripture was sound: He "has declared his belief that the Bible, the entire Bible, is inspired of God." To the Norwegian, Briggs' "only crime" was that "he disagrees with the majority in the Presbyterian church regarding the way inspiration was given." Jernberg then defined for his Danish and Norwegian readers what he believed was the essence of higher criticism of the Old Testament. "For him [Briggs] and his like-minded colleagues, God's inspiring work can best be seen in the historical development of the Jewish people. They believe the Old Testament's ideas sprang from the soil of the Jewish nation, but they also stress that this soil was cultivated by the spirit of God." Jernberg insisted that Briggs' interpretation of the Old Testament posed no threat to Christianity. "On the contrary!" he declared. "Only after one understands it, and then studies the Bible does God's way of doing things become clear, and one is impressed by how closely God's work in the book corresponds to God's work in nature."[18]

Two years later Jernberg published an article by T. C. Reade titled "Min uforandrede Bibel" [My Unchanged Bible]. The author neither condemned nor condoned higher criticism. He acknowledged that science had appeared to threaten Christianity in recent years, but denied that it had shaken his faith in the Scriptures. "I have never been very concerned about the human authorship of the various books of the Bible," Reade affirmed, "because I believe God is the actual author of them." Current debates over the precise nature of the literary vehicle of God's message were irrelevant to the larger issue of its divine origin. "I have never spent much time trying to discern when and where these books were written by people," he declared, "no more than I would trouble myself trying to discover the age and name of the telegrapher who delivers a message from my best friend."[19]

Certainly Jernberg's approach to the Bible had more in common with the hermeneutics of some late nineteenth-century Congregationalist scholars than with those of Scandinavian millenarians. Unlike some of the other clergymen in the Eastern and Western Evangelical Free Church Associations, he apparently believed that the ethics of the Sermon on the Mount formed the heart of the Gospel. Scandinavian millenarians did not ignore the moral imperatives of Jesus, of course, but the written works of such Darbyites as Franson and Princell reveal relatively little concern with personal ethics and even less with social ethics. But to the amillennial Jernberg, ethics and not systematic theology of any sort seemed central.

In a long article which he wrote in 1900, Jernberg unveiled his willingness to accommodate certain nineteenth-century Protestant revisions of the faith. He assured his readers that what he termed "the new theology" and identified with the school commonly known as "Progressive Orthodoxy" was "much less dangerous than we believe." The motto of this school, Jernberg stated, was

"Back to Christ." He believed this was also the core of recent Scandinavian revivalism. "The same thought found expression twenty years ago among our Swedish friends in the words: "Where is it written?'" Jernberg not only repeated Waldenström's famous question, but shared the Swede's aversion to creeds, as well. He praised Newell Hillis, the former Presbyterian who succeeded Lyman Abbott in the pulpit of Plymouth Congregational Church in Brooklyn, as a man who was "compelled by his conscience to say goodbye to his spiritual mother when he could no longer agree with some of the [Westminster] Confession's phrases." Jernberg similarly lauded the Social Gospeler Charles Parkhurst, who had referred to certain parts of that creed, including those dealing with predestination, as inhumane and blasphemous.[20] In the second half of this article, published a week later, Jernberg added Jesus to his list of religious leaders who opposed creedal statements and stressed the primacy of ethics in Christianity. "One need not have a great knowledge of Jesus' teachings to see that they are not based on philosophy, but rather on morals. To him the important thing was not what his disciples thought, but rather what they are." But "if we turn to confessions of faith," Jernberg claimed, "we find ourselves in a completely different world. Here nothing is asked about the character of people. . . . They do not demand character; in fact, they do not even mention it." The "new theology," however, wants "to supplant Moses and the intellectuals with Jesus. It wants the church and the world to listen to his word, not to human decrees."[21]

Jernberg's accommodation of higher criticism and Progressive Orthodoxy, like his indifferent attitude toward millenarianism, was an anomaly among the forebears of the Evangelical Free Church of America, and neither his moderate liberalism nor his opposition to creedal statements became normative among these Nordic immigrants. Despite his important role in the formation of the Eastern and Western Evangelical Free Church Associations, Jernberg's influence waned quickly after he resigned as editor of Evangelisten. C. T. Dyrness, a thoroughly millenarian Norwegian who had studied at Chicago Theological Seminary and was pastor of First Congregational Church of Chicago, became editor of that newspaper in 1904. It thereupon became preoccupied with eschatology. In 1909 the Western Evangelical Free Church Association opened its own seminary at Rushford, Minnesota. Seven years later this school was moved to Minneapolis, where it trained most of the denomination's ministers until the seminary which later developed into Trinity Evangelical Divinity School was founded in Chicago. The Dano-Norwegian Institute of Chicago Theological Seminary ceased in 1915; Jernberg and the other faculty members who educated men for bilingual ministries united to form Union Theological College, but this institution closed its doors in the 1930's. Jernberg moved to Los Angeles in 1923 and became a librarian at the Divinity School of the University of Southern California.[22]

Jernberg's attempt to combine the free church ideal of Scandinavian revivalism with the moderate liberalism which characterized much of American Congregationalism failed. His impact on the theology of the scattered Norwegian and Danish free church congregations which he gathered together in the 1890's was short-lived. After the turn of the century these immigrants became just as vociferous in their attacks on higher criticism as both the Mission Covenant of America and Princell's millenarian party had always been. Shortly after Jernberg resigned as editor of Evangelisten, that newspaper carried a lengthy article praising the Scriptural emphasis of Moody Bible Institute. "The Bible is practically the only school book [there]," wrote Otto Grauer. He lauded the Institute's curriculum as one which focused on "a precise examination of the Bible's words . . . and a consideration of the Bible's principal teachings."[23]

Millenarianism, however, continued to separate the Swedish immigrants in the Mission Covenant from the various free church Scandinavian-Americans. As we have seen, the wave of revivalistic Darbyism which swept across the Nordic countries and also stimulated immigrants like Princell and Franson was the chief root of the Norwegian and Danish Mission Covenants as well as Princell's Swedish Evangelical Free Church. Waldenström, however, stiffly resisted this new eschatological current and, although a handful of his fellows in the Swedish Mission Covenant, most notably its president, E. J. Ekman, became millenarians, the denomination as a whole did not. In the New World, I wish now to demonstrate, the ethnic counterparts of the three Scandinavian Mission Covenants generally adhered to the same positions on this issue which the parent bodies in northern Europe had taken. No one of these immigrant communions spoke with one voice, however. Jernberg dissented from the futurist millenarianism which was strong among the Norwegian and Danish immigrants whose ministers he educated. And the American Covenant, although generally heeding Waldenström's advice to shun millenarianism, counted a few apocalypticists in its ranks. Princell's group remained solidly Darbyite, and through its occasional prophetic conferences played a key role in keeping before Nordic immigrants the belief in an imminent Second Coming. The newspaper of this party, Chicago-Bladet, became a verbal weapon which its editors used to criticize the indifference or hostility of Waldenström and most of his followers to their millenarianism.

Although the Covenant newcomers who edited Missions-Vännen published articles by both millenarians and nonmillenarians, their continued reliance on Waldenström's judgment and their eagerness to reprint articles from his newspaper in Sweden made the organ of the American Covenant generally unfriendly to current eschatological topics. In 1886 and 1887 Missions-Vännen reported at great length the speeches given at the Second International Prophetic Conference in Chicago. But only a few months earlier it had carried Waldenström's warnings that many millenarians had misinterpreted the beast of Revelation 17. "For the most part, people have understood the monster to signify the fallen church . . . the Catholic church, or this church and the Protestant state churches," the Swedish Covenanter wrote.

Instead of this "partisan standpoint" of historicist millenarians, Waldenström advanced the view that "the beast does not represent only the Catholic church, but rather the worldly church in general."[24]

Writing editorially in the same newspaper, Otto Högfeldt complained that the preoccupation of some Christians with millenarianism had distorted their perception of the Bible. "In our times one often hears about people who insist . . . that they can predict coming things," he lamented. Högfeldt admitted that the eschatological sections of Scripture were important, but regretted that "various persons misinterpret and use the prophetic parts of God's Word in the wrong way." This may have been an oblique reference to Princell and Franson, who were still at odds with the Mission Covenant and employed millenarian rhetoric to chastise the new denomination. Högfeldt reminded his Covenant readers that "all of God's Word is given to us for our edification and use, and it is certainly not the Lord's intention that we should read one part of His Word and ignore another."[25]

The following year the editors of Missions-Vännen published an attack on Darbyism. C. B. Johnson, a Covenant pastor in Iowa, denounced the idea that Christ might come at "any moment." Johnson believed this central tenet of Darbyism made the date of the Second Coming arbitrary, a charge which futurist millenarians hotly denied. "It is one thing to expect the return of Jesus, because nobody knows the time," Johnson asserted, "but it is another matter to say that he can come at any time. The first view is Biblical; the second is unbiblical."[26]

A controversy between Waldenström and Otto Witt over millenarianism had repercussions in the United States, where the Covenant's journalists naturally sided with their mentor while the Chicago-Bladet defended his adversary. Witt, a Swedish missionary, became a futurist millenarian while overseas and propagated his eschatological views upon returning to his homeland. In his efforts to prove that Christ's return was imminent, he reproduced many of the arguments then current among Scandinavian millenarians, including those involving calculations of pyramids and the rise of Zionism. To Waldenström, Witt's attempts to predict the date of the Second Advent ignored Christ's statement in Mark 13 that only God knew when that event would occur. Responding to one of the missionary's appearances in Stockholm, Waldenström contended that "Witt's lecture is just another indication which direction the trend . . . must lead when the faithful are not satisfied with the Lord's answer to his twelve: 'It is not for you to know the times or hours which the Father has determined in his own power.'"[27]

John Martenson and his fellow Darbyites at Chicago-Bladet challenged Waldenström's contention immediately, terming his criticism of Witt's eschatology "superficial." The response of Swedish Covenanters to the current millenarian fervor was inconsistent, they wrote. Waldenström had denounced as "perverse Biblical research" a millenarian treatise on pyramids which had recently been translated into Swedish. They added that the editors of Missions-Vännen, who generally opposed millenarianism, had published the Swedish version of this book.[28] Chicago-Bladet later carried lengthy excerpts from E. J. Ekman's millenarian treatise, De yttersta tingen [The Final Things].[29]

The publication of Waldenström's Swedish translation of Paul's letters to the Philippians, Colossians, and Thessalonians provided another opportunity for Chicago-Bladet's editors to find fault with his eschatology. The second epistle to the Thessalonians had long been an important source of millenarian thought. Waldenström's translation of it failed to satisfy the Darbyites in the Evangelical Free Church, who charged that he had made Paul appear to oppose the Thessalonians' hope of Christ's imminent return. According to Princell's reading of the Greek text, the apostle had admonished the church not to be confused by claims that the day of the Lord was approaching, whereas Waldenström's translation declared "that their minds were confused because some asserted that the time for the Lord's return was immediately at hand." "And as a result of this explaining away of 'the day of the Lord,' it follows that Paul's hope [expressed in I Thessalonians] was a misunderstanding which he had to correct."[30]

The same Swedish Evangelical Free Church editors rejected Waldenström's denial that Revelation was divinely inspired, because it was not written by an apostle. In the final fascicle of his translation of the New Testament the Swedish Covenant leader described Revelation as a product of its times -- i.e., the second century A.D. Waldenström's denigration of the book struck at the heart of the faith of these millenarians. They responded by accusing Waldenström of echoing Dionysius, the third-century Christian who doubted that Jesus' disciple was the author of Revelation. If the writer were not the disciple, they asked, why did he refer to himself as a slave of Christ?[31]

Undaunted by Waldenström's low regard of their millenarianism, the Swedish Evangelical Free Church's leaders remained exponents of Darbyite futurism. At a prophetic conference held at Rockford, Illinois in 1891, Princell and his wife Josephine admitted that interest in millenarianism had recently waned among Scandinavian immigrants. They insisted, of course, that the decline of fervor did not lessen its importance to Christians.[32] But several events of the decade which Fredrik Franson wove into his eschatological framework also stimulated a renewed millenarian interest among his and Princell's followers in the United States. They perceived such phenomena as the Russian pogroms against the Jews and the emergence of Zionism as signs of Christ's imminent return. Prophetic conferences held by Scandinavians in Europe and the United States helped keep millenarian fervor high,[33] as did Franson's book, Himlauret, which Princell's colleagues published in Chicago in 1898. Treatises on historicist millenarianism, especially those by H. Grattan Guinness, which kept interest in the Second Advent strong in Scandinavia,[34] also made an impact on Nordic Americans before the end of the century. Like their ally Franson, the immigrant leaders of the Evangelical Free Church criticized the historicist approach, but nevertheless tried to combine some of the prophetic signs which the historicists perceived with their own Darbyite belief in the any-moment coming.[35] Probably owing to Franson's influence and the rapidity with which Darbyite and historicist millenarian books were arriving in the Nordic countries, the leaders of the Norwegian and Danish Mission Covenants also attempted to accommodate both of these incongruous eschatologies.[36] At the beginning of the twentieth century, however, the Swedish Evangelical Free Church and its newspaper remained essentially Darbyite. When the Swedish-American Covenanter Axel Mellander denied that "Christ's return [i.e., the secret rapture] and revelation are not two chronologically separated events," a sharp reply appeared in Chicago-Bladet. Its writer agreed with Mellander's assertion that nobody knows the precise moment of the Second Advent, but defended the Darbyite understanding of the apocalyptic sequence of rapture, great tribulation, the appearance of Antichrist, and God's final judgment of the world.[37]

The Eastern and Western Evangelical Free Church Associations, which encompassed many of the scattered Norwegian and Danish immigrant congregations which traced their roots to Franson's trans-Atlantic revivals of the 1880's, presented a less fervently millenarian image during the last decade of the century. As we have noted in an earlier chapter, Franson acquainted them with Darbyite futurism in the early 1880's when he made the first of his evangelistic crusades in Scandinavia.[38] They stayed in close touch with the Danish and Norwegian Mission Covenants in the 1880's and 1890's and clearly shared the trans-Atlantic millenarian community which the Swedish-American revivalist was helping to create. Their ministers frequently participated in the prophetic conferences which Princell held, making those gatherings pan-Scandinavian, although their leadership was predominantly Swedish. There is no reason, therefore, to believe that these Norwegians and Danes lost interest in the Second Coming of Christ during the 1890's.

The leading role which the Congregationalist Reinert Jernberg played in the Eastern and Western Evangelical Free Church Associations allows the impression that these twin bodies were only lukewarm toward millenarianism. Their newspaper, Evangelisten, which Jernberg edited and which is one of the few extant sources of their history, carried a few Darbyite articles before the turn of the century, but Jernberg declined to commit the journal to any one eschatological position. Indeed, he did not print a millenarian sermon until July, 1890, six months after Evangelisten appeared. The anonymous author explained that Paul's words in I Thessalonians 5:2 ("For you yourselves know very well that the Day of the Lord will come like a thief comes at night") referred to the any-moment coming. In Darbyite fashion he told his congregation that "to all readers of the Bible, it is clear that the return of Jesus Christ will take place suddenly, without any signs other than the prophetic and apostolic warnings." His ecclesiology was also taken from the tradition of Darby. He described the remnant to be saved as a spiritual, invisible body comprising "some few souls spread around, unheeded or despised by the masses. . . ."[39]

Such material, however, did not appear frequently in Evangelisten. The Nordic immigrants who read Jernberg's newspaper seldom found articles to match the millenarian zeal of the publications of the Danish and Norwegian Mission Covenants. One powerful exception was a hymn composed by Jernberg's colleague, John Hanson, who warned that

> In power and majesty the Son of God comes,
> The world flees from its place at full speed;
> Oh, sinner, tremble and quake!
> See, from the vault of the clouds
> The Lord of Heaven himself brings you your due.[40]

Jernberg published a description of various types of millenarianism in 1891. Taken verbatim from The Independent, the article asserted that Christ would return "to judge the human race and receive all his people and bless them for eternity." Following Paul's letter to the Thessalonians, its writer stated that "both classes [of saved Christians] -- the risen dead and the transformed living -- will be elevated together to the clouds to meet the Lord." Beyond these assertions, which most millenarians and indeed some nonmillenarians could accept, the author said little which reflected the eschatological currents of his times. Nothing in the article suggests an awareness of or commitment to Darbyite millenarianism. Its appearance in Evangelisten should probably be attributed to Scandinavian-Americans' strong interest in the topic at that time, not to a change in the editor's personal stance on eschatological questions.[41]

Despite Jernberg's lack of interest in eschatology, the Eastern and Western Evangelical Free Church Associations which he helped to organize were avowedly millenarian bodies. Severin K. Didriksen, the Norwegian immigrant who had earlier cooperated with Franson in Christiania, preached the sermon at the former association's annual convention in 1893. He made it clear that he expected the Second Advent to occur soon. Like most other millenarians, Didriksen acknowledged Christ's admonition that the day and hour of his return were known only to God. But, characteristic of his denomination's millenarian zeal, he quoted Jesus, John the Baptist, and other New Testament figures to corroborate his belief that "the Kingdom of God is near."[42]

The Midwestern cousins of these Norwegians and Danes revealed more explicitly their conviction that the Second Coming was imminent. Meeting at Wesley, Iowa in 1894, the Western Evangelical Free Church Association discussed vigorously the question: "How shall we understand the doctrine of Christ's Second Coming and the thousand-year reign?" Hans Josephsen, a Norwegian who had cooperated in gathering the Norwegian Lutheran Free Church of Milwaukee in 1887 and graduated from Chicago Theological Seminary a few months before the 1894 convention, moderated the discussion. He stressed three points which, he believed, were matters of consensus among Scandinavian free church immigrants and therefore should be discussed by the Association. First, among apostolic Christians "the hope of the Lord's rapid return ignited their love and enthusiasm for the Lord and the advancement of his Kingdom." Secondly, he noted, "the Lord's return has become a very popular matter in our time and because of this ought to be considered." Finally, Josephsen regretted that "the doctrine of Christ's return and the thousand-year reign has been falsely presented and thus perverted, so that to many, such a teaching suggests a picture of terror, while to others it seems to be nothing more than fanaticism."

The other ministers who participated in the discussion apparently shared these observations and added some of their own. One theme which ran consistently through their comments was joy over the anticipated return of Christ. These ministers were apocalypticists, but their millenarianism precipitated neither fatalism nor despair. Charles J. Jensen (1873-1940), an immigrant carpenter who was also a minister in northern Wisconsin, addressed himself to a common misperception about their eschatology. "Many believe that when Christ comes, the whole world will collapse," he observed. To Jensen this was an unchristian fear, because with the Second Advent "a glorious time will begin for God's people, while the ungodly will meet their judgment." Charles Nelson, a young Evangelical Free Church clergyman who later served Lutheran Free congregations in Wisconsin and Illinois, agreed wholeheartedly, remarking that "talk of the Lord's return is the finest music to my ears." Nelson concurred with Josephsen that the Bible should be the only source of millenarian doctrines, as did Niels Julius Bing, an equally young immigrant. This Dane, who served briefly as minister of the Scandinavian Congregational Church of Britt, Iowa before joining the ministerium of the United Danish Lutheran Church, combined millenarianism and Lutheran eucharistic theology. For a reason which he did not explain, belief in "the blessing and greatness that the Lord himself will come" reminded Bing "of the Lord's presence in communion."

Some of the ministers who attended this conference agreed with Josephsen that recent interest in millenarianism meant the recovery of a long ignored Christian teaching. K. Knudsen observed, perhaps a bit anachronistically, that "it is seldom that such a topic is taken up for discussion." Bing echoed this belief, blaming the rigidity of the Old World churches for neglecting the doctrine of the Second Coming. "I am glad the brethren here expect the Lord soon," he told his colleagues, "and that the old dogmas of the state church no longer blind the people."[43]

After Reinert Jernberg relinquished the editorship of Evangelisten, that newspaper became a herald of the futurist millenarianism which was widespread among the Norwegian and Danish immigrants whom it served. A flurry of Darbyite articles filled its pages at the turn of the century. On January 3, 1900 the new editor admonished his readers to consider the signs of Christ's imminent return. "The Bible is full of prophecies regarding our Lord's Second Coming," he wrote, "and we can rest assured that these prophecies will find literal fulfillment, just like those which proclaimed his first coming." Among these he numbered such phenomena as the progress which such faiths as Christian Science, the Church of Jesus Christ of Latter-day Saints, and spiritism were making, the general restlessness of humanity, and Zionism. These were the same portents which many other millenarians of that decade perceived, including Fredrik Franson, whose Himlauret the editor had apparently read. To this list the new editor added "false teachers, who deny Christ and deny that the Bible is God's inspired Word." Unwittingly reproducing the gist of an argument which Martin Luther had made in an Advent sermon nearly four centuries previously, the editor hailed modern technology as another sign. "Our ocean liners and railroad trains dart back and forth day and night," he remarked. "These are also days of great knowledge, many books, newspapers, discoveries, and inventions." These signs, the editor concluded, indicate that "the age of the heathen is approaching its end, and that the Lord's return is near."[44] A writer pursued this theme in a subsequent issue, describing the events of the Second Coming in purely Darbyite terms. Christ would actually return twice, he emphasized. "The first time he will come for his saints, and later with his saints." Following Darby, the writer stated that the first of these comings would be the secret rapture, when the true, spiritual church would ascend to meet Jesus in the clouds. This rapture, moreover, would precede the great tribulation.[45]

Thus, Darbyite futurism, which had furnished much of the impetus for the revivalism which led to the Mission Covenants in Norway and Denmark, had clearly become the prevailing eschatology in the Eastern and Western Evangelical Free Church Associations by 1900. But, as among other Scandinavians in both the Old World and the New, historicist millenarianism continued to influence their thinking, as well. Although the editors of Evangelisten continued to be preoccupied with the works of such Darbyites as Franson, the newspaper occasionally carried excerpts from the popular books of H. Grattan Guinness. In 1901, for example, readers were treated to the Anglican's historicist explication of certain Pauline epistles and other books of Scripture.[46] Such articles were exceptions, however, and suggest that some of these Nordic immigrants ignored the ultimate incompatibility of divergent millenarianisms whose details they perhaps had not thoroughly analyzed.

The eschatology and Biblicism of the Scandinavian newcomers who created the religious bodies eventually known as the Evangelical Covenant Church and the Evangelical Free Church of America were largely formed by the early years of the twentieth century. The American Mission Covenant and the various "Free" associations underwent many changes during the subsequent years, of course, and the present denominations have not allowed their general conservatism to spell stagnation. But it is clear that by about 1905 such nineteenth-century forces as Scandinavian pietism, Lutheran and Anglo-American revivalism, and millenarianism had combined with traditional Biblicism to make enduring imprints on them. The Mission Covenant of America had weathered the storm of coerced assimilation by retaining much of its Swedish Lutheran legacy and following closely the leadership of Paul Waldenström. Princell's Swedish Evangelical Free Church and the Eastern and Western Evangelical Free Church Associations, on the other hand, were millenarian bodies, even during the 1890's when Reinert Jernberg gave the latter two a different journalistic image. The eschatological cosmology of these Scandinavian newcomers inspired the Danish and Norwegian Mission Covenants, with whom Darbyite Danes and Norwegians in the United States remained in close touch. While the nonmillenarian Covenanters in Sweden influenced heavily their counterparts in America, millenarian Scandinavian immigrants transmitted Anglo-American religious currents to Nordic Christians who stayed in their native lands. Despite their eschatological differences, however, both the Mission Covenant and Evangelical Free Churches displayed by the beginning of the twentieth century the markings which now brand them as "conservative."

CHAPTER XII

CONCLUSION

This analysis of the development of conservative factors in the Evangelical Free and Swedish Mission Covenant traditions need not proceed beyond the early years of the twentieth century. There were, to be sure, significant theological developments after that time. In the 1920's, for example, some Swedish-Americans of the latter tradition adopted millenarianism, which the previous generation of Covenanters had generally scorned. Later, neo-orthodoxy also made minor inroads into the Evangelical Covenant Church. But neither became a main current among Covenanters in the United States, although considerable theological diversity has arisen among their spiritual cousins in Sweden. Among the various Scandinavians who constitute the Evangelical Free Church of America, there appears to have been even less theological change after 1900 than among the Covenanters. In both traditions World War I marked the beginning of the major shift from the Scandinavian languages to English, a process which did not approach completion until a quarter of a century later. For the Nordic-Americans in the Evangelical Free tradition, this aspect of Americanization facilitated even more theological borrowing from conservative Anglo-American Protestantism and thereby further cemented their own evangelical faith. The Biblicism of these Scandinavians, for instance, which in earlier times was essentially a traditional acceptance of the vernacular texts, began to rest on the Princeton theology of the verbal inerrancy of the original autographs. For the most part, events of the twentieth century have confirmed the conservatism which gave rise to these two traditions in the 1870's and 1880's. They inherited traditional Protestant teachings, but some of the chief roots of their current conservatism -- revivalism, Biblical literalism, and, for some of them, millenarianism -- lay in the prolific religious soil of the nineteenth century.

The immigrant adherents of these two Scandinavian free church traditions and their spiritual progeny have never constituted more than a small segment of the mosaic of conservative Protestantism in the United States, but their story nevertheless challenges several widely held notions about that wing of American Christianity. It should be apparent that none of the older theories of the origins of "fundamentalism" fits the Nordic denominations under consideration. Moreover, the recent study by Ernest Sandeen, who emphasized millenarianism as the chief root of "fundamentalism" or "evangelicalism," fails to explain the genesis of the Swedish Covenant and is only partially applicable to the Evangelical Free Church.

Perhaps the misperception whose absurdity these Scandinavian denominations most obviously unveil is the myth of Bible Belt fundamentalism. If, as such scholars as Richard Hofstadter and H. Richard Niebuhr maintained, fundamentalism was a product of the rural South, why did so many Scandinavians in the Midwest, the Pacific Northwest, and other regions of the United States, and indeed in Europe, display the kind of Biblical, millenarian faith whose origins supposedly lay below the Mason-Dixon line? Few Nordic immigrants settled in the South, and the Biblicism, eschatology, and other attributes of their conservatism were evident decades before such phenomena as the "Scopes monkey trial" of 1925 molded that region's image as a stronghold of "fundamentalism."

A closely related and equally fallacious notion which the present study contradicts is the alleged anti-intellectualism of conservative Protestantism. It is true, of course, that neither of these free church traditions was borne by intellectuals as was, for example, Unitarianism. But the Scandinavians of various educational backgrounds who developed the Mission Covenants and the Evangelical Free Church expressed deep interest in and advocated the same textual criticism of the Bible and shared a wide range of millennial and millenarian views which many well-educated Christians espoused. Moreover, in the United States immigrants of both traditions founded several educational institutions, such as North Park College. A corollary of this misinterpretation purports that "fundamentalism" was principally the fight of unenlightened Christians against Darwinian theories of natural selection and the origins of mankind. As we have seen, Scandinavians in both the Swedish Covenant and Evangelical Free traditions defended the Genesis account of Creation and opposed evolutionary theories which contradicted it. The *raison d'etre* of these new denominations was not, however, the fight against new intellectual currents. Although none of the communions in these traditions was formally constituted until 1878, nearly a quarter of a century after Darwin's Origin of Species was published, they were not born as reactions to that or any other book. Their leaders' arguments against evolution were not original, but rather derived from British and American sources. Furthermore, at no time did the controversy over Darwinism occupy a central place in the thought or activities of these Nordic Christians. A review of the Scandinavian free church press on both sides of the Atlantic indicates that they were concerned about critics of Christianity, such as Robert Ingersoll and Bjørnstjerne Bjørnson, but their responses to these men came after the denominations under consideration were already organized or about to be organized. Hence, radical intellectual currents cannot be regarded as factors in their births.

Higher criticism has often been thought of as another challenge to traditional Protestantism which elicited a defensive conservative response, and verbal inspiration of the Scriptures was one of the five fundamentals which Stewart Cole believed to constitute the creed of all "fundamentalists." The various Nordic Christians discussed in this thesis opposed radical Biblical scholarship but, again, their opposition to it came several years after the various Covenants and the Evangelical Free Church were founded. Moreover, as was the case in their hostility to Darwinism and other radical currents of that day, these Scandinavians made practically no original contribution to the rhetorical warfare. Their arguments, except those of Paul Peter

Waldenström, whose views of the Scriptures were thoroughly rooted in European Lutheran scholarship, came from Anglo-American sources. The Scandinavian free churches were committed to the primacy of the Bible in religious matters from their inception, and the devotion of their adherents to Scriptural authority played an important role in their founding. But this reliance on the Bible, although not accompanied by an articulated doctrine of literal inspiration, was well entrenched before the works of Julius Wellhausen and other higher critics were known in Scandinavia.

If the older interpretations of conservative Protestantism by such scholars as Cole, Furniss, and Niebuhr fail to explain the existence of the Mission Covenants and the Evangelical Free Church, how helpful is Sandeen's recent study of The Roots of Fundamentalism? Sandeen, it will be recalled, found the chief root of modern evangelical Protestantism in nineteenth-century British and American millenarianism, especially the futurism which John Nelson Darby brought to the United States. His thesis fits splendidly when extended to the forebears and founders of the Evangelical Free Church. As I have argued in Chapters V and VII, the Mission Covenants of Denmark and Norway stemmed in large part from the millenarian revivals which Fredrik Franson, a Darbyite who had worked with Dwight Moody in Chicago, held in Scandinavia during the 1880's. These two denominations and the like-minded Danish and Norwegian-Americans who formed the Eastern and Western Evangelical Free Church Associations during the following decade were thoroughly millenarian. They were, in fact, an extension of the Anglo-American millenarian community which Sandeen analyzed. Furthermore, the Swedish Evangelical Free Church, which Franson's associate John Princell organized in 1884, was a Darbyite body, one which helped spread this form of eschatology among Nordic immigrants both before and after the beginning of the twentieth century. The present Evangelical Free Church of America, like the Danish and Norwegian Mission Covenants, continues to emphasize the imminent return of Christ.

One encounters considerable difficulty, however, when one attempts to apply the Sandeen thesis to the origins of the Swedish Mission Covenant and its American cousin, the Evangelical Covenant Church. Admittedly, few Covenanters in either country would label their denomination "fundamentalist;" but they are among the professed "evangelicals" whose roots Sandeen seeks to analyze. More important than their nomenclature, though, is their theology, which has seldom been millenarian. In Sweden, as in the other Nordic countries, the Mission Covenant traces its beginnings in part to mid-century revivalism and the ideal of pure congregations. But in contrast to the Covenants of Norway and Denmark, that of Sweden was a permanent fixture on the religious landscape of Scandinavia before the streams of Darbyism and other forms of eschatology flowed from British and American sources to northern Europe. While a few Swedish Covenanters became millenarians, most notably Andreas Fernholm and Erik Ekman, both of whom rejected Lutheranism and had close ties with Reformed Protestantism abroad, the denomination as a whole rejected these new eschatological currents. In both the United States and Sweden Covenanters criticized the Darbyites for allegedly overemphasizing the Second Coming at the expense of other dimensions of Christian faith. The chief roots of the Swedish Mission Covenant and its American counterpart did not lie in millenarianism, but rather in Lutheran pietism which had been a main current in northern European religious life since the end of the seventeenth century.

The differences between these two traditions can be partially seen in their differing relations with Dwight Moody. In 1971 Karl Olsson, historian of the Evangelical Covenant Church, wrote that he had "the impression . . . that Moody Bible Institute, Moody Church, and Wheaton College played a more determinative role in the [Evangelical] Free Church than in the Covenant, once the language barrier was removed."[1] Olsson's suspicion was undoubtedly correct, although my own study suggests that it was equally true of the period before English became the primary language of both traditions in the United States. Indeed, it is not too much to say that the Evangelical Free Church owes much of its theology and revival methods to Moody and his followers in Chicago. Both Darbyite millenarianism and Anglo-American forms of evangelization were passed from Moody and his co-workers to Swedes in Chicago, such as Franson and Princell, who in turn spread them among other Scandinavians in Europe and the United States. The Moody coterie also influenced Swedes of the Covenant tradition, just as the renowned Chicago evangelist had gained great popularity among Christians of many denominations throughout northern Europe.

But for several reasons, Moody's influence was not nearly so profound among the Swedish Covenanters as it was among the Evangelical Free. First, in both the United States and Sweden congregations which eventually became constituents of the Covenant were organized in the 1860's, several years before the revivalist from the Windy City was well known in Europe or America. These small churches shared Moody's enthusiasm (if not his methods) for effecting conversions, but they drew on a revival tradition which had been present in Sweden since the era of pietism. And, as we have noted, they generally rejected his millenarianism when it became a major issue among Scandinavian Christians on both sides of the Atlantic.

These two Nordic free church traditions reveal not only something of the heterogeneity of conservative Protestantism in the United States, but also something of the varied responses of immigrant communions to Americanization, both religious and secular. For several decades the myth of the readily assimilable Nordic immigrant was a standard feature of Scandinavian-American historiography. Historians writing from within the Nordic immigrant community developed this myth to stave off the nativist criticism which had battered other ethnic groups, especially those from southern and eastern Europe, who allegedly resisted New World ways while clinging to those of the Old. More recently, however, historians have begun to take a more critical look at Scandinavian acculturation and assimilation in the United States, and have discovered that not all Nordic newcomers willingly shed their native languages and northern European customs in favor of American English and the ways of Yankee society. I have not sought to prove that Scandinavian immigrants in general or even those of the free church traditions under consideration remained actively hostile to assimilation in the nineteenth century. Such a generalization would have no more validity than the myth of their willingness to assimilate. A comparison of the Mission Covenant and Evangelical Free Church leaders' responses to the waves of American ideas and institutions which inundated them in the New World reveals that Scandinavian immigrants did not speak with one voice on this question.

The Evangelical Free were clearly more enthusiastic about Americanization than were the Covenanters. Many of the leaders and allies of the Free, such as Princell, Franson, and Reinert Jernberg, had come to the United States as boys or young men who had not played significant parts in the religious life of Scandinavia. They were bilingual, of course, and occasionally expressed their love of, but not a close attachment to, their native lands. They were primarily Americans. Jernberg, the Norwegian Yale _alumnus_ who taught at Chicago Theological Seminary, urged his fellow Norwegian-Americans to assimilate rapidly, a conviction which was echoed for Swedish immigrants in the pages of _Chicago-Bladet_. Although Princell studied at a Swedish Lutheran seminary in the United States, he and his confederates derived much of their theology and revival methods from Yankee sources. Strictly speaking, their millenarianism did not harmonize well with their frequent praise of American institutions, but this incongruity did not prevent them from proclaiming the imminent return of Christ and the end of the world while extolling American civilization as the summit of history.

In terms of national and cultural loyalties, the leaders of the Mission Covenant were a different breed. Unlike most of their counterparts in the antecedents of the Evangelical Free Church, many of them had been active in the free churches of their homeland. E. August Skogsbergh, Carl Björk, David Nyvall, and Axel Mellander were four of the most important Covenanters who had been involved in Sweden. The Swedish Mission Covenant had an important theologian, the Lutheran Paul Waldenström, to whom American Covenanters looked for answers to doctrinal questions until well into the twentieth century. The Evangelical Free, on the other hand, took their theological guidance from millenarians like John Nelson Darby and conservative American Congregationalists like Moody and Reuben Torrey. Consequently, the Free, many of whom had been baptized in Lutheran churches, were quite un-Lutheran in such matters as sacramental theology. The American Covenanters' reliance on Waldenström's guidance, its leaders' misperceptions about the extent of liberalism among Yankee Protestants, and their loyalty to Swedish culture prevented them from developing close contacts with other denominations after the abortive cooperation at Chicago Theological Seminary ended. Their relative isolation from other communions also distinguished the Covenanters from the

Evangelical Free. Intimately related to their spiritual dependence on Swedish Christianity was their desire to retain their Old World ways in the New. While Reinert Jernberg was boasting about the secular contributions which rapidly assimilating Scandinavians had made to American society, David Nyvall urged members of the Mission Covenant to retain their "Swedishness." The Covenant's conservatism, then, involved both the religious and cultural heritage of its members.

But was the Protestantism of these two Scandinavian-American traditions, both of which are now firmly in the "evangelical" camp, thoroughly conservative during the fourth quarter of the nineteenth-century? This question must be answered with a qualified No. This does not mean, of course, that Nordic immigrants adopted the liberalism which leaders of the former denomination accused the Congregationalists of propagating. They regarded their movements as attempts to restore forgotten or neglected dimensions of Christianity. But these newcomers and like-minded Christians in Scandinavia departed from the relatively rigid Lutheranism of Scandinavia in several respects. They insisted that the ecclesiology of the New Testament was incompatible with the inclusive parish system of the state churches. Some, most notably Waldenström, rejected the satisfaction theory of the atonement. Members of the Danish and Norwegian Mission Covenants and the immigrant antecedents of the Evangelical Free Church of America were preoccupied with Darbyite millenarianism, which also influenced many members of the established churches but never became normative in them. Finally, on both sides of the Atlantic members of both free church traditions rejected higher criticism of the Scriptures, much of which was eventually accepted in the theology faculties of the state churches. In the Nordic countries they incurred the wrath of Lutheran clergymen who regarded them as radicals who threatened Scandinavia's religious stability. But if we are seeking the roots of twentieth-century conservative Protestantism in America, we must look at both the Evangelical Free and Mission Covenant traditions. In terms of revivalism, Christology, the ideal of the pure visible church, eschatology, and reliance on the Bible, both were by 1900 what they are today -- segments of the intricate mosaic of conservative Protestantism in America.

REFERENCE NOTES

Chapter I

1. Ernest R. Sandeen, The Roots of Fundamentalism: British and American Millenarianism, 1800-1930 (Chicago: University of Chicago Press, 1970), p. 246.

2. Sandeen, The Roots of Fundamentalism, xiv-xv.

3. "Fundamentalism," Encyclopædia of the Social Sciences, Vol. V, 1944 ed., pp. 526-27.

4. New Haven: Yale University Press, 1954.

5. George Marsden, "Defining Fundamentalism," Christian Scholar's Review, I (Winter, 1971), 141-51.

6. Actually, there is a third "American" denomination in the International Federation of Free Evangelical Churches, the Evangelical Covenant Church of Canada. This body is affiliated with the Evangelical Covenant Church of America. The present study, however, is limited to the backgrounds of the denominations in the United States.

REFERENCE NOTES

Chapter II

1. See, for example, William Warren Smith, Revivalism in America (Gloucester, Massachusetts: P. Smith, 1944).

2. Johannes Pedersen, Den danske kirkes historie, Vol. V (København: Gyldendalske Boghandel, 1951), p. 116.

3. Fridtjof Valton, De norske vekkelsers historie (Oslo: (Filadelfiaforlaget, 1942), p. 64.

4. Quoted in Karl A. Olsson, By One Spirit (Chicago: Covenant Press, 1962), pp. 26-27.

5. Pedersen, Den danske kirkes historie, Vol. V, p. 201.

6. Søren Anton Sørensen, Zioniterne. En religiøs Bevægelse i Drammen og Omegn (Kristiania: Cammermeyer, 1904). See also articles on "Sioniterne i Norge" in Unions-Banneret, March 1, April 1, April 15, and June 1, 1886.

7. George M. Stephenson, The Religious Aspects of Swedish Immigration (Minneapolis: University of Minnesota Press, 1932), pp. 6-7.

8. Einar Molland, Fra Hans Nielsen Hauge til Eivind Berggrav, 3rd ed. revised (Oslo: Gyldendal Norsk Forlag, 1972). The standard work on Hauge is Andreas Aarflot, Tro og lydighet. Hans Nielsen Hauges Kristendomsforståelse (Oslo: Universitetsforlaget, 1969).

9. Stephenson, <u>The Religious Aspects of Swedish Immigration</u>, pp. 34-36.

10. The most comprehensive study of Scott's activities in Sweden and their repercussions is Gunnar Westin, <u>George Scott och hans verksamhet i Sverige</u> (Stockholm: Svenska Kyrkans Diakonistyrelses Bokförlag, 1938).

11. Michael Neiiendam, <u>Frikirker og Sekter</u>, 3rd ed. (København: G. E. C. Gads Forlag, 1948), p. 241.

12. J. F. Balling and P. G. Lindhardt, <u>Den nordiske kirkes historie</u>, 3rd ed. (København: Nyt Nordisk Forlag, 1973), p. 209.

13. Helge Rasmussen, "Historisk tilbageblik på danske vækkelser og vækkelsesbevægelser," p. 13, in Helge Rasmussen, ed., <u>En dansk vækkelsesbevægelse</u> (København: Missionsforbundets Forlag, 1963).

14. Balling and Lindhardt, <u>Den nordiske kirkes historie</u>, 3rd ed., p. 208.

15. See, for example, <u>Aftonbladet</u>, September 6 and 7, 1842.

16. Balling and Lindhardt, <u>Den nordiske kirkes historie</u>, 3rd ed., p. 208.

17. E. J. Ekman, <u>Den inre missionens historie</u>. 5 vols. (Stockholm: E. J. Ekmans Förlagsexpedition, 1896-1902).

REFERENCE NOTES

Chapter III

1. Berndt Gustafson, _Svensk kyrkohistoria_ (Stockholm: AB Tryckmans, 1973), pp. 215-16.

2. Einar Molland, _Fra Hans Nielsen Hauge til Eivind Berggrav_, 3rd ed. (Oslo: Gyldendal Norsk Forlag, 1972), pp. 100-01. For a survey of the coming of religious toleration to Norway, see Molland's article, "Problemet religionsfrihet i norsk politikk og lovgivning 1814-1964," in Per-Olov Ahrén, _et al_, eds., _Kyrka folk stat_ (Lund: Gleerups, 1967), pp. 143-58.

3. A fine study of these reforms is Aage Skullerud, _Bondeopposisjonen og religionsfriheten i 1840-årene_ (Bergen: Universitetsforlaget, 1971).

4. Claus Winther Hjelm, _Betænkning og Forslag til Lov om Grændserne for Religionsfriheden, og navnlig om Separatister og gudelige Forsamlinger_ (Christiania: Chr. Grøndahl, 1840).

5. Nils Bloch-Hoell, "Forholdet mellom Den norske kirke og Den romersk-katolske kirke i Norge i tiden 1843-1892," _Norsk teologisk tidsskrift_, LIX (1958), 90-121.

6. A comprehensive study of the 1845 dissenter law, the controversy surrounding its enactment, and its aftermath is Knut Rygnestad, _Dissentarspørsmålet i Noreg frå 1845 til 1891_ (Oslo: Lutherstiftelsens Forlag, 1955).

7. Norges officielle Statistik, Tredie Række, No. 284. Oversigt over de vigtigste Resultater af de statistiske Tabeller vedkommende Folketælling i Kongeriget Norge i Januar 1891. Sjette Afsnit: Befolkningens Fordeling efter Trosbekjendelse, pp. 112-13.

8. Skullerud, Bondeopposisjonen og religionsfriheten i 1840-årene, pp. 39-73.

9. William Mulder, Homeward to Zion (Minneapolis: University of Minnesota Press, 1957), pp. 7-29.

10. Mulder, Homeward to Zion, p. 34.

11. Mulder, Homeward to Zion, p. 37.

12. Mulder, Homeward to Zion, p. 105.

13. Mulder, Homeward to Zion, p. 107.

14. Jørgen W. Schmidt, Oh, Du Zion i Vest (København: Rosenkilde og Bagger, 1965), p. 15.

15. Rygnestad, Dissentarspørsmålet i Noreg frå 1845 til 1891, pp. 353-55-

16. Luthersk Kirketidende, June 2, 1867. For further examples of similar persecutions see Gjøvik Blad, June 28, 1861 and Adressetidende for Brevig, October 31, 1860.

17. Morgenbladet, February 23, 1855.

18. Martin L. Leuschner, "North American Baptist General Conference," in Davis C. Woolley, ed., Baptist Advance:

The Achievements of the Baptists of North America for a Century and a Half (Nashville: Broadman Press, 1964), p. 228.

19. Michael Neiiendam, Frikirker og Sekter, 3rd ed. (København: G. E. C. Gads Forlag, 1948), p. 80.

20. Unions-Banneret, May 15, 1887; Banneret, April 15, 1895.

21. Erik Nyhlén, Svensk frikyrka (Stockholm: Bokförlaget Prisma, 1964), p. 142.

22. Nyhlén, Svensk frikyrka, p. 142.

23. Nyhlén, Svensk frikyrka, p. 142; Banneret, April 15, 1895.

24. Infra, pp. 49-50.

25. Luthersk Kirketidende, May 21, 1865.

26. De norske Baptisters første almindelige Conference i Bergen den 6te, 7de og 8de Juli 1877, p. 3.

27. Banneret, April 30, 1900.

28. See, for example, Luthersk Kirketidende, November 24, 1867.

29. Storthings Forhandlinger 1888 Indst. O. IX "Indstilling fra Kirkekomiteen i Anledning forskjellige private Forslag til Forandringer i Dissenterloven af 16de Juli 1845," p. 4.

30. Norges officielle Statistik, Tredie Række, No. 284, pp. 112-13.

31. Neiiendam, Frikirker og Sekter, 3rd ed., pp. 145-46.

32. Nyhlén, Svensk frikyrka, pp. 204-05.

33. Nyhlén, Svensk frikyrka, p. 205.

34. Neiiendam, Frikirker og Sekter, 3rd ed., pp. 228-35.

35. Karl M. Kofod, P. C. Trandberg (København: O. Lohse, 1925), p. 111.

36. Kofod, P. C. Trandberg, p. 119.

37. Kofod, P. C. Trandberg, p. 143.

38. A well-written biography is Emil Larsen, Urovækkeren Mogens Abraham Sommer (København: G. E. C. Gads Forlag, 1963).

39. Emil Larsen, "Det danske Missionsforbunds forhistorie," in Helge Rasmussen, ed., En dansk vækkelsesbevægelse (København: Missionsforbundets Forlag, 1963), p. 22.

40. Andreas Aarflot, Norsk kirkehistorie, Vol. II (Oslo: Lutherstiftelsens Forlag, 1967), p. 365.

41. Ingulf Diesen, Det Norske Misjonsforbunds historie (Oslo: Det Norske Misjonsforbunds Teologiske Seminar, 1971), p. 20. See also Erling Danbolt, Presten G. A. Lammers for og mot frimenighetstanken (Oslo: Universitetsforlaget, 1963).

42. Tromsø Stiftstidende, March 9, 1884.

43. *Protocol for Tromsø frie apostolisk christelige Menighed*, 1856-1892.

44. "Bidrag til den tromsøiske 'Vækkelses' Historie," *Theologisk Tidsskrift for den evangelisk-lutherske Kirke i Norge*, II (1859), 456-57. Blom's chronology was imperfect; the first number of *Øjeblikket* appeared on May 24, 1855.

45. "*Meddelelser*" *til og fra de frie apostolisk christelige Menigheder*, February, 1859.

46. *Tromsø Stiftstidende*, March 9, 1884.

47. *Medlemsprotokoll for Bergen frie apostolisk christelige Menighed*, 1858-1923.

48. "*Meddelelser*" *til og fra de frie apostolisk christelige Menigheder*, December, 1860.

49. *Protocol, vedkommende den frie apostolisk christelige Menighed i Skien*.

50. For Franson's influence, see Chapter VII.

51. *Tromsø Tidende*, June 26, 1857.

52. *Luthersk Kirketidende*, January 24, 1864.

53. *Luthersk Kirketidende*, January 21, 1866.

54. See, for example, *Luthersk Kirketidende*, August 14, 1864 and October 18, 1863.

55. Dagfinn Mannsåker, *Det norske presteskapet i det 19. hundreåret* (Oslo: Det norske Samlaget, 1954), pp. 70, 76.

56. *Infra*, pp. 57-58.

57. Vilhelm Beck, *Memoirs* (Philadelphia: Fortress Press, 1965), pp. 91-92. This is the American edition of Vilhelm Beck, *Erindringer fra mit Liv* (København: Kirkelig Forening for Indre Mission, 1902).

58. Molland, *Fra Hans Nielsen Hauge til Eivind Berggrav*, 3rd ed. revised, p. 42. The standard history of the Norwegian Luther Society is Ola Rudvin, *Indremisjons-selskapets historie*. Vol. I: *Den norske Lutherstiftelse 1868-1891* (Oslo: Lutherstiftelsens forlag, 1967).

59. *Dansk Kirketidende*, September 24, 1871.

60. Paul Nyholm, "Introduction," in Beck, *Memoirs*, p. 25. K. M. Eckhoff, *Home Missions and Colportage in Norway* (Edinburgh: Lorimer and Gillies, 1883), pp. 5-8.

61. An important recent study of a local Lutheran free congregation is Tormod Hægeland, *Evangelisk luthersk dissens i en evangelisk luthersk statskirke* (Oslo: Universitetsforlaget, 1976). The more general history of the Lutheran Free Church is told in Andreas Holm, *et al.*, eds., *Kristus er Herre. Den Evangelisk Luthersk Frikirke 1877-1977* (Oslo: Norsk Luthersk Forlag, 1977).

62. Aarflot, *Norsk kirkehistorie*, Vol. II, p. 491.

63. P. G. Lindhardt, _Den danske kirkes historie_, Vol. VII (København: Gyldendalske Boghandel, 1958), p. 108.

64. Beck, _Memoirs_, pp. 54-55.

65. Harald Beyer, _Søren Kierkegaard og Norge_ (Kristiania: H. Aschehoug & Co., 1924) is generally reliable, although in some respects outdated for general information on the reception of Kierkegaard's works in Norway.

66. Sven Gustafsson, _Nyevangelismens kyrkokritik_ (Lund: Gleerups Förlag, 1962), pp. 112-13.

67. _Nordisk Teologisk Leksikon_, Vol. III, 1957 ed., pp. 420-24.

68. Gustafsson, _Svensk kyrkohistoria_, p. 237.

69. Quoted in Molland, _Fra Hans Nielsen Hauge til Eivind Berggrav_, 3rd ed. revised, p. 54.

70. Lindhardt, _Den danske kirkes historie_, Vol. VII, pp. 191-92.

71. The most complete study of Heuch is Knut Rygnestad, _Johan Christian Heuch. Apologet og stridsmann_ (Trondheim: Globus-forlaget, 1966).

72. Carl Fredrik Wisløff, _Norsk kirkehistorie_, Vol. III (Oslo: Lutherstiftelsens Forlag, 1971), p. 18.

73. Molland, _Fra Hans Nielsen Hauge til Eivind Berggrav_, 3rd ed. revised, pp. 54-55.

74. Per Amdam, _Bjørnson og kristendommen_ (Oslo: Universitetsforlaget, 1969).

75. See William R. Hutchison, *The Transcendentalist Ministers* (New Haven: Yale University Press, 1959), p. 108.

76. Wisløff, *Norsk kirkehistorie*, Vol. III, p. 14; Molland, *Fra Hans Nielsen Hauge til Eivind Berggrav*, 3rd ed. revised, pp. 56-57.

77. *Om artenes uppkomst* (Stockholm: Hiertas förlagsexpedition, 1871); *Om Artenes Oprindelse og Kvalitetsvalg* (København: Gyldendal, 1872).

78. *Dansk Kirketidende*, July 23, 1871.

79. Wisløff, *Norsk kirkehistorie*, Vol. III, p. 13.

REFERENCE NOTES

Chapter IV

1. Albert Schweitzer, Geschichte der Leben-Jesu-Forschung (Tübingen: J. C. B. Mohr, 1913), pp. 13-26.

2. Berndt Gustafsson, Svensk kyrkohistoria (Stockholm: AB Tryckmans, 1973), pp. 167-68.

3. Svenska Män och Kvinnor, Vol. VIII, 1955, pp. 528-29.

4. Budbæreren (Red Wing, Minnesota), August, 1878.

5. Einar Molland, Fra Hans Nielsen Hauge til Eivind Berggrav, 3rd ed. revised (Oslo: Gyldendal Norsk Forlag, 1972), p. 27.

6. Andreas Aarflot, Norsk kirkehistorie, Vol. II (Oslo: Lutherstiftelsens Forlag, 1968), pp. 282-83.

6a. Frederick Metcalfe, The Oxonian in Norway; or Notes of Excursions in that Country in 1854-1855 (London: Hurst and Blackett, Publishers, 1856), pp. 94-95. See Kirkelig Maanedstidende, January, 1856, for statistics and other information concerning the increasing distribution of Bibles in the Tromsø discese in the 1850's.

6b. Budbæreren (Red Wing, Minnesota), January, 1878.

7. Claude Welch, Protestant Thought in the Nineteenth Century, Vol. I (New Haven: Yale University Press, 1972), p. 195. Hengstenberg's conservatism also extended into the political arena. An unabashed spokesman for the union of throne and altar in Prussia, he cooperated with such political

reactionaries as the Gerlach brothers to oppose the mid-century wave of liberalism in Germany.

8. Norsk Biografisk Leksikon, Vol. II, 1925, p. 494.

9. Balling and Lindhardt, Den nordiske kirkes historie, 3rd ed. (København: Nyt Nordisk Forlag, 1973), p. 206.

10. Quoted in Andreas Aarflot, "Skriftsynet i norsk lekmanns-tradisjon i det 19. århundre," in Ole Øystese, ed., Bibelsyn og bibelgransking (Stavanger: Nomi Forlag, 1966), p. 242.

11. Norsk Biografisk Leksikon, Vol. X, 1949, p. 66.

12. Schweitzer, Geschichte der Leben-Jesu-Forschung, pp. 98-123.

13. Stephen Neill, The Interpretation of the New Testament, 1861-1961 (London: Oxford University Press, 1964), p. 13.

14. George M. Stephenson, The Religious Aspects of Swedish Immigration (Minneapolis: University of Minnesota Press, 1932), p. 30.

15. Tidskrift for udenlandsk theologisk Litteratur, Vol. I (1833), i-xxiv.

16. Frants Buhl, "Naar er femte Mosebog affatter?" Theologisk Tidskrift for den danske Folkekirke (1878), 129-68, 193-227.

17. Buhl's transition can be seen in a pair of his articles, both titled "Den nye Pentateuchkritiks Ret og Uret," Theologisk Tidskrift for den danske Folkekirke, II (1885), 256-82 and III (1886), 250-77.

18. Vilhelm Beck, Memoirs (Philadelphia: Fortress Press, 1965), pp. 174-75.

19. Norsk Biografisk Leksikon, Vol. XI, 1952, pp. 37-42.

20. Luthersk Ugeskrift, August 6, 1887.

21. Grete Tufte Bakken, "M. J. Færden: Bibelkritikkens foregangsmann i vårt land," Norsk teologisk tidsskrift, LXVIII (1967), 75.

22. Gustafsson, Svensk kyrkohistoria, p. 213.

23. Svenska Män och Kvinnor, Vol. V, 1949, p. 365.

24. Ingemar Lindén, Biblicism apokalyptik utopi (Uppsala: Acta Universitatis Upsaliensis, 1971), p. 230.

25. Stephenson, The Religious Aspects of Swedish Immigration, p. 34.

26. Svenska Män och Kvinnor, Vol. VII, 1954, p. 182.

27. Infra, pp. 154-56.

REFERENCE NOTES

Chapter V

1. In the present study, "millenarianism," often called "premillennialism," refers to the belief that the Second Coming of Christ will precede his thousand-year reign on earth. It is distinguished from "postmillennialism," the belief that the Second Advent will follow a thousand years of worldly bliss.

2. Quoted in Hugh T. Kerr, ed., A Compend of Luther's Theology (Philadelphia: The Westminster Press, 1943), pp. 246-47.

3. LeRoy Edwin Froom, The Prophetic Faith of Our Fathers, Vol. III (Washington, D. C.: Review and Herald, 1946), pp. 297-99.

4. C. C. Goen, "Jonathan Edwards, A New Departure in Eschatology," Church History, XXVIII (1959), 25-40. Froom, however, stresses the continuity of millenarianism in colonial America; see The Prophetic Faith of Our Fathers, Vol. III, Pt. I.

5. Ernest R. Sandeen, The Roots of Fundamentalism: British and American Millenarianism, 1800-1930 (Chicago: University of Chicago Press, 1970), p. 7.

6. For a concise treatment of Irving, see Sandeen, The Roots of Fundamentalism: British and American Millenarianism, 1800-1930, pp. 14-29.

7. Almindelig Kirketidende, March, 1863.

8. _Dansk Kirketidende_, October 6, 1861.

9. Michael Neiiendam, _Frikirker og Sekter_, 4th ed. revised (København: G. E. C. Gads Forlag, 1958), p. 208.

10. _Almindelig Kirketidende_, July 1, 1885.

11. _Almindelig Kirketidende_, March, 1863.

12. _Dansk Kirketidende_, October 6, 1861.

13. _Dansk Kirketidende_, February 16, 1862.

14. _Dansk Kirketidende_, July 28, 1867.

15. Karl M. Kofod, _P. C. Trandberg_ (København: O. Lohse, 1925), p. 207. See also Trandberg's _Kalenderoptegnelser_, Copenhagen Royal Library, _Ny kongelige Samling_, 2789, June 1, 1870; August 29-31, 1870; September 9, 1871; October 1, 6, 10, and 11, 1878; March 31, 1879; April 5, 1879.

16. Trandberg, _Kalenderoptegnelser_, June 12, 1870; June 26, 1870. Because Trandberg was no longer a member of the Danish state church, his preaching was free from episcopal review. But even in the state church the lectionary was no longer binding; the clergy had been given the freedom to use their own discretion in selecting texts, or to preach from Luther's catechisms. Ironically, this latitude had been given so that the state church's pastors could more effectively counter free church preaching. See P. G. Lindhardt, _Den danske kirkes historie_, Vol. VII (København: Gyldendalske Boghandel, 1958), p. 35.

17. Bornholms Avis, January 18, 1872.

18. Kofod, P. C. Trandberg, pp. 237, 250. Trandberg continued to study Irvingite millenarianism and worship throughout the 1870's. But in April, 1879 he heard what he termed a "wretched" sermon in the Copenhagen Catholic Apostolic Church. Trandberg wrote that this sermon alienated him from the sect. See Kalenderoptegnelser, April 20, 1879 and Kofod, P. C. Trandberg, p. 248.

19. This was not the first time that Thomsen and Blædel had clashed over the latter's ambivalent attitude toward the Catholic Apostolic Church. In the 1860's Thomsen had participated in theological discussions at Blædel's home, but was declared persona non grata after accusing his host of abandoning belief in the imminent Second Advent for fear of ostracization. See Peter Schindler, ed., Efterladte Papirer af Martin Schneekloth 1844-1871 (København: Nyt Nordisk Forlag, 1942), pp. 43-45.

20. Dansk Kirketidende, September 24, 1871.

21. Michael Neiiendam, Frikirker og Sekter, 3rd ed. (København: G. E. C. Gads Forlag, 1948), p. 189.

22. Erik Nyhlén, Svensk frikyrka (Stockholm: Bokförlaget Prisma, 1964), pp. 225-26.

23. Froom, The Prophetic Faith of Our Fathers, Vol. IV, p. 462. Winthrop S. Hudson, however, suggests that Miller "probably found the clue which pointed to 1843 in the Publications of the British Continental Society;" see Religion in America, 2nd ed. revised (New York: Charles Scribner's Sons, 1973), p. 194. But Sandeen counters that "Hudson's

attribution of Continental Society influence was based upon the similarity of their argument and not upon any direct influence;" see The Roots of Fundamentalism, p. 50.

24. Religion in America, 2nd ed. revised, p. 196.

25. Francis D. Nichol, Midnight Cry: A Defense of William Miller and the Millerites (Washington, D. C.: Review and Herald, 1944).

26. Matteson's autobiography is Mattesons Liv og Adventbevægelsens Begyndelse blandt Skandinaverne (College View, Nebraska: International Publishing Association, 1908).

27. Lutheraneren, April, 1872.

28. Augustana, November 3, 1874.

29. Augustana, January, 1870.

30. Meddelelser fra den dansk-amerikanske Mission, III (1870), 40.

31. Den danske Evangelist, February, 1873.

32. Den danske Evangelist, April, 1873.

33. Ingemar Lindén, Biblicism apokalyptik utopi (Uppsala: Acta Universitatis Upsaliensis, 1971), p. 204.

34. "As early as 1874 the Review and Herald reports a letter from a woman named Reirsen in Norway telling that she and her husband had begun to keep the Seventh-day Sabbath and that several others were interested as a result of having read

Advent Tidende." Don F. Neufeld, _et_ _al_., _Seventh-day Adventist Encyclopedia_ (Washington, D. C.: Review and Herald Publishing Association, 1966), p. 896. Matteson received a similar letter from a Dane in 1872 and several more in subsequent years; see _Seventh-day Adventist Encyclopedia_, p. 338.

35. Quoted in Lindén, _Biblicism apokalyptik utopi_, p. 236.

36. Øivind Gjertsen, "The Seventh-day Adventist Church in Norway: A Factual Account," in Sigmund Skard, ed., _Americana Norvegica: Norwegian Contributions to American Studies_, II (Philadelphia: University of Pennsylvania Press, 1968), p. 79.

37. Matteson, _Mattesons Liv_, pp. 211-12.

38. See, for example, the account in _Budbæreren_ (Red Wing, Minnesota), August, 1879.

39. Matteson, _Mattesons Liv_, p. 212.

40. _Budbæreren_ (Red Wing, Minnesota), August, 1879.

41. Gjertsen, "The Seventh-day Adventist Church in Norway," p. 82.

42. Protokol for Den første Syvende-dags Adventistmenighed i Kristiania; _Review and Herald_, February 13, 1879.

43. Protokoll for Syvende-Dags Adventistmenigheten i Hadsel, 1889-1897, State Archives in Trondheim.

44. _Budbæreren_ (Red Wing, Minnesota), August, 1879.

45. See, for example, January 18, 1879; May 8, 1886; May 29, 1886; July 3, 1886; July 10, 1886; and June 25, 1887.

46. Gjertsen, "The Seventh-day Adventist Church in Norway," p. 81.

47. Morgenbladet, January 21, 1879. For a Methodist critique of the Adventists' Sabbatarianism, see Kristelig Tidende, April 17, 1885.

48. Unions-Banneret, February, 1881. See also Unions-Banneret, October, 1880, for a Baptist critique of Sabbatarianism.

49. Ingemar Lindén, Biblicism apokalyptik utopi, p. 257.

50. Gjertsen, "The Seventh-day Adventist Church in Norway," p. 84.

51. Lindén, Biblicism apokalyptik utopi, p. 443.

52. Lindén, Biblicism apokalyptik utopi, p. 228.

53. Gjertsen, "The Seventh-day Adventist Church in Norway," p. 84.

54. Mrs. E. G. White, "Visit to Scandinavia," in Historical Sketches of the Foreign Missions of the Seventh-day Adventists (Basle: Imprimerie Polyglotte, 1886), p. 194.

55. Protokoll for Syvende-Dags Adventistmenigheten i Hadsel, 1889-1897.

56. Adventistmenigheten i Arendal 1892-1895 Menighetsprotokoll, State Archives in Kristiansand.

57. Gjertsen, "The Seventh-day Adventist Church in Norway," p. 84.

58. Sandeen, _The Roots of Fundamentalism_, p. 97.

59. Philadelphia: J. S. Claxton, 1867

60. Philadelphia: J. S. Claxton, 1867. Baxter wrote several prophetic books focusing on Louis Napoleon in the 1860's. The first was _Louis Napoleon the Infidel Antichrist_ (Toronto: M. Shewan, 1861). In subsequent works he sequentially set the date of the Second Advent at "about 1863," "about the period 1869-1870," "about or soon after 1870," and "about or soon after 1873."

61. _Firti kommende Undere i de 10-12 Aar_ (Christiania: G. Hüberts Forlag, 1887).

62. _Norsk Biografisk Leksikon_, Vol. V, 1931, pp. 365-67.

63. Bergen: Bernhard Wærøs Bogtrykkeri, 1922

64. _Från ljus till ljus_ (Stockholm: P. Palmquist, 1883).

65. _Ljus for den sista tiden!_ (Stockholm: P. A. Huldbergs Bokförlag, 1895).

66. _Lys for de sidste Dage_ (Kristiania: G. Hüberts Forlag, 1888).

67. Paul Wettergreen, _Opbyggelige Foredrag over Johannes's_

Aabenbaring (Arendal: Chr. Christensens Forlag, 1883), iv, pp. 253, 259-62, 266-391.

68. See, for example, January 15, 1889; February 1, 1889; February 15, 1889; July 15, 1889; and August 1, 1889.

69. Lys for den sidste Tid (Rønne: Chr. Møller, 1896)

70. De Helliges Taalmodighed og Tro (København: Kirkelig Forening for den indre Mission, 1884)

71. Det tusenåriga riket och begynnelsen till en ny tid (Stockholm: P. A. Huldbergs Förlag, 1893)

72. An illuminating obituary for Guldberg is in Folkebladet, August 31, 1896.

73. Hans Guldberg, "Forord," in James Keith, Egyptens store Pyramide(Kristiania: G. Hüberts Forlag, 1887), pp. 3-4.

74. Norsk biografisk leksikon, Vol. VII, 1936, pp. 161-62.

75. For a prime example, see Thorstein Gunnarson, Dommedagsventing. Millennismen og dens innslag i norsk Kristendom (Bergen: A/S Lunde & Co.s Forlag, 1928), p. 88.

76. The most concise, yet most comprehensive, statement of Guldberg's eschatology is found in his Vægter, hvor langt paa Natten? Et Midnatsraab (Kristiania: E. C. Bjørnstad & Co.s Bogtrykkeri, 1887).

77. Den bestemte tid (Faribault, Minnesota: O. A. Østbys Forlag, 1896).

78. Den bestämte tiden (Minneapolis: Sanning och friheds förlag, 1897)

79. En ny Tid er nær! (Laurvik: M. Andersens Forlag, 1894); En ny tid är nära! (Stockholm: P. A. Huldbergs Bokförlag, 1893)

80. George Needham, ed., Prophetic Studies of the International Prophetic Conference (Chicago: Fleming H. Revell, 1896).

81. Kristelig Tidende, March 4, 1887. All of the speeches were printed in Paul Wettergreen and P. Tallaksen, eds., Er Kristi Tilkommelse nær? (Kristiania: A. W. Brøggers Bogtrykkeri, 1887).

82. Wettergreen and Tallaksen, eds., Er Kristi Tilkommelse nær?, p. 86.

83. For a concise analysis of Darby's eschatology see Sandeen, The Roots of Fundamentalism, chap. III.

84. Dwight L. Moody: American Evangelist, 1837-1899 (Chicago: University of Chicago Press, 1969), p. 251.

85. Sandeen, The Roots of Fundamentalism, pp. 174-76.

86. For an illuminating discussion of Moody's influence in Sweden, see Ernst Newman, "Dwight L. Moody och hans inflytande i Sverige," in Från skilde tider. Studier tillägnade Hjalmar Holmquist (Stockholm: Svenska Kyrkans Diakonistyrelses Bokförlag, 1938), pp. 368-404.

87. Franson's revivals in Scandinavia and his role in the founding of the Norwegian and Danish Mission Covenants

will be analyzed in Chapter VII.

88. Fredrik Franson, ed., Utförligt referat öfwer forhandlingerna wid den för de profetiska ämnenas studier afsedda konferensen i Chicago (Kristinehamn: F. Broström & Kini, 1882).

89. Himlauret eller det profetiska ordet (Chicago: Chicago-Bladets Förlag, 1898)

90. Franson, Himlauret, pp. 219-20.

91. Emanuel Linderholm, Pingströrelsen i Sverige (Stockholm: Albert Bonniers Förlag, 1925), p. 20.

92. Kort öfwersikt öfwer Uppenbarelseboken (Kristinehamn: F. Broström & Kini, 1882)

93. Franson, Himlauret, p. 250.

94. Franson, Himlauret, p. 203.

95. Franson, Himlauret, pp. 205-06, 275-76.

96. Linderholm, Pingströrelsen i Sverige, p. 35.

97. O. F. Myrberg, Johannis Uppenbarelse med ledning af Gamla Testamentets profetia och verlds- och kyrkohistorien förklarad (Stockholm: Z. Hæggströms Förlag, 1888), pp. 212, 277.

98. Lindén, Biblicism apokalyptik utopi, p. 238.

99. Christi gjenkomst til Tusindårsriget (Bergen: H. Grønsdals forlag, 1887), pp. 60-61.

100. Grønsdal, Christi gjenkomst til Tusindårsriget, pp. 91, 140-41.

101. Livet efter Døden og Gudsrigets Fremtid (Stavanger: L. C. Kiellands Bogtrykkeri, 1893)

102. Life after Death and the Future of the Kingdom of God (Edinburgh: T. & T. Clark, 1896)

103. Life after Death and the Future of the Kingdom of God, p. 229.

104. Life after Death and the Future of the Kingdom of God, p. 305.

105. Life after Death and the Future of the Kingdom of God, pp. 350-52.

106. Life after Death and the Future of the Kingdom of God, p. 314.

107. Luthersk Ugeskrift, May 10, 1884.

108. Luthersk Ugeskrift, June 23, 1888.

109. Luthersk Kirketidende, September 11, 1886.

110. Til Minde om Pastor Ipsen (København: Missionstrykkeriet, 1897), p. 7.

111. This opposition will be discussed in Chapter XI.

112. Gunnarson, Dommedagsventing, p. 39.

113. The most erratic may have been Aanen Reinertsen, a returned Norwegian emigrant who believed that Christ had already returned in him. This self-styled Messiah established a harem in southern Norway and published a long series of periodicals in which he proclaimed confused eschatological ideas and denounced the Lutheran clergy in vituperative terms. Committed twice to mental hospitals, Reinertsen died in 1891, shortly after his harem was discovered. Surprisingly, practically no research has been done on Reinertsen. The most revealing contemporary accounts are in Kragerø Tidende, September 22, 24, and 27, 1887, and July 19, 1888; Kristelig Tidende, April 18, 1890; Luthersk Ugeskrift, August 8, 1891; Luthersk Kirketidende, August 6, 1887 and April 26, 1890; and Den vestlandske Tidende, April 10, 1890.

114. Gunnarson, Dommedagsventing, p. 62.

REFERENCE NOTES

Chapter VI

1. Oscar Lövgren, _Oscar Ahnfelt_ (Stockholm: Svenska Missionsförbundets Förlag, 1932), pp. 105-13.

2. Lövgren, _Oscar Ahnfelt_, p. 126.

3. Bror Walan, _Församlingstanken i Svenska Missionsförbundet_ (Stockholm: Gummessons Bokförlag, 1964), p. 74.

4. Karl A. Olsson, _By One Spirit_ (Chicago: Covenant Press, 1962), p. 89.

5. Quoted in David Nyvall, _My Father's Testament_ (Chicago: Covenant Press, 1974), p. 126.

6. Quoted in Nyvall, _My Father's Testament_, pp. 128-29.

7. William Bredberg, _P. P. Waldenströms verksamhet till 1878_ (Stockholm: Missionsförbundets Förlag, 1948) is an excellent study of Waldenström's early career.

8. Olsson, _By One Spirit_, pp. 91-92. According to Bredberg, pastors of the state church had officiated at communion in the Uppsala Mission Society's chapel on previous occasions without suffering any consequences; see _P. P. Waldenströms verksamhet till 1878_, p. 320.

9. Bredberg, _P. P. Waldenströms verksamhet till 1878_, p. 341.

10. William Bredberg and Oscar Lövgren, eds., Genom Guds nåd. Svenska Missionsförbundet under 75 år (Stockholm: Missionsförbundets Förlag, 1953), pp. 77-83, quoted in Olsson, By One Spirit, p. 96.

11. Olsson, By One Spirit, p. 96.

12. Infra, pp.200-01.

13. Bror Walan, Fernholm och frikyrkan (Stockholm: Gummessons Bokförlag, 1962), especially Chap. XII.

14. Bredberg, P. P. Waldenströms verksamhet till 1878, p. 88.

15. Waldenström, September 9, 1879, to C. Jansson, in Waldenström Archives.

16. Nyvall, My Father's Testament, p. 104.

17. Walan, Församlingstanken i Svenska Missionsförbundet, pp. 224-28.

18. Walan, Församlingstanken i Svenska Missionsförbundet, p. 228; Hemlandsvännen, February 3, 1881.

19. P. Waldenström, Biblisk troslära, 2nd ed. (Stockholm: Svenska Missionsförbundets Förlag, 1915), pp. 110, 112.

20. Waldenström, Biblisk troslära, 2nd ed., p. 113.

21. Tidens Tecken, 1873, p. 138 and 1876, p. 36, quoted in Walan, Fernholm och frikyrkan, pp. 67-68.

22. Förbundet, August, 1880.

23. Förbundet, May, 1880.

24. Förbundet, August, 1880.

25. Förbundet, August, 1881.

26. Hemlandsvännen, December 16, 1886.

27. Olsson, By One Spirit, pp. 102-03.

28. Nyvall, My Father's Testament, p. 108. Tischendorf, then professor of New Testament at the University of Leipzig, was not a radical Biblical scholar, but rather a textual, or "lower" critic, best known for his discovery of the codex sinaiticus, the second oldest extant Greek text of the New Testament.

29. Nyvall, My Father's Testament, p. 171.

30. Pietisten, March and June, 1872.

31. For the largely hostile reaction to Waldenström's atonement theory, see Bredberg, P. P. Waldenströms verksamhet till 1878, pp. 150-63.

32. Walan, Församlingstanken i Svenska Missionsförbundet, p. 105.

33. Prädikantmötet i Stockholm den 15-18 Augusti 1876, II, p. 23, quoted in Bredberg, P. P. Waldenströms verksamhet till 1878, p. 239.

34. Prädikantmötet i Stockholm den 15-18 Augusti 1876, II, pp. 4-5, quoted in Walan, Församlingstanken i Svenska Missionsförbundet, pp. 105-06.

35. Prädikantmötet i Stockholm den 15-18 Augusti 1876, II, p. 23, quoted in Bredberg, P. P. Waldenströms verksamhet till 1878, p. 239.

36. William Ohrman, "Bibeltillämpning och bibeluppfattning inom Svenska missionsförbundet 1883-1897 med särskild hänsyn till P. P. Waldenström" (unpublished licentiate thesis, University of Uppsala, 1972), p. 6.

37. Andreas Fernholm, July 24, 1884, to M. W. Montgomery, in M. W. Montgomery, A Wind from the Holy Spirit in Sweden and Norway (New York: American Home Missionary Society, 1885), p. 55.

38. Nyvall, My Father's Testament, p. 188.

39. Svenska Morgonbladet, January 11, 1893.

40. P. Waldenström and E. Tegnér, Bibelkommissionens öfversättning af gamla testamentet (Stockholm: Aktiebolaget Normans Förlag, 1902), p. 5.

41. Waldenström and Tegnér, Bibelkommissionens öfversättning af gamla testamentet, p. 6.

42. Waldenström and Tegnér, Bibelkommissionens öfversättning af gamla testamentet, p. 8.

43. Waldenström and Tegnér, Bibelkommissionens öfversättning af gamla testamentet, p. 9.

44. Waldenström and Tegnér, *Bibelkommissionens öfversättning af gamla testamentet*, pp. 10-11, 20-22.

45. Waldenström and Tegnér, *Bibelkommissionens öfversättning af gamla testamentet*, p. 27.

46. Waldenström, January 4, 1894, to Frederick Emrich, in Waldenström Archives.

47. P[aul] W[aldenström], *Låt oss behålla vår gamla bibel* (Stockholm: Aktiebolaget Normans Förlag, 1902), p. 14.

48. Waldenström, *Låt oss behålla vår gamla bibel*, p. 42.

49. Waldenström, *Låt oss behålla vår gamla bibel*, p. 6.

50. Waldenström, *Låt oss behålla vår gamla bibel*, pp. 32-33.

51. Waldenström, *Låt oss behålla vår gamla bibel*, p. 29.

52. Waldenström, *Låt oss behålla vår gamla bibel*, p. 20.

53. Waldenström, December 31, 1892, to Svening Johansson, in Waldenström Archives.

54. *Svenska Morgonbladet*, January 17, 1894.

REFERENCE NOTES

Chapter VII

1. Ingulf Diesen, *Det Norske Misjonsforbunds historie* (Oslo: Det Norske Misjonsforbunds Teologiske Seminar, 1971), pp. 36-38. For a more detailed description of Franson's revivals in Norway, see John Christensen, *Verdensmisjonæren Fredrik Franson* (Oslo: Det Norske Misjonsforbunds Forlag, 1927).

2. Christensen, *Verdensmisjonæren Fredrik Franson*, p. 59.

3. *Luthersk Kirketidende*, May 23, 1885. Moody's revivals were also severely criticized abroad by more traditional churchmen who disliked his "indifference to forms;" see James F. Findlay, *Dwight L. Moody: American Evangelist, 1837-1899* (Chicago: University of Chicago Press, 1969), pp. 145, 157.

4. Findlay, *Dwight L. Moody*, p. 262.

5. Findlay, *Dwight L. Moody*, pp. 263, 265-66, 330-31.

6. *Luthersk Kirketidende*, May 30, 1885.

7. *Morgenrøden*, April 15, 1884.

8. *Morgenrøden*, April 15, 1884.

9. Leif Eeg-Olofsson, *Olle i Kroken. Olof Olofsson, förkunnare och frikyrkooriginal* (Stockholm: Svenska Missionsförbundet, 1957), p. 30.

10. Ingulf Diesen, Fem foredrag om Det Norske Misjonsforbund (Oslo: Det Norske Misjonsforbunds Teologiske Seminar, 1974), pp. 10-11; Diesen, Det Norske Misjonsforbunds historie, pp. 43-46.

11. Findlay, Dwight L. Moody, p. 216.

12. Christensen, Verdensmisjonær Fredrik Franson, p. 81.

13. Missonæren, September 6, 1890.

14. Luthersk Kirketidende, March 22, 1884. The letter originally appeared in the Methodist periodical, Kristelig Tidende, March 7, 1884. See also Kristelig Tidende, December 21, 1883 and February 15, 1884 for further examples of Methodist hostility to Franson.

15. Emil Larsen, Historiske studier over kirkelige og frikirkelige brydninger (København: Tro og Liv, 1965), p. 86.

16. For Lang's relation to Sommer's movement, see Emil Larsen, Urovækkeren Mogens Abraham Sommer (København: G. E. C. Gads Forlag, 1963), pp. 107-10. Larsen has also analyzed Lang's activities in Denmark in his article, "Det danske Missionsforbunds forhistorie" in Helge Rasmussen, ed., En dansk vækkelsesbevægelse (København: Missionsforbundets Forlag, 1963), pp. 24-25.

17. Kristelige Talsmand, September 23, 1938 and February 2, 1943, quoted in Larsen, Historiske studier over kirkelige og frikirkelige brydninger, p. 85.

18. _Holbæk_ _Amtstidende_, February 21, 1945.

19. Vilhelm Beck, _Memoirs_ (Philadelphia: Fortress Press, 1965), pp. 125, 146.

20. _Den_ _indre_ _Missions_ _Tidende_, December 14, 1885.

21. _Den_ _indre_ _Missions_ _Tidende_, March 8, 1885.

22. _Luthersk_ _Kirketidende_, March 14, 1885.

23. _Den_ _indre_ _Missions_ _Tidende_, March 8, 1885.

24. _Den_ _indre_ _Missions_ _Tidende_, August 16, 1885.

25. _Holbæks_ _Amtstidende_, February 21, 1945.

26. Larsen, _Historiske_ _studier_ _over_ _kirkelige_ _og_ _fri-kirkelige_ brydninger, p. 130.

27. This is not to deny the considerable degree of freedom in the Mission Covenants of Norway and Denmark. Not all of those two denominations' members are revivalistic Darbyites, but revivalism remains a strong current in both, and Franson's futurist millenarianism is still the normative eschatology.

28. _Morgenrøden_, April 15, 1883.

29. _Morgenrøden_, April 15, 1883.

30. _Morgenrøden_, April 15, 1884.

31. Morgenrøden, April 15, 1884.

32. Morgenrøden, April 15, 1884; May 1, 1884; May 15, 1884; June 1, 1884.

33. Morgenstjernen, August 1, 1889.

34. Morgenstjernen, July 1, 1893.

35. Morgenstjernen, April 1, 1893.

36. Morgenstjernen, April 1, 1884.

37. Morgenrøden, May 1, 1884.

38. Morgenrøden, May 15, 1884.

39. Morgenrøden, May 15, 1884.

40. Morgenstjernen, October 1, 1889.

41. Morgenstjernen, October 15, 1889.

42. Morgenstjernen, November 15, 1892.

43. See, for example, Missionæren, May 3, 1900 and June 23, 1900.

44. Ernest R. Sandeen, The Roots of Fundamentalism: British and American Millenarianism, 1800-1930 (Chicago: University of Chicago Press, 1970), p. 111. Sandeen has also pointed out that these millenarians occasionally interpreted Biblical texts, such as the Song of Solomon, figuratively; p. 109.

45. F. Franson, Bibelns lära om Antikrist (Hedemora: A. F. Lidmans boktryckeri, 1886), pp. 2-4.

46. Morgenrøden, February 1, 1884.

47. Luthersk Kirketidende, March 22, 1884.

48. St. Louis Globe-Democrat, December 3, 1879, quoted in Findlay, Dwight L. Moody, p. 259.

49. Morgenstjernen, September 1, 1890.

50. For a prime example, see Morgenstjernen, April 1, 1890.

51. Morgenrøden, June 1, 1883; June 15, 1883. An abridged and revised version of Hastings' address appeared in the newspaper of the Danish Mission Covenant, Morgenstjernen, February 15, 1889.

52. Findlay, Dwight L. Moody, p. 246.

53. Morgenrøden, November 15, 1883. Norwegian Methodists and Baptists naturally disagreed; see Kristelig Tidende, December 21, 1883 and Unions-Banneret, March 1, 1884.

54. Morgenrøden, February 1, 1884.

55. Morgenrøden, August 15, 1884.

56. Report of the Theological Conference of The International Federation of Free Evangelical Churches (1971), p. 4.

57. Morgenstjernen, January 1, 1889.

58. Viggo Ramsvold, "Det første halve sekel," in Rasmussen, ed., *En dansk vækkelsesbevægelse*, p. 43.

59. *Morgenstjernen*, January 1, 1889; February 1, 1889.

60. Ramsvold, "Det første halve sekel," p. 44.

REFERENCE NOTES

Chapter VIII

1. The best study of the Augustana Synod is G. Everett Arden, _Augustana Heritage: A History of the Augustana Lutheran Church_ (Rock Island, Illinois: Augustana Press, 1963).

2. Samuel S. Schmucker, _The American Lutheran Church, Historically, Doctrinally, and Practically Delineated, in Several Occasional Discourses_, 5th ed. (Philadelphia: E. W. Miller, 1852), pp. 237-42. For a more general study of American Lutheranism, see Vergilius Ferm, _The Crisis in American Lutheran Theology_ (New York: The Century Co., 1927).

3. Ferm, _The Crisis in American Lutheran Theology_, p. 194.

4. _Augustanasynodens protokoll_, 1874, p. 10.

5. _Augustanasynodens protokoll_, 1870, pp. 7-8.

6. _Augustanasynodens protokoll_, 1870, pp. 47-48.

7. Gunnar Westin, ed., _Emigranterna och kyrkan_ (Stockholm: Svenska Kyrkans Diakonistyrelses Bokförlag, 1932), pp. 237-38, 410.

8. Karl A. Olsson, _By One Spirit_ (Chicago: Covenant Press, 1962), pp. 104-05. The most comprehensive study of Hasselquist is Oscar Fritiof Ander, _T. N. Hasselquist. The Career and Influence of a Swedish-American Clergyman, Journalist, and Educator_ (Rock Island, Illinois: Augustana Historical Society, 1931).

9. C. J. Nyvall, _Travel Memories from America_ (Chicago: Covenant Press, 1959), p. 120.

10. Karl A. Olsson, "Paul Peter Waldenström and Augustana," in J. Iverne Dowie and Ernest M. Esperlie, eds., _The Swedish Immigrant Community in Transition_ (Rock Island, Illinois: Augustana Historical Society, 1963), pp. 107-20.

11. Olsson, _By One Spirit_, pp. 198-201.

12. Quoted in Olsson, _By One Spirit_, p. 202. George M. Stephenson attributed the Augustana Synod's opposition to revivalism to the fact that such awakenings were often part of proselytizing by other communions; see _The Religious Aspects of Swedish Immigration_ (Minneapolis: University of Minnesota Press, 1932), p. 386. But sectarianism and revivalism had often gone hand-in-hand in Sweden, as well. In the 1860's, when Hasselquist began to polemicize against revivalism, it was an attribute of Swedish Christians who were seceding from the Augustana Synod.

13. _Gamla och nya hemlandet_, March 16, 1869.

14. _The Lutheran Observer_, December 18, 1868; _The Lutheran and Missionary_, March 25, 1869.

15. Olsson, By One Spirit, pp. 230, 698.

16. Olsson, By One Spirit, p. 212.

17. Olsson, By One Spirit, p. 244.

18. Zions Banér, February, 1874.

19. David Nyvall, My Father's Testament (Chicago: Covenant Press, 1975), pp. 173, 213.

20. Nyvall, Travel Memories from America, pp. 51, 35.

21. Missions-Wännen, January, 1879.

22. Josephine Princell, ed., J. G. Princells levnadsminnen (Chicago: Chicago-Bladets tryckeri, 1916) remains the best study of this controversial Swedish-American pastor, although Mrs. Princell's estimation of her husband, written shortly after his death, is a very biased account. Princell's father, who emigrated from Sweden, was named Magnus Gudmundson, but changed the family name to Gummeson after arriving in the United States. "Princell" was derived from Princeton, Illinois, John's boyhood home; see Stephenson, The Religious Aspects of Swedish Immigration, p. 427.

23. Quoted in Roy A. Thompson, "Origin and Development of the Evangelical Free Church of America," in H. Wilbert Norton, et al., The Diamond Jubilee Story of the Evangelical Free Church of America (Minneapolis: Free Church Publications, 1959), p. 135.

24. Chicago-Bladet, April 8, 1881.

25. _Chicago-Bladet_, July 8, 1881.

26. _Chicago-Bladet_, August 9, 1881.

27. _Chicago-Bladet_, April 29, 1881.

28. J. G. Princell, "Waiting, Watching, Working," in George Needham, ed., _Prophetic Studies of the International Prophetic Conference_ (Chicago: Fleming H. Revell, 1886), p. 207.

29. _Frihet och Frid_, November 30, 1889.

30. _Frihet och Frid_, November 15, 1892.

31. _Chicago-Bladet_, April 28, 1885.

32. Karl A. Olsson has described Princell's determined opposition to the formation of the Mission Covenant; see _By One Spirit_, pp. 288-93.

33. Olsson, _By One Spirit_, p. 728.

34. _Missionæren_, July 6, 1890.

35. _Morgenstjernen_, April 1, 1890.

36. _Morgenrøden_, October 15, 1884.

37. _Morgenstjernen_, March 1, 1890; March 15, 1890; _Missionæren_, July 6, 1890.

38. _Evangelisten_, July 15, 1890.

39. *Evangelisten*, April 1, 1897.

40. *Evangelisten*, April 1, 1890.

41. M. W. Montgomery, *The Work among the Scandinavians* (New York: American Home Missionary Society, 1888), p. 19.

42. R. Arlo Odegaard, *With Singleness of Heart* (Minneapolis: Free Church Press, n.d.), pp. 101-02.

43. Montgomery, *The Work among the Scandinavians*, pp. 16-17.

44. *Evangelisten*, February 1, 1890.

45. *Morgenstjernen*, March 15, 1890.

46. *Morgenstjernen*, August 1, 1894.

47. Odegaard, *With Singleness of Heart*, p. 560; *Evangelisten*, February 1, 1890.

48. Odegaard, *With Singleness of Heart*, p. 565.

REFERENCE NOTES

Chapter IX

1. James F. Findlay, _Dwight L. Moody: American Evangelist, 1837-1899_ (Chicago: University of Chicago Press, 1969), p. 204; Aaron I. Abell, _The Urban Impact upon American Protestantism_ (Cambridge, Massachusetts: Harvard University Press, 1943), pp. 31-32; _supra_, p. 166.

2. Quoted in Matthew Spinka, ed., _A History of Illinois Congregational and Christian Churches_ (Chicago: The Congregational and Christian Conference of Illinois, 1944), p. 284.

3. _Minnesota General Association Minutes_, 1868, p. 19.

4. _The Home Missionary_, December, 1878.

5. _Minnesota General Association Minutes_, 1874, p. 7.

6. _Minnesota General Association Minutes_, 1875, p. 7.

7. Quoted in Paul R. Lucas, "The Church and the City: Congregationalism in Minneapolis, 1850-1890," _Minnesota History_, XLIV (Summer, 1974), 63.

8. Lucas, "The Church and the City," 65-66.

9. Quoted in Karl A. Olsson, _By One Spirit_ (Chicago: Covenant Press, 1962) p. 271.

10. Contributions to the Ecclesiastical History of Connecticut, Vol. II (n.p., Connecticut Conference of the United Church of Christ, 1967), p. 324; P. Waldenström, Genom Norra Amerikas Förenta Stater (Stockholm: Pietistens Expedition, 1890), p. 142.

11. The Tabernacle Church included immigrants from the British Isles, Norway, Sweden, Denmark, Finland, Germany, The Netherlands, Switzerland, Iceland, France, and Italy; see Winfred Rhoades, Frederick Ernest Emrich (Boston: The Pilgrim Press, 1933), pp. 25-26.

12. William M. Taylor, Not Ashamed of the Gospel (New York: American Home Missionary Society, 1881), p. 15.

13. General Congregational Association of Illinois Minutes, 1894, p. 83.

14. General Congregational Association of Illinois Minutes, 1894, pp. 83-84.

15. Amherst College Biographical Record of the Graduates and Non-Graduates (Amherst, Massachusetts: Amherst College, 1927), p. 268.

16. Edward Hitchcock, Reminiscences of Amherst College (Northampton, Massachusetts: Bridgman and Childs, 1863) pp. 190-93.

17. General Congregational Association of Illinois Minutes, 1894, p. 84.

18. Yale Obituary Record, 1894, p. 268.

19. *Kansas General Association Minutes*, 1879, pp. 19, 42.

20. M. E. Eversz, "The Late Superintendent Montgomery," *The Home Missionary*, May, 1894.

21. *The Pilgrim*, September, 1883.

22. *The Pilgrim*, April, 1886.

23. *The Pilgrim*, June, 1886.

24. *The Pilgrim*, May, 1886.

25. *Minnesota General Association Minutes*, 1882, p. 14.

26. *The Pilgrim*, October, 1882.

27. *Minnesota General Association Minutes*, 1882, pp. 16-17.

28. *The Pilgrim*, June, 1882.

29. *The Pilgrim*, September, 1883.

30. *The Pilgrim*, February, 1884.

31. Marcus Whitman Montgomery, *A Wind from the Holy Spirit in Sweden and Norway* (New York: American Home Missionary Society, 1885), pp. 3-5.

32. Montgomery, *A Wind from the Holy Spirit in Sweden and Norway*, p. 15.

33. Montgomery, _A Wind from the Holy Spirit in Sweden and Norway_, pp. 17-18.

34. Montgomery, _A Wind from the Holy Spirit in Sweden and Norway_, p. 18.

35. Montgomery, _A Wind from the Holy Spirit in Sweden and Norway_, pp. 15-16.

36. Montgomery, _A Wind from the Holy Spirit in Sweden and Norway_, p. 19.

37. Montgomery, _A Wind from the Holy Spirit in Sweden and Norway_, p. 22.

38. Montgomery, _A Wind from the Holy Spirit in Sweden and Norway_, p. 34.

39. _Minnesota General Association Minutes_, 1882, 1883.

40. _Congregational Year-Book_, 1885, p. 177.

41. Montgomery, _A Wind from the Holy Spirit in Sweden and Norway_, p. 33.

42. Montgomery, _A Wind from the Holy Spirit in Sweden and Norway_, p. 21.

43. Montgomery, _A Wind from the Holy Spirit in Sweden and Norway_, p. 24.

44. _Morgenrøden_, June 15, 1884.

45. John R. Bodo, <u>The Protestant Clergy and Public Issues, 1812-1848</u> (Princeton: Princeton University Press, 1954), pp. 37-39.

46. Montgomery, <u>A Wind from the Holy Spirit in Sweden and Norway</u>, p. 23.

47. A. H. Darling, <u>An Account of the Spiritual State of Norway</u> (London: Yapp and Hawkins, 1874), p. 40.

48. Darling, <u>An Account of the Spiritual State of Norway</u>, pp. 30-40.

49. <u>The Pilgrim</u>, July, 1884.

50. Marcus Whitman Montgomery, "The Free Church Movement in Sweden," <u>The Andover Review</u>, II (October, 1884), 411.

51. Montgomery, <u>A Wind from the Holy Spirit in Sweden and Norway</u>, p. 33.

52. Montgomery, <u>A Wind from the Holy Spirit in Sweden and Norway</u>, p. 34.

53. Montgomery, <u>A Wind from the Holy Spirit in Sweden and Norway</u>, p. 89.

54. Abell, <u>The Urban Impact upon American Protestantism</u>, p. 182.

55. Montgomery, <u>A Wind from the Holy Spirit in Sweden and Norway</u>, p. 111.

56. C. V. Bowman, <u>The Mission Covenant of America</u> (Chicago: The Covenant Book Concern, 1925), p. 162.

57. Olsson, _By One Spirit_, p. 316.

58. Olsson, _By One Spirit_, p. 335.

59. Olsson, _By One Spirit_, pp. 272-73.

60. Robert M. Anderson, "An Analysis of Congregational Aid to Scandinavian Churches"(unpublished Bachelor of Divinity thesis, North Park Theological Seminary, 1960), p. 39.

61. P. Richard Lindstrom, "The Risberg School" (unpublished Bachelor of Divinity thesis, North Park Theological Seminary, 1966), pp. 74-75.

62. _The Pilgrim_, January, 1886.

63. Montgomery, _A Wind from the Holy Spirit in Sweden and Norway_, p. 6.

64. _The Pilgrim_, October, 1885.

65. _The Pilgrim_, October, 1886.

66. _The Home Missionary_, January, 1889.

67. _The Pilgrim_, October, 1886.

68. _The Pilgrim_, January, 1885.

69. See especially Miller's _Orthodoxy in Massachusetts, 1630-1650_ (Cambridge, Massachusetts: Harvard University Press, 1933).

REFERENCE NOTES

Chapter X

1. *Supra*, pp. 234-36.

2. M. W. Montgomery, *The Work among the Scandinavians* (New York: American Home Missionary Society, 1888), p. 18.

3. P. C. Trandberg, *Afskeden og dens Grunde* (Chicago: Luther Society's Trykkeri, 1890), pp. 9-10.

4. Trandberg, *Afskeden og dens Grunde*, p. 10.

5. Trandberg, *Afskeden og dens Grunde*, p. 5.

6. Trandberg, *Afskeden og dens Grunde*, p. 10.

7. Anonymous at Chicago Theological Seminary, October 21, 1889, to M. W. Montgomery, in Chicago Theological Seminary archives.

8. Samuel Ives Curtiss, February 6, 1890, to Peter Christian Trandberg, in Chicago Theological Seminary archives.

9. Trandberg, *Afskeden og dens Grunde*, p. 6.

10. Trandberg, *Afskeden og dens Grunde*, pp. 19-20, 22.

11. *Missions-Vännen*, November 13, 1889.

12. *Minutes of the National Council*, 1889, pp. 175-76.

13. *Minutes of the National Council*, 1889, p. 276.

14. *Missions-Vännen*, December 4, 1889.

15. *Missions-Vännen*, January 29, 1890.

16. *Missions-Vännen*, February 12, 1890.

17. For a brief and relatively sympathetic treatment of Mellander, see A. Milton Freedholm, "Axel Mellander," *The Covenant Quarterly*, XXIV (1966), 19-27.

18. In a eulogy to Mellander, David Nyvall wrote that he "was a genuine denominational man, who saw questions first and last from the point of view of the denomination, at the same time that he was a man of conscience who firmly held to what he believed was right;" see *Missions-Vännen*, December 5, 1922.

19. To Mellander, dancing was anathema. While a pastor in Massachusetts during the 1880's he had actively opposed dancing by Swedish youth. See Freedholm, "Axel Mellander," 21.

20. *Missions-Vännen*, January 22, 1890.

21. *Missions-Vännen*, January 1, 1890.

22. Joseph B. Clark to M. W. Montgomery, in *Letter Books of the American Home Missionary Society*, 1889-1890, III, No. 8260, quoted in Robert M. Anderson, "An Analysis of Congregational Aid to Scandinavian Churches" (unpublished Bachelor of Divinity thesis, North Park Theological Seminary, 1960), p. 35.

23. /M. W. Montgomery, ed./, Frukterna (New York: American Home Missionary Society,/1890/), pp. 6-7.

24. Frukterna, p. 16.

25. Frukterna, p. 7.

26. Frukterna, p. 10.

27. Frukterna, p. 15.

28. P. Waldenström, Genom Norra Amerikas Förenta Stater (Stockholm: Pietistens Expedition, 1890), p. 309.

29. P. Waldenström, Nya färder i Amerikas Förenta Stater (Stockholm: Aktiebolaget Normans Förlag, 1902), p. 197.

30. Waldenström, Nya färder i Amerikas Förenta Stater, pp. 199, 202.

31. Waldenström, Genom Norra Amerikas Förenta Stater, p. 266.

32. Waldenström, Genom Norra Amerikas Förenta Stater, p. 558. See also Karl A. Olsson, By One Spirit (Chicago: Covenant Press, 1962), p. 159.

33. Frukterna, p. 18.

34. Chicago-Bladet, October 13, 1891.

35. Chicago-Bladet, February 13, 1894.

36. Evangelisten, November 15, 1890; June 1, 1890.

37. Evangelisten, October 20, 1895.

38. Evangelisten, September 10, 1895.

39. "Statement of Doctrine," May 16, 1886, in Gilbert MSS, Chicago Theological Seminary archives.

40. G. H. Gilbert, "Biblical Theology: Its History and Its Mission," The Biblical World, VI (November, 1895), 361.

41. G. H. Gilbert, "The Apostles' Creed According to the Teachings of Jesus," The Biblical World, XII (September, 1898), 160.

42. Advance, January 26, 1899.

43. Advance, February 2, 1899.

44. Robert William Tully, "The 'Heresy' of George Holley Gilbert" (unpublished Bachelor of Divinity thesis, Chicago Theological Seminary, 1955), pp. 56, 64.

45. Chicago-Bladet, October 31, 1899.

46. The Northwestern Congregationalist, January 15, 1900.

47. A. Mellander, Betänkande i Kongregationalistfrågan (Chicago: Missionärens Tryckeri, 1900), pp. 9-12, 16, 22.

48. Nya Österns Veckoblad, December 21, 1898.

49. Chicago-Bladet, October 31, 1899.

50. P. Richard Lindström, "The Risberg School" (unpublished Bachelor of Divinity thesis, North Park Theological Seminary, 1966), pp. 138-40.

51. Tully, "The 'Heresy' of George Holley Gilbert," pp. 65-66.

52. H. M. Scott and Samuel Ives Curtiss, February 11, 1902, to Rev. D. Nyvall, in Chicago Theological Seminary archives.

53. H. M. Scott, April 26, 1907, to E. G. Hjerpe, in Chicago Theological Seminary archives.

54. _Missions-Vännen_, May 8, 1889.

REFERENCE NOTES

Chapter XI

1. *Missions-Vännen*, November 19, 1884; November 26, 1884; December 3, 1884.

2. *Missions-Vännen*, January 21, 1885.

3. *Chicago-Bladet*, January 21, 1885.

4. *Supra*, p. 125.

5. *Chicago-Bladet*, August 9, 1881.

6. *Chicago-Bladet*, May 16, 1893.

7. *Chicago-Bladet*, July 16, 1895; July 23, 1895.

8. *Chicago-Bladet*, July 11, 1899.

9. *Chicago-Bladet*, May 4, 1897.

10. *Chicago-Bladet*, December 3, 1901.

11. P. Waldenström, *Genom Norra Amerikas Förenta Stater* (Stockholm: Pietistens Expedition, 1890), pp. 591-92.

12. *Missions-Vännen*, August 21, 1889.

13. *Supra*, pp. 154-56.

14. *Missions-Vännen*, October 18, 1898; July 4, 1899; July 11, 1899; July 18, 1899.

15. *Supra*, p. 252.

16. *Supra*, pp. 157-59.

17. *Missions-Vännen*, July 7, 1902; July 14, 1902.

18. *Evangelisten*, June 8, 1893.

19. *Evangelisten*, April 20, 1895.

20. *Evangelisten*, July 4, 1900.

21. *Evangelisten*, July 11, 1900.

22. *The Year Book of the Congregational Christian Churches of the United States of America*, 1942, p. 46.

23. *Evangelisten*, March 13, 1901.

24. *Missions-Vännen*, April 8, 1885.

25. *Missions-Vännen*, May 21, 1890.

26. *Missions-Vännen*, May 27, 1891.

27. *Missions-Vännen*, February 24, 1892.

28. *Chicago-Bladet*, March 1, 1892.

29. *Chicago-Bladet*, January 16, 1894.

30. Chicago-Bladet, August 16, 1892.

31. Chicago-Bladet, April 10, 1894.

32. Chicago-Bladet, July 28, 1891.

33. Chicago-Bladet, September 24, 1895; October 1, 1895; August 25, 1896.

34. Supra, pp. 115-16.

35. See, for example, Chicago-Bladet, May 12, 1891 and July 5, 1892.

36. Supra, pp. 176-78.

37. Chicago-Bladet, July 15, 1902.

38. Supra, pp. 161-76.

39. Evangelisten, July 1, 1890.

40. Evangelisten, July 23, 1891.

41. Evangelisten, July 30, 1891.

42. Evangelisten, October 19, 1893.

43. Evangelisten, September 15, 1894.

44. Evangelisten, January 3, 1900.

45. Evangelisten, January 10, 1900.

46. Evangelisten, January 30, 1901.

REFERENCE NOTES

Chapter XII

1. Karl Olsson, "Similarities and Differences in the Churches of the Federation -- America," in *Report of the Theological Conference of the Free Evangelical Churches, August 29 - September 4, 1971*, pp. 13-14.

BIBLIOGRAPHY

Articles

Bakken, Grete Tufte. "M. J. Færden: Bibelkritikkens foregangsmann i vårt land," Norsk teologisk tidsskrift, LXVIII (1967), 65-90.

Beck, Robert N. "Brief History of the Swedes in Worcester," Swedish Pioneer Historical Quarterly, X (July, 1959), 105-16.

Bergendoff, Conrad. "The Swedish Immigrant and the American Way," Swedish Pioneer Historical Quarterly, XIX (July, 1968), 143-57.

Bjork, Kenneth O. "A Covenant Folk with Scandinavian Colorings," Norwegian-American Studies, XXI (1962), 212-51.

Buhl, Frants. "Naar er femte Mosebog affattet?" Theologisk Tidskrift for den danske Folkekirke, (1878), 129-68, 193-227.

Buhl, Frants. "Den nye Pentateuchkritiks Ret og Uret," Theologisk Tidskrift for den danske Folkekirke, II (1885), 256-82 and III (1886), 250-77.

Eklund, Emmet. "Swedish Lutheran Congregations of the Boston Area: 1867-1930," Swedish Pioneer Historical Quarterly, XVI (April, 1965), 56-75.

Fevold, Eugene L. "The Norwegian Immigrant and His Church," Norwegian-American Studies, XXIII (1967), 3-16.

Freedholm, A. Milton. "Axel Mellander," The Covenant Quarterly, XXIV (1966), 19-27.

Goen, C. C. "Jonathan Edwards, A New Departure in Eschatology," Church History, XXVIII (1959), 25-40.

Hovde, Brynjolf J., trans. and ed. "Chicago as Viewed by a Norwegian Immigrant in 1864," Norwegian-American Studies and Records, III (1928), 65-72.

Lund, Doniver A. "Educational Experience in America: Immigrant and Native-Born," Swedish Pioneer Historical Quarterly, XVIII (January, 1967), 13-31.

Marsden, George. "Defining Fundamentalism," Christian Scholar's Review, I (Winter, 1971), 141-51.

Marti, Donald B. "The Puritan Tradition in a 'New England of the West,'" Minnesota History, XL (Spring, 1966), 1-11.

Montgomery, M. W. "Mormonismens Vederstyggeligheder afsløreede," Den indre Missions Tidende, XXXV (August 5, 1888), 497-507; (August 12, 1888), 513-22); (August 19, 1888), 533-39.

Norseen, Oscar G. "The First Swedes to Locate in Worcester, Massachusetts," Swedish Pioneer Historical Quarterly, IV (October, 1953), 11-16.

Peterson, Bernard. "Swedish Pioneers in the Greater Boston Area," Swedish Pioneer Historical Quarterly, II (Summer, 1951), 15-23.

Preus, J. C. K. "From Norwegian State Church to American Free Church," Norwegian-American Studies, XXV (1972), 186-224.

Sandeen, Ernest R. "Defining Fundamentalism: A Reply to Professor Marsden," Christian Scholar's Review, I (Spring, 1971), 227-32.

Westin, Gunnar. "Emigration and Scandinavian Church Life," Swedish Pioneer Historical Quarterly, VIII (April, 1957), 35-49.

Books

Aarflot, Andreas. Norsk kirkehistorie. Vol. II. Oslo: Lutherstiftelsens Forlag, 1967.

Abell, Aaron I. The Urban Impact on American Protestantism, 1865-1900. Cambridge, Massachusetts: Harvard University Press, 1943.

Amherst College Biographical Record of Graduates and Non-Graduates. Amherst, Massachusetts: Amherst College, 1927.

Ander, Oscar Fritiof. T. N. Hasselquist. The Career and Influence of a Swedish-American Clergyman, Journalist, and Educator. Rock Island, Illinois: Augustana Historical Society, 1931.

Arden, G. Everett. Augustana Heritage: A History of the Augustana Lutheran Church. Rock Island, Illinois: Augustana Press, 1963.

Balling, J. F. and Lindhardt, P. G. Den nordiske kirkes historie. 3rd ed. Copenhagen: Nyt Nordisk Forlag, 1973.

Baxter, Michael. Coming Wonders Expected between 1867 and 1875. Philadelphia: J. S. Claxton, 1867.

Baxter, Michael. Firti kommende Undere i de 10-12 Aar. Christiania: G. Hüberts Forlag, 1887.

Baxter, Michael. Louis Napoleon, the Destined Monarch of the World and Personal Antichrist. Philadelphia: J. S. Claxton, 1867.

Beck, Vilhelm. Erindringer fra mit Liv. København: Kirkelig Forening for Indre Mission, 1902.

Beck, Vilhelm. Memoirs. Philadelphia: Fortress Press, 1965.

Beck, Vilhelm. Til Minde om Pastor Ipsen. København: Missionstrykkeriet, 1897.

Bergmann, Leola Nelson. Americans from Norway. Philadelphia: J. B. Lippincott Company, 1950.

Blegen, Theodore C. Norwegian Migration to America. Vol. I: 1825-1860. Vol. II: The American Transition. Northfield, Minnesota: The Norwegian-American Historical Association, 1931, 1940.

Bjork, Kenneth O. West of the Great Divide. Northfield, Minnesota: The Norwegian-American Historical Association, 1958.

Bodo, John R. The Protestant Clergy and Public Issues, 1812-1848. Princeton: Princeton University Press, 1954.

Bowman, C. V. The Mission Covenant of America. Chicago: The Covenant Book Concern, 1925.

Bredberg, William. P. P. Waldenströms verksamhet till 1878. Stockholm: Missionsförbundets Forlag, 1948.

Bredberg, William and Lövgren, Oscar, eds. Genom Guds nåd. Svenska Missionsförbundet under 75 år. Stockholm: Svenska Missionsförbundets Förlag, 1953.

Christensen, John. Verdensmisjonæren Fredrik Franson. Oslo: Det Norske Misjonsforbunds Forlag, 1927.

Contributions to the Ecclesiastical History of Connecticut. Vol. II. n.p., Connecticut Conference of the United Church of Christ, 1967.

Darling, A. H. An Account of the Spiritual State of Norway. London: Yapp and Hawkins, 1874.

Diesen, Ingulf. Fem foredrag om Det Norske Misjonsforbund. Oslo: Det Norske Misjonsforbunds Teologiske Seminar, 1975.

Diesen, Ingulf. Det Norske Misjonsforbunds historie. Oslo: Det Norske Misjonsforbunds Teologiske Seminar, 1971.

Dimbleby, Jabez Bunting. The Appointed Time. London: E. Nister, 1895.

Dimbleby, Jabez Bunting. Den bestemte tid. Faribault, Minnesota: O. A. Østbys forlag, 1896.

Dimbleby, Jabez Bunting. Den bestämte tiden. Minneapolis: Sanning och friheds förlag, 1897.

Dimbleby, Jabez Bunting. The Bible's Astronomical Chronology Evolution and the Higher Criticism. Glasgow: David Bryce & Son, 1905.

Dimbleby, Jabez Bunting. The New Era at Hand. 3rd ed. revised. London: Book Society, 1893.

Dimbleby, Jabez Bunting. En ny tid er nær! Faribault, Minnesota: O. A. Østbys forlag, 1895; Laurvik: M. Andersens Forlag, 1894.

Dimbleby, Jabez Bunting. En ny tid är nära! Stockholm: P. A. Bokförlag, 1893.

Dimbleby, Jabez Bunting. Signs of the Second Advent and the New Era Begun. 15th ed. London: E. Nister, 1898.

Dowie, J. Iverne and Esperlie, Ernest M., eds. The Swedish Immigrant Community in Transition. Rock Island, Illinois: Augustana Historical Society, 1963.

Eeg-Olofsson, Leif. Olle i Kroken. Olof Olofsson, förkunnare och frikyrkooriginal. Stockholm: Svenska Missions-förbundet, 1957.

Ekman, E. J. Den inre missionens historia. 5 vols. Stockholm: E. J. Ekmans Förlagsexpedition, 1896-1902.

Ferm, Vergilius. The Crisis in American Lutheran Theology. New York: The Century Co., 1927.

Findlay, James F. Dwight L. Moody: American Evangelist, 1837-1899. Chicago: University of Chicago Press, 1969.

Franson, F. Bibelns lära om Antikrist. Hedemora: A. F. Lidmans boktryckeri, 1886.

Franson, Fredrik. Himlauret eller det profetiska ordet. Chicago: Chicago-Bladets Förlag, 1898.

Franson, Fredrik. Kort öfwersikt öfwer Uppenbarelseboken. Kristinehamn: F. Broström & Kini, 1882.

Franson, Fredrik, ed. Utforligt referat öfwer forhandlingarna wid den för de profetiska ämnenas studier afsedda konferensen i Chicago. Kristinehamn: F. Broström & Kini, 1882.

Froom, LeRoy Edwin. The Prophetic Faith of Our Fathers. 4 vols. Washington, D. C.: Review and Herald, 1946-54.

Från skilda tider. Studier tillägnade Hjalmar Holmquist. Stockholm: Svenska Kyrkans Diakonistyrelses Bokförlag, 1938.

Furniss, Norman. The Fundamentalist Controversy, 1918-1931. New Haven: Yale University Press, 1954.

Gaustad, Edwin Scott, ed. The Rise of Adventism. New York: Harper and Row, 1974.

Gilbert, George H. The Student's Life of Jesus. Chicago: Press of Chicago Theological Seminary, 1896.

Goodykoontz, Colin B. Home Missions on the American Frontier. Caldwell, Idaho: The Caxton Printers, Ltd., 1939.

Guinness, H. Grattan. Från ljus till ljus. Stockholm: P. Palmquist, 1883.

Guinness, H. Grattan. Ljus för den sista tiden! Stockholm: P. A. Huldbergs Bokförlag, 1895.

Guinness, H. Grattan. Lys for de sidste Dage. Kristiania: G. Hüberts Forlag, 1888.

Guinness, H. Grattan. Lys for den sidste Tid. Rønne: Chr. Møller, 1896.

Gunnarson, Thorstein. Dommedagsventing. Millennismen og dens innslag i norsk Kristendom. Bergen: A/A Lunde & Co.s Forlag, 1928.

Gustafsson, Berndt. Svensk kyrkohistoria. Stockholm: AB Tryckmans, 1973.

Harms, Theodor. De sidste Ting. Chicago: J. T. Relling & Co., 1882, 1889.

Hitchcock, Edward. Reminiscences of Amherst College. Northampton, Massachusetts: Bridgman and Childs, 1863.

Holm, Andreas, ed. Den norske evangelisk lutherske frikirke gjennom 75 år. Oslo: EKB Boktrykkeri, 1952.

Hudson, Winthrop. Religion in America. 2nd. ed. revised. New York: Charles Scribner's Sons, 1973.

Hutchison, William R. The Transcendentalist Ministers. New Haven: Yale University Press, 1959.

Hvidt, Kristian. Flugten til Amerika. Aarhus: Universitetsforlaget i Aarhus, 1971.

Ipsen, O. C. De Helliges Taalmodighed og Tro. København: Kirkelig Forening for den indre Mission, 1884.

Janson, Florence Edith. The Background of Swedish Immigration. Chicago: University of Chicago Press, 1931.

Jernberg, Reinert August. A Nation in the Loom. The Scandinavian Fibre in Our Social Fabric. Chicago: P. F. Pettibone & Co., 1895.

Keijer, Augustinus, ed. Evangelicals, American and European. Stockholm: The International Federation of Free Evangelical Churches, 1966.

Keith, James. Egyptens store Pyramid. Kristiania: G. Hüberts Forlag, 1887.

Kerr, Hugh T., ed. A Compend of Luther's Theology. Philadelphia: The Westminster Press, 1943.

Knudsen, Johannes. Frikirkedannelse. Træk af Amerikas kirkehistorie. Kolding: Konrad Jørgensens Bogtrykkeri, 1965.

Kofod, Karl M. P. C. Trandberg. København: O. Lohse, 1925.

Larsen, Emil. Historiske studier over kirkelige og frikirkelige brydninger. København: Tro og Liv, 1965.

Larsen, Emil. Urovækkeren Mogens Abraham Sommer. København: G. E. C. Gads Forlag, 1963.

Lindberg, John S. The Background of Swedish Emigration to the United States. Minneapolis: University of Minnesota Press, 1930.

Lindén, Ingemar. Biblicism Apokalyptik Utopi. Uppsala: Acta Universitatis Upsaliensis, 1971.

Linderholm, Emanuel. Pingströrelsen i Sverige. Stockholm: Albert Bonniers Förlag, 1925.

Lindhardt, P. G. Den danske kirkes historie. Vol VII. København: Gyldendaksle Boghandel, 1958.

Lövgren, Oscar. Oscar Ahnfelt. Stockholm: Svenska Missionsförbundets Förlag, 1932.

McGiffert, Arthur Cushman, Jr. No Ivory Tower. Chicago: The Chicago Theological Seminary, 1965.

Mellander, Axel. Betänkande i Kongregationalist-frågan. Chicago: Missionärens Tryckeri, 1900.

Miller, Perry. Orthodoxy in Massachusetts, 1630-1650. Cambridge, Massachusetts: Harvard University Press, 1933.

Molland, Einar. Fra Hans Nielsen Hauge til Eivind Berggrav. 3rd ed. revised. Oslo: Gyldendal Norsk Forlag, 1972.

[Montgomery, M. W., ed.] Frukterna. New York: American Home Missionary Society, [1890].

Montgomery, Marcus Whitman. A Wind from the Holy Spirit in Sweden and Norway. New York: American Home Missionary Society, 1885.

Montgomery, M. W. The Work among the Scandinavians. New York: American Home Missionary Society, 1888.

Mulder, William. Homeward to Zion. Minneapolis: University of Minnesota Press, 1957.

Myrberg, O. F. Johannis Uppenbarelse med ledning af Gamla Testamentets profetia och verlds- och kyrkohistorien förklarad. Stockholm: Z. Hæggströms Förlag, 1888.

Needham, George, ed. Prophetic Studies of the International Prophetic Conference. Chicago: Fleming H. Revell, 1886.

Neiiendam, Michael. Frikirker og Sekter. 3rd ed. København: G. E. C. Gads Forlag, 1948.

Neiiendam, Michael. Frikirker og Sekter. 4th ed. revised. København: G. E. C. Gads Forlag, 1958.

Neill, Stephen. The Interpretation of the New Testament, 1861-1961. London: Oxford University Press, 1964.

Nelson, A. P. Puritanernas och Pilgrimernas historia. Boston: The Pilgrim Press, 1901.

Nelson, A. P. Svenska Missionsvännernas historia i Amerika. Minneapolis: published by the author, 1906.

Nelson, E. Clifford and Fevold, Eugene L. The Lutheran Church among Norwegian-Americans. Vol. I. Minneapolis: Augsburg Publishing House, 1959.

Norton, H. Wilbert, et al. The Diamond Jubilee Story of the Evangelical Free Church of America. Minneapolis: Free Church Publications, 1959.

Nyhlén, Erik. Svensk frikyrka. Stockholm: Bokförlaget Prisma, 1964.

Nyvall, C. J. Travel Memories from America. Chicago: Covenant Press, 1959.

Nyvall, David. My Father's Testament. Chicago: Covenant Press, 1974.

Odegaard, R. Arlo. With Singleness of Heart. Minneapolis: Free Church Press, n. d.

Olsson, Karl A. By One Spirit. Chicago: Covenant Press, 1962.

Pedersen, Johannes. Den danske kirkes historie. Vol. V. København: Gyldendalske Boghandel, 1951.

Princell, Josephine, ed. J. G. Princells levnadsminnen. Chicago: J. V. Martensons Tryckeri, 1916.

Qualey, Carlton C. Norwegian Settlement in the United States. Northfield, Minnesota: The Norwegian-American Historical Association, 1938.

Rasmussen, Helge, ed. En dansk vækkelsesbevægelse. København: Missionsforbundets Forlag, 1963.

Reinertsen, Aanen. En kort Afhandling om det tusindaarige Rige og dens 1ste Opstandelses Hemmelighed. Kragerø: n.d., n. publ.

Rhoades, Winfred. Frederick Ernest Emrich. Boston: Pilgrim Press, 1933.

Rudvin, Ola. Indremisjonsselskapets Historie. Vol. I. Oslo: Lutherstiftelsens Forlag, 1967.

Rygnestad, Knut. Dissentarspørsmålet i Noreg frå 1845 til 1891. Oslo: Lutherstiftelsens Forlag, 1955.

Sandeen, Ernest R. The Roots of Fundamentalism: British and American Millenarianism, 1800-1930. Chicago: University of Chicago Press, 1970.

Schindler, Peter, ed. Efterladte Papirer af Martin Schneekloth 1844-1871. København: Nyt nordisk forlag, 1942.

Schmidt, Jørgen W. Oh, Du Zion i Vest. København: Rosenkilde og Bagger, 1965.

Schmucker, Samuel S. The American Lutheran Church, Historically, Doctrinally, and Practically Delineated, in Several Occasional Discourses. 5th ed. Philadelphia: E. W. Miller, 1852.

Schweitzer, Albert. Geschichte der Leben-Jesu-Forschung. Tübingen: J. C. B. Mohr, 1913.

Semmingsen, Ingrid. Veien mot vest: Utvandringen fra Norge til Amerika. 2 vols. Oslo: H. Aschehoug & Co., 1942, 1950.

Stephenson, George. The Religious Aspects of Swedish Immigration. Minneapolis: University of Minnesota Press, 1932.

Spinka, Matthew, ed. A History of Illinois Congregational and Christian Churches. Chicago: The Congregational and Christian Conference of Illinois, 1944.

Swanson, John F. A Missionary Statesman. Chicago: The Scandinavian Alliance Mission of North America, 1945.

Taylor, William M. Not Ashamed of the Gospel. New York: American Home Missionary Society, 1881.

Totten, C. A. L. Det tusenåriga riket och begynnelsen till en ny tid. Stockholm: P. A. Huldbergs Förlag, 1893.

Trandberg, Peter Christian. En aaben Erklæring. Chicago: R. Egebergh Bogtrykkeri, 1889.

Trandberg, Peter Christian. Afskeden og dens Grunde. Chicago: Luther Society's Trykkeri, 1890.

Trandberg, Peter Christian. Deliverance from Babylon and Its Foreshadowings. Chicago: N. O. Moore, Printer, 1888.

Trandberg, Peter Christian. Hvad jeg vil. Chicago: C. Rasmussens Trykkeri, 1886.

Valton, Fridtjof. De norske vekkelsers historia. Oslo: Filadelfiaforlaget, 1942.

Walan, Bror. Fernholm och frikyrkan. Stockholm: Gummessons Bokförlag, 1962.

Walan, Bror. Församlingstanken i Svenska Missionsförbundet. Stockholm: Gummessons Bokförlag, 1964.

Waldenström, P. Biblisk troslära. 2nd ed. Stockholm: Svenska Missionsförbundets Förlag, 1915.

Waldenström, P. Genom Norra Amerikas Förenta Stater. Stockholm: Pietistens Expedition, 1890.

Waldenström, Paul. Låt oss behålla vår gamla bibel. Stockholm: Aktiebolaget Normans Förlag, 1902.

Waldenström, P. Nya färder i Amerikas Förenta Stater. Stockholm: Aktiebolaget Normans Forlag, 1902.

Waldenström, P. and Tegnér, E. Bibelkommissionens öfversättning af gamla testamentet. Stockholm: Aktiebolaget Normans Förlag, 1902.

Welch, Claude. Protestant Thought in the Nineteenth Century. Vol. I. New Haven: Yale University Press, 1972.

Westin, Gunnar, ed. Emigranterna och kyrkan. Stockholm: Svenska Kyrkans Diakonistyrelses Bokförlag, 1932.

Westin, Gunnar. George Scott och hans verksamhet i Sverige. Stockholm: Svenska Kyrkans Diakonistyrelses Bokförlag, 1938.

Wettergreen, Paul. Opbyggelige foredrag over Johannes's Aabenbaring. Arendal: Chr. Christensen, 1883.

Wisløff, Carl Fredrik. Norsk kirkehistorie. Vol. III. Oslo: Lutherstiftelsens Forlag, 1971.

Øystese, Ole, ed. Bibelsyn og Bibelgransking. Stavanger: Nomi Forlag, 1966.

Unpublished Research

Anderson, Robert M. "An Analysis of Congregational Aid to Scandinavian Churches." Unpublished Bachelor of Divinity thesis, North Park Theological Seminary, 1960.

Diesen, Tor Ingulf. "The Background and Development of the Free Church Movement in Norway." Unpublished Bachelor of Divinity thesis, Trinity Seminary and Bible College, 1957.

Hale, Frederick Allen. "The Scandinavian Departments of Chicago Theological Seminary." Unpublished Master of Arts thesis, University of Minnesota, 1974.

Lindstrom, P. Richard. "The Risberg School." Unpublished Bachelor of Divinity thesis, North Park Theological Seminary, 1966.

Ohrman, William. "Bibeltillämpning och bibeluppfattning inom Svenska Missionsförbundet 1883-1897 med särskild hänsyn till P. P. Waldenström." Unpublished licentiate thesis, University of Uppsala, 1972.

Tully, Robert William. "The 'Heresy' of George Holley Gilbert." Unpublished Bachelor of Divinity thesis, Chicago Theological Seminary, 1955.

Report

Report of the Theological Conference of The International Federation of Free Evangelical Churches. 1971.

SCANDINAVIANS IN AMERICA

An Arno Press Collection

Ander, O. Fritiof. **The Cultural Heritage of the Swedish Immigrant:** Selected References. [1956]

Ander, Oscar Fritiof. **T.N. Hasselquist:** The Career and Influence of a Swedish American Clergyman, Journalist and Editor. 1931

Barton, H. Arnold, editor. **Clipper Ship and Covered Wagon:** Essays From the *Swedish Pioneer Historical Quarterly*. 1979

Blegen, Theodore C. and Martin B. Ruud, editors and translators. **Norwegian Emigrant Songs and Ballads.** Songs harmonized by Gunnar J. Maimin. 1936

Christensen, Thomas Peter. **A History of the Danes in Iowa.** 1952

Duus, Olaus Fredrik. **Frontier Parsonage:** The Letters of Olaus Fredrik Duus, Norwegian Pastor in Wisconsin, 1855-1858. Translated by the Verdandi Study Club of Minneapolis. Edited by Theodore C. Blegen. 1947

Erickson, E. Walfred. **Swedish-American Periodicals:** A Selective Bibliography. 1979

Gjerset, Knut. **Norwegian Sailors in American Waters:** A Study in the History of Maritime Activity on the Eastern Seaboard. 1933

Gjerset, Knut. **Norwegian Sailors on the Great Lakes:** A Study in the History of American Inland Transportation. 1928

Hale, Frederick. **Trans-Atlantic Conservative Protestantism in the Evangelical Free and Mission Covenant Traditions** (Doctoral Thesis, The Johns Hopkins University, 1976, Revised Edition). 1979

Hogland, A. William. **Finnish Immigrants in America:** 1880-1920. 1960

Hokanson, Nels. **Swedish Immigrants in Lincoln's Time.** With a Foreword by Carl Sandberg. 1942

Hummasti, Paul George. **Finnish Radicals in Astoria, Oregon, 1904-1940:** A Study in Immigrant Socialism (Doctoral Dissertation, University of Oregon, 1975, Revised Edition). 1979

Hustvedt, Lloyd. **Rasmus Bjørn Anderson:** Pioneer Scholar. 1966

Jenson, Andrew. **History of the Scandinavian Mission.** 1927

Kolehmainen, John I. **Sow the Golden Seed:** A History of the Fitchburg (Massachusetts) Finnish American Newspaper, Raivaaja, (The Pioneer), 1905-1955. 1955

Kolehmainen, John I. and George W. Hill. **Haven in the Woods:** The Story of the Finns in Wisconsin. 1965

Koren, Elisabeth. **The Diary of Elisabeth Koren:** 1853-1855. Translated and Edited by David T. Nelson. 1955

Larson, Esther Elisabeth. **Swedish Commentators on America, 1638-1865:** An Annotated List of Selected Manuscript and Printed Materials. 1963

Lindeström, Peter. **Geographia Americae With An Account of the Delaware Indians.** 1925

Marzolf, Marion Tuttle. **The Danish Language Press in America** (Doctoral Dissertation, the University of Michigan, 1972). 1979

McKnight, Roger. **Moberg's Emigrant Novels and the *Journals* of Andrew Peterson:** A Study of Influences and Parallels (Doctoral Thesis, the University of Minnesota, 1974). 1979

Mattson, Hans. **Reminiscences:** The Story of an Immigrant. 1891

Mortenson, Enok. **Danish-American Life and Letters:** A Bibliography. 1945

Nelson, Helge. **The Swedes and the Swedish Settlements in North America.** 1943. 2 vols. in 1

Nielson, Alfred C. **Life in an American Denmark.** 1962

Olson, Ernst W., Anders Schon and Martin J. Engberg, editors. **History of the Swedes of Illinois.** 1908. 2 vols.

Puotinen, Arthur Edwin. **Finnish Radicals and Religion in Midwestern Mining Towns,** 1865-1914 (Doctoral Dissertation, the University of Chicago, 1973). 1979

Raaen, Aagot. **Grass of the Earth:** Immigrant Life in the Dakota Country. 1950

Scott, Franklin D. **Trans-Atlantica:** Essays on Scandinavian Migration and Culture. 1979

Strombeck, Rita. **Leonard Strömberg—A Swedish-American Writer** (Doctoral Thesis, the University of Chicago, 1975, Revised Edition). 1979

Svendsen, Gro. **Frontier Mother:** The Letters of Gro Svendsen. Translated and edited by Pauline Farseth and Theodore C. Blegen. 1950

Vogel-Jorgensen, T[homas]. **Peter Lassen Af California.** 1937

Waerenskjold, Elise. **The Lady with the Pen:** Elise Waerenskjold in Texas. Edited by C.A. Clausen with a foreword by Theodore C. Blegen. 1961

Weintraub, Hyman. **Andrew Furuseth:** Emancipator of the Seamen. 1959

Winther, Sophus Keith. **Mortgage Your Heart.** 1937